Residential Soccer Performance Center
Self Teaching Method

by

Alex von Ludwig

The contents of this work, including, but not limited to, the accuracy of events, people, and places depicted; opinions expressed; permission to use previously published materials included; and any advice given or actions advocated are solely the responsibility of the author, who assumes all liability for said work and indemnifies the publisher against any claims stemming from publication of the work.

All Rights Reserved
Copyright © 2020 by Alex Ludwig

No part of this book may be reproduced or transmitted, downloaded, distributed, reverse engineered, or stored in or introduced into any information storage and retrieval system, in any form or by any means, including photocopying and recording, whether electronic or mechanical, now known or hereinafter invented without permission in writing from the publisher.

Dorrance Publishing Co
585 Alpha Drive
Suite 103
Pittsburgh, PA 15238
Visit our website at *www.dorrancebookstore.com*

ISBN: 978-1-6491-3326-7
eISBN: 978-1-6491-3293-2

Residential Soccer Peformance Center

Alex Ludwig

347 different exercises

The way around Alex Ludwig soccer Academy 3 weeks residential camp special program for special players who would like to be growing very quick amazingly fast, high -level skills understand very quality Individual tactics, position tactics and team tactics.

I did work over 12 years in residential soccer camps in the USA and other 20 years in professional and National level head coaching in Europe and the USA and 7 years coach in the Boys U 18 National team in Hungary, then 3 years Assistant Coach in the Canadian Women's National team players in Vancouver with Metro Gerala.

With my technical skill system, you going to learn everything what you can do with the ball in the soccer game.

In the individual week, the program focuses learning skills, technic, shooting, finishing, small sided positional games.

Positional 2nd week focus on positional technic, skill and strategy, Defense-Offense- in position Defender, Midfielder and Forward. (small sided games -4v4,5v5,6v6,7v7,8v8,9v9)

Team week 3rd week, team skills, technics, and tactics. In 11 side.

After every week you come to a deeply knowledgeable soccer player but after the tree weeks you become a Knowledgeable and experienced soccer player who understand very well the soccer game.

Dear Coaches and Director Coaches I do guarantee if you learn this Performer Center Program

You going to teach your players different, noticeably short time develop to the next level your team and individual your players.

In the next pages I am going to represent my special Performance Center Programs. Enjoy it!

Alex Ludwig

Master Coach

SUNDAY

(DAY CAMP PICK-UP 8:45 PM):

1:00 pm - Players arrive/Check-in

3:00 pm - Camp Introduction

4:00 pm - Training Session

5:30 pm   Dinner in dining hall

6:45 pm   Warm ups

7:00-9:30 pm Training

9:45-10:45 pm Meeting

11:00 pm   Lights out

SATURDAY

DAILY SCHEDULE (DAY CAMP): 8:45 am - 12:00 pm

DAILY SCHEDULE (RESIDENTIAL CAMP):

8:45 am - Warm-ups

9:00-11:30 am Training

12:00 pm Players Check-out

MONDAY-FRIDAY

(DAY CAMP PICK-UP 8:45 PM):

DAILY SCHEDULE RESIDENTIAL CAMP):

6:15-7:00 - Soccer aerobic (technical

7:30 am - Breakfast

8:45am - Warm-ups

9:00-11:30 am   Training

12:00 pm Lunch

1.00-1.30pm Mandatory rest

1:45pm - Warmups

2:00-4:30 pm   Training

5;30pm   Dinner Dining Hall

6.00-6.30pm Mandatory rest

6;45 pm Warmups

7:00-8:30 pm   Training

9:25-10:45pm   Meeting

11:00 pm   Lights out

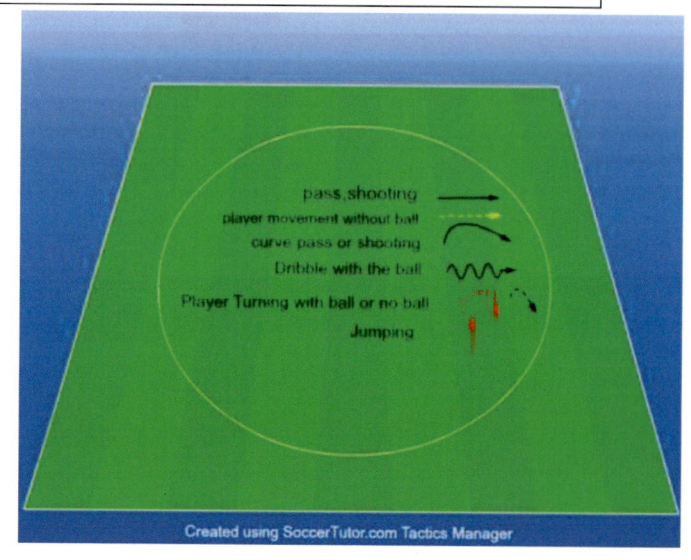

Performance Center First Week- Individual Program!

Sunday.

2-3.4.00 Registration, distribute the room keys and uniform

4.30-5.00 field Instructions and group building
after team building the players meet with the coaches getting know each other all simple volume up and passing games then cool down and going to the dinner.

6:45 to 8:30 PM

the teams going on the field and doing small side games. The formation going to build up after the numbers because a small side games is very important To understand the triangles which is very important key in soccer games .playing 3 players again 3 players 4 against 4 with goalkeepers .the key the players have to know each other the coach have to know the players and if this possible keep the team together .selecting the players later evening by evening's meeting the cultures came together and if they have a players who fit not very good in the group we're looking for that person a group where they could fit better to the future learning system .

Before the games starting 15 to 20 minutes shooting exercise shooting technique

The coach explains and demonstrate the correct shooting technique with the shoelace this is power shot technique. **The keywords are.**

- **Happy feet (Which is helping you make your body ready for shooting .and coming in the right shooting position to the ball.)**
- **Opposite footstep to the ball -no shooting foot- by the side from the ball away from the ball on your shoe size**
- **Opposite foot toes facing the target**
- **By the shooting foot the shoelace the Sheen and the knee facing the target facing the ball**
- **By the shooting foot ankle locked and the toes done**
- **Before you hit the ball, your hip must come up**
- **run to the ball and hit the ball important follow through the direction where you shoot**
- **After you hit the ball a little magic hope forward is optimal getting a good position after the shot**
- **Important head forward chest over the ball before the shot look up where you would like to hit the ball**

The players going every day shooting 3 * 30 minutes sessions and the coaches must correct every single time if they are missing some keys from the shooting technic

Every morning sessions the early morning sessions called soccer Aerobic the most outdoor could be indoor it's a bottom of session -dribbling technic ,fitness .depends what the player need to be ready to go for the long day sessions .The sessions are 30-45 minutes. Then breakfast

After warming up we are breaking down 4 groups goalkeepers, technical session. tactical session and trebling session. Goalkeepers stay with the goalkeeper coach until 11:00 AM after the moving to the teams in 30 minutes shooting finishing session.

Monday Morning.

8.45-9.00 Group warmups funny warmups make the kids ready for the focus on the sessions 9.00-11.30am start main training session

Technical Station: Passing and Receiving, the stations 30min long then switch Stations!

 15 Center line pass to outside line, receive and dribble try to beat the center line then pass to the other outside line, they receive it and pass to the center line, pass back the outside line dribble ....

!. 15 min2.   15min

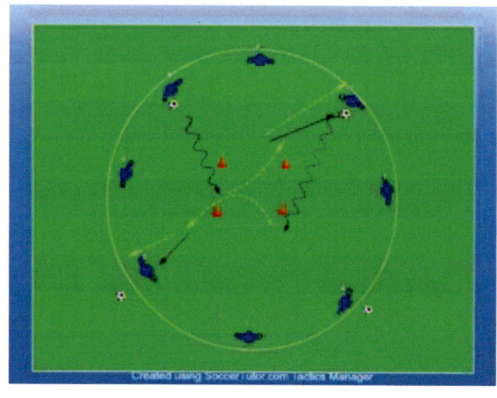

3. PASSING AND DRIBBLING II

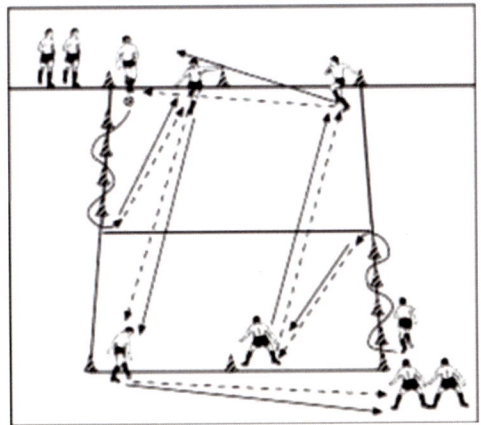

Set Up

 Exercise 2.

Sequence

, except now, after the second diagonal pass, the player at the corner cone kicks a square pass along the end line (to the other group).

- As above, all players follow their passes to their next positions. **Focus on:**

- Practicing dribbling
- Accurate passes over short and long distances
- Combining dribbling and passing as the situation requires

2. 20'(min) Circle passing

This is a good drill to use as a warm up before a match or training session or as part of a basic skills practice.

Start with 5 players in a circle with a 20 yard diameter. Then have another player behind each of these players. See diagram below

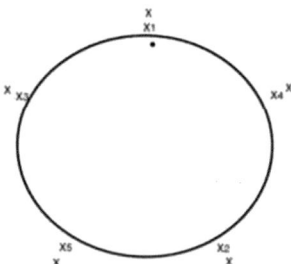

X1 starts with the ball and passes to X2. X1 then sprints behind X2 (so it's a pass and follow the pass). X2 then passes to X3 and sprints and follows the pass. X 3 then passes to X 4 and does the same. X 4 passes to X5 and then X5 passes to X1. After each pass the player follows the pass and goes to the back of that line.

Do this for 2-3 minutes and then add a second ball. Now the balls start with X1 and X4. While X1 is passing to X2, X4 is passing to X5. This will require a lot of movement, hard sprints, communication and vision.

Next add one defender in the middle. The difference now is the players can pass in any direction they want. However, they still must follow their pass.

Next add a second defender so it's sort of a 5 v 2 game but with much more movement and confusion than normal (must like a real game of soccer)..

4. 15 min.

2. PASSING AND DRIBBLING I

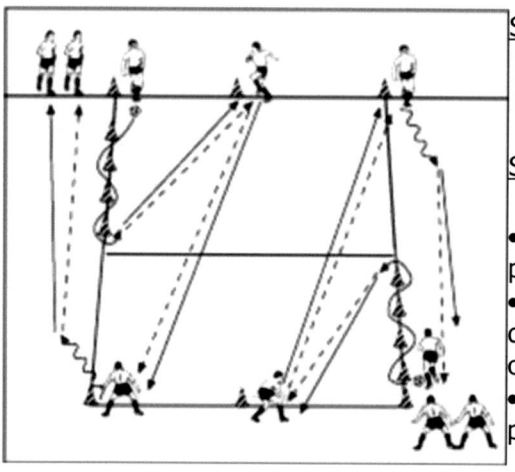

Set Up

Exercise 1.

Sequence

- Players dribble through the slalom and pass diagonally back to the end line.
- The player on the end line passes diagonally forwards to the cone at the far end of the near sideline.
- All players follow their passes to their next positions.

Focus On

- Practicing dribbling

- Accurate passes over short and long distances

Combining dribbling and passing as the situation requires
5. 15 min

3. Match Related   30 min -1 v 1 + 1 ---- than 20' min 2 v 2 + 1

Creativity to beat player 1 v 1
Players in groups of 4. 2 players participate in a 1 v 1 game to line. The players in support cannot attack or defend

Movement of players at angles -they can only provide support.

Scores pass to the player on the goal line.

6. 10 min

Passes thru a gate – players in move, receiving then dribbling and pass thru one other gate.

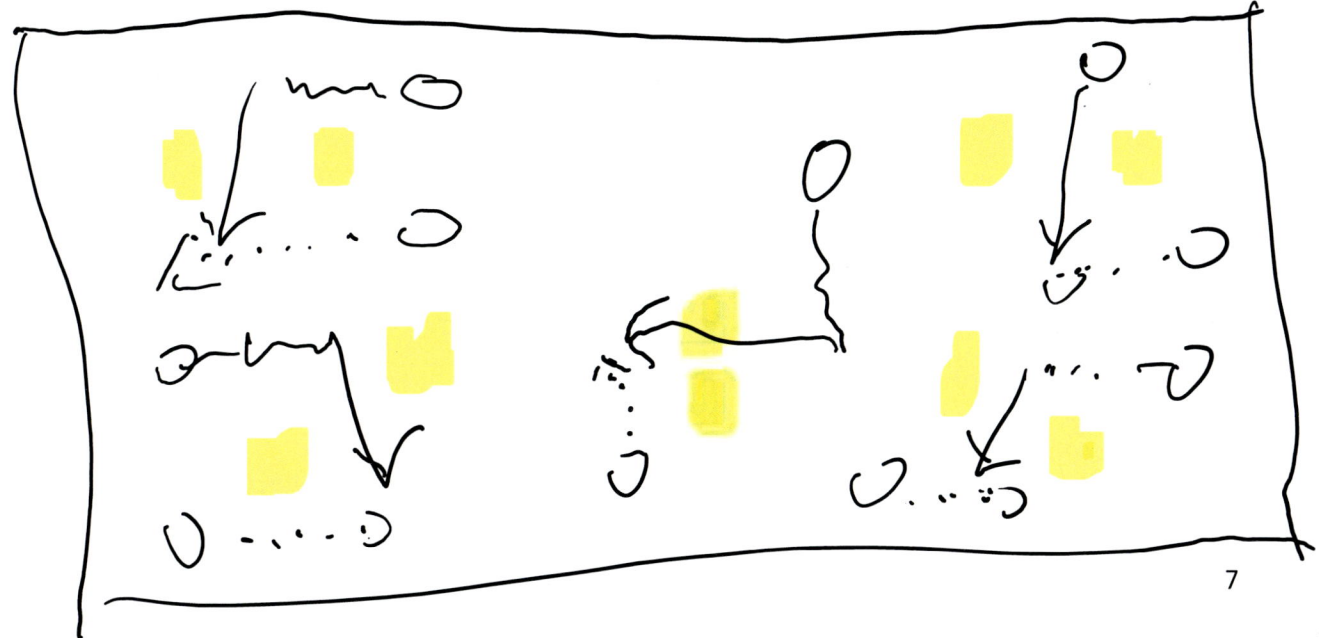

Dribbling Station: Faces in groups, Individual with defenders and without defenders.

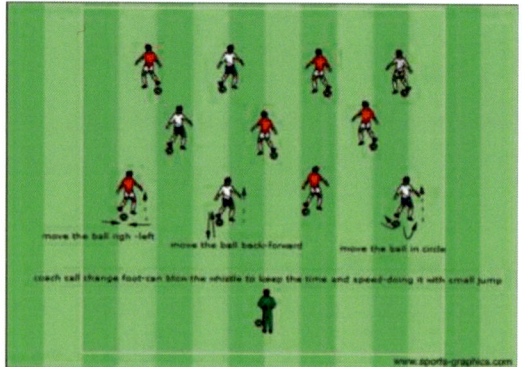

warm up dribbling with outside and inside with the foot
-The player's sole on the ball and they move it right to left
 Next they move the ball with the sole back and forward
 Then they wright a circle with the sole of the foot
- The next step all 3 exercise get down with small jumping rhythm
 Coach use whistle or count (one –two)
 This exercise I do every practice with the dribbling inside toe and outside toe 15' to 2

In move dribbling with the inside then outside foot, strait dribbling with outside foot (Break away)
Dribbling with heads up, changing directions, stopping then accelerate.

Fake number one:

Dribbling with the outside foot, then stop the ball with the right foot jump over the ball forward, in the air you do a half turn left hand, then take the ball with the left outside foot, accelerate.

Do it both ways.

Fake number two:

Dribbling with the outside food ,then speed it up ,the next do a fake kick with the right foot, roll the ball back, between you do a half turn Coming up in the air ,and the rolling foot taking the ball and accelerate .Is very important to sell the fake Kick and you're doing everything with one foot.

Fake number three:

Dribbling with the outside food then, right footstep to the ball from the left site, then left foot go inside Caesar around the ball, then turn and take the ball with the right inside foot then accelerate.

Coach must make sure the kids learning everything correctly and fix every mistake right away!

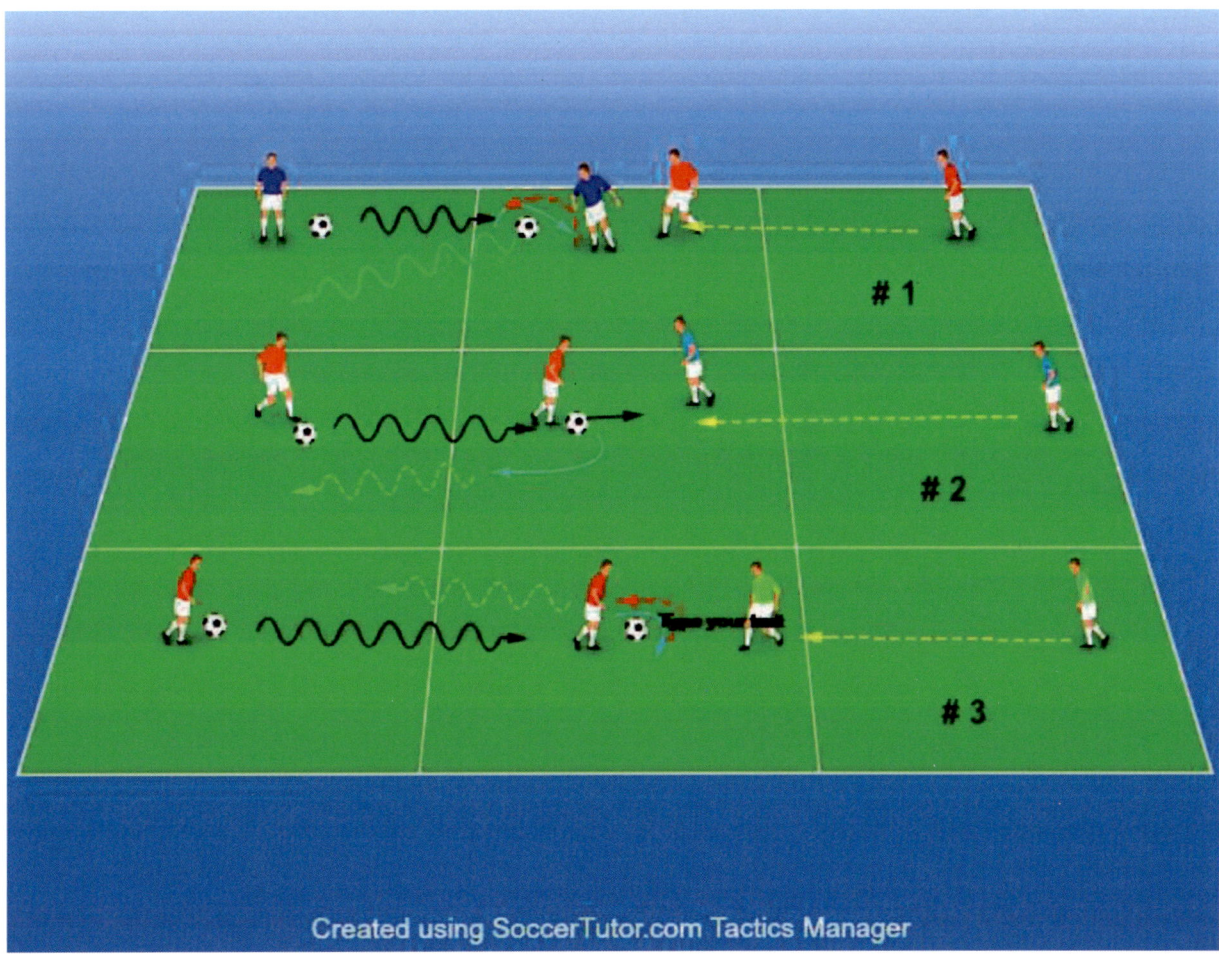

Tactical stations.

The topic is shielding and one versus 1

Volume up between two players 1 ball with passing exercise in motion receiving the ball inside foot outside foot turns and important communication between the two players

1.Exercise: Shielding!

The shielding is very important the offensive player stay between the ball and the defensive player, arm which is between the Defensive player site bend it and put it away from the body , Move the ball with dribbling and stay always closer to the ball than the opponent.

1/a The players believe the shielding 2 minutes defender 2 minutes open superior every time the coach is walking around and try fix and help positions how do you move the ball are you acting with body positions it's very important the players have to understand Which way he can develop himself to correct shielding position.

1/b Coach Kicking the ball into the field and call numbers example number one ,two players coming in one red 1 blue and they play shielding and try to beat the opponent and tables through the goal line then scored 1 point important coaches have to fix the position mistake shielding and dribbling mistakes

1/c Two players on the Center two players on the goal line, Players from the goal line passing the ball into the field to his partner and inside the two players shielding play Beat the opponent , try to score dribbling over the goal line, one time the player has a possibility to play back to his partner who passed the ball to him just help out if the defender is too strong

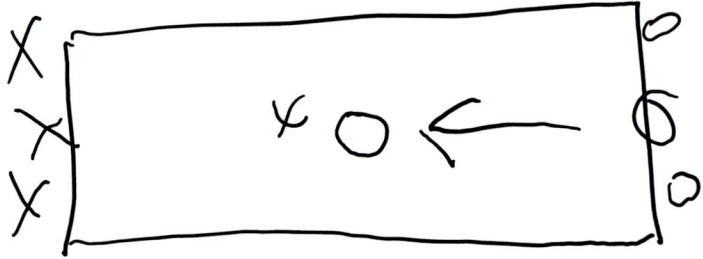

1/d 1 versus 1 trebling shielding for a big goal 2 players can go in the same time One Direction One Direction only the different there still the ball game is over changing positions

Coaches must look for intensity and use goalie or no Goalkeeper

11.00 Am The players going to group from the evening games and looking for the evening coaches going to one goal and shooting technique finishing 30 minutes against goalkeeper, the shooting technique But we have to teach with the shoelace following the technique instructions. First day first time shooting we must try to teach the players from shooting from the hand the key not always the power but the target the direction.

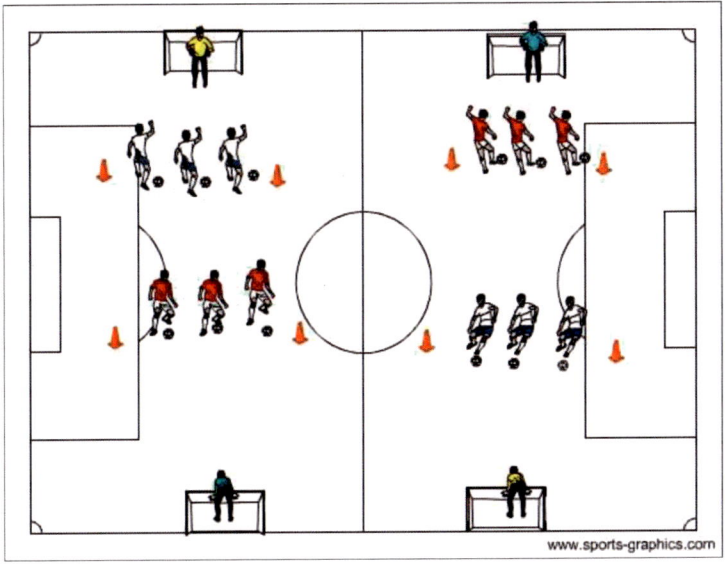

11.30 Session is finished players going to Eat lunch.

Monday afternoon:

1.45-2.00 pm

Group volume up for the volume up make the kids ready for the main session

2.00-4.30pm Start the main training session

Technical station:

1. Players working- being up couple of minutes with the ball three blinks stepovers turns.

2. Players pick up the ball in hand start jogging and right knee touch the ball catch it left knee touch the ball catch it in the air, Important the ball have to go forward and the player helped to catch before the ball come to the ground it's important the happy feet. Keeps keeping and very quick feet.

3. players kick the ball up in the air with the full shoelace one time right foot to catch the ball next time left foot catch the ball important the ball doesn't go too high good when the ball go until the head high. everything in motion no standing position.

4. The next players combine the 2nd and the 3rd exercise which is right foot right knee catch left foot left the catch then right foot left foot right knee left knee catch and right knee left knee right foot left foot catch what do you send from the combination important the kids have to keep the ball in the air the ball can't touch the ground.

5. And the last five 6 minutes practice the shooting technique with the full shoelace following the shooting technique keywords important the coach have to very careful every single step let the players understand Exactly how they have to hold the foot or they have to hold the body position.

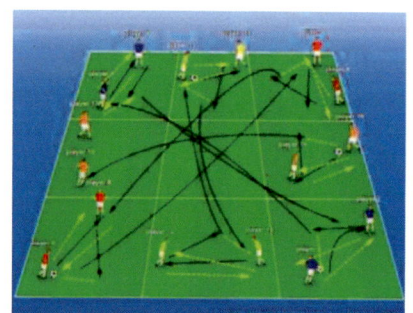

Tactical station; Topic shielding and two versus 1 In a small sided game situation

Players warming up with passing receiving using inside foot outside foot crossing the body move away from the body with outside food.

1.= 10. min. The first exercise the players going through in the morning learned shielding rules. Coach asking the players repeat the important parts from the exercise. Repeating the morning sessions shielding exercise especially important the periods must know exactly how you use your body when you shield the ball.

2. = 15 min. 2 versus 1 shielding using goalkeeper and finishing

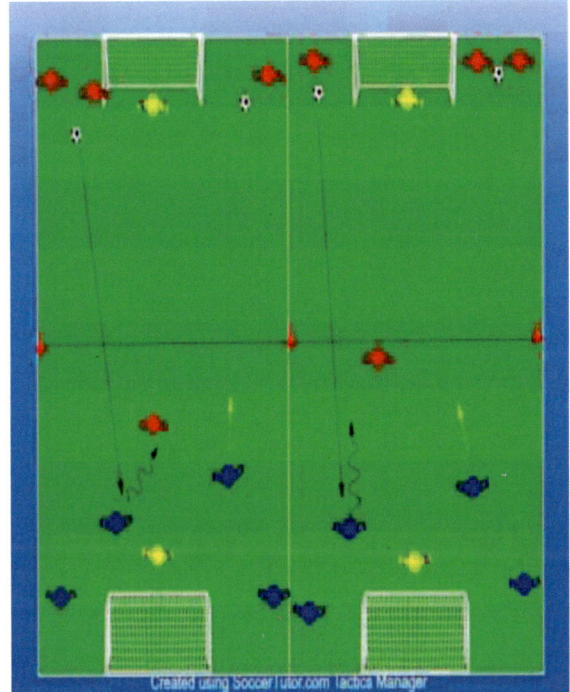

Important players one side passing the ball and this player who did pass the ball become the defender and the other two coming against the one player Shield the ball and passing and beat the one player and after finishing against the goalkeeper. the key in the exercise how are you shield the ball how are you using your partner in offense. In defense the player does not have to commit too early do not open too much space behind. Try to Take your time and be active defense and this possibility to stop the ball or clear it. Important the coach must change positions everybody have to be defense, and everybody must be offense

3. 15 min.

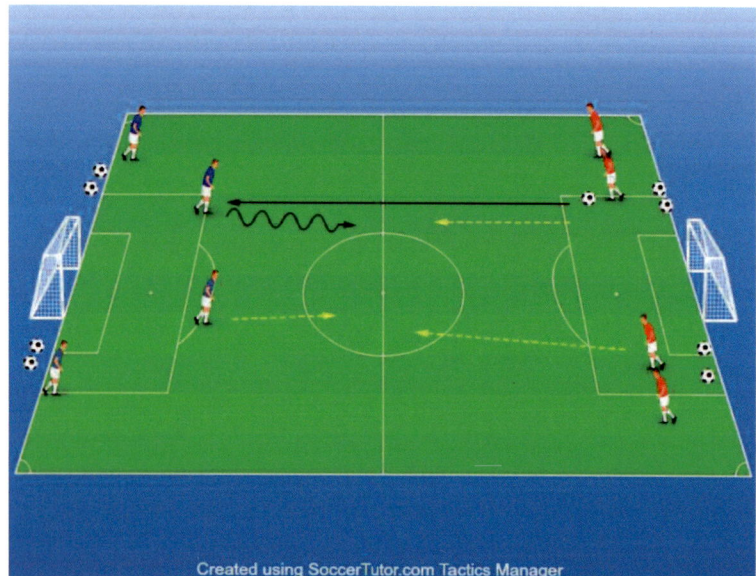

2 v 2 Shielding and passing and position pressure in harbor. Net player does pass the ball to blue player then the same player going and give pressure on the blue player, the other let player moves up and taking position in cover.

3/a

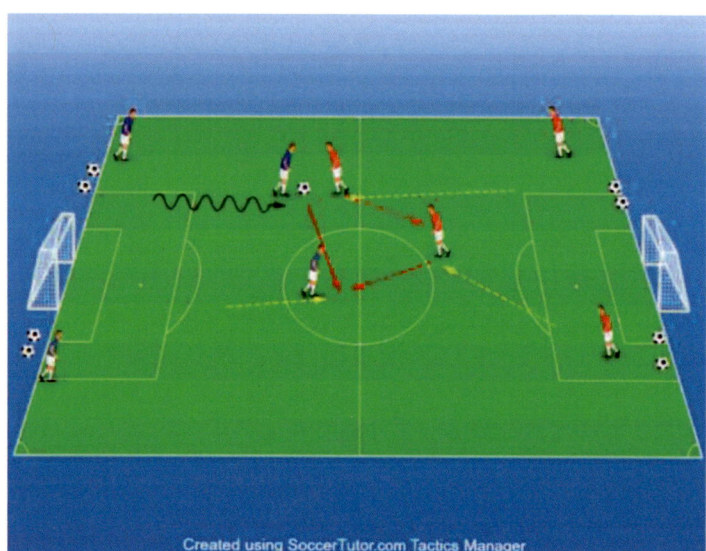

After red player did Passing the ball, he moved up quickly and giving them pressure and the second red player taking cover position you can see in a picture. The blue Bay are Passing to the partner in that case the second red player giving the pressure and the first that player taking a cover position you can see by the Red Arrows. Coaches must **explain how and why important the pressure and cover** because without cover the true pass could be a killer boss and big advantage for the offensive team.

Dribbling station; 30 min.

The players going to repeat it in the morning they learned fake number 1 fake number 2 and fake 3.

Whenever the players understand and know the fakes then we going to doing against each other tours each other and do the fakes and turn.

If the players they learned and know very well the fake number one #2 #3 then they going dribble against an opponent against each other towards each other and on the middle one 1 1/2 yards from the opponent doing the face and dribbling back it's very important the timing the players can't heat each other or touch each other or kicking each other ball away .

Shooting finishing:

4.00 pm The players going to group from the evening games and looking for the evening coaches going to one goal and shooting technique finishing 30 minutes against goalkeeper, the shooting technique But we have to teach with the shoelace following the technique instructions. First day first time shooting we must try to teach the players from shooting from the hand the key not always the power but the target the direction. The coaches can decide it if the group is advanced with their technique then they can start Monday afternoon shooting from the ground.

4.00-4.30pm Shooting session

First day in the camp in the morning 11:00 AM visual team only from the hand explaining the shooting technique incredibly careful very under stable for the players. Afternoon shooting the beginning from the hand if the players are the ones we can start on the ground but you see in a picture very simple in a first day evening before the shorts side games the shooting a same way from the ground simple.

Monday evening session.

6.45 -7.00 pm warm up

7.00-7.30 pm Shooting finishing

7.30-8.30pm evening small sided games; 4 v 4; 5 v 5; 6 v 6; 7 v 7.

The evening games must have a lot of fun and try everything what you did learn the morning and afternoon sessions.

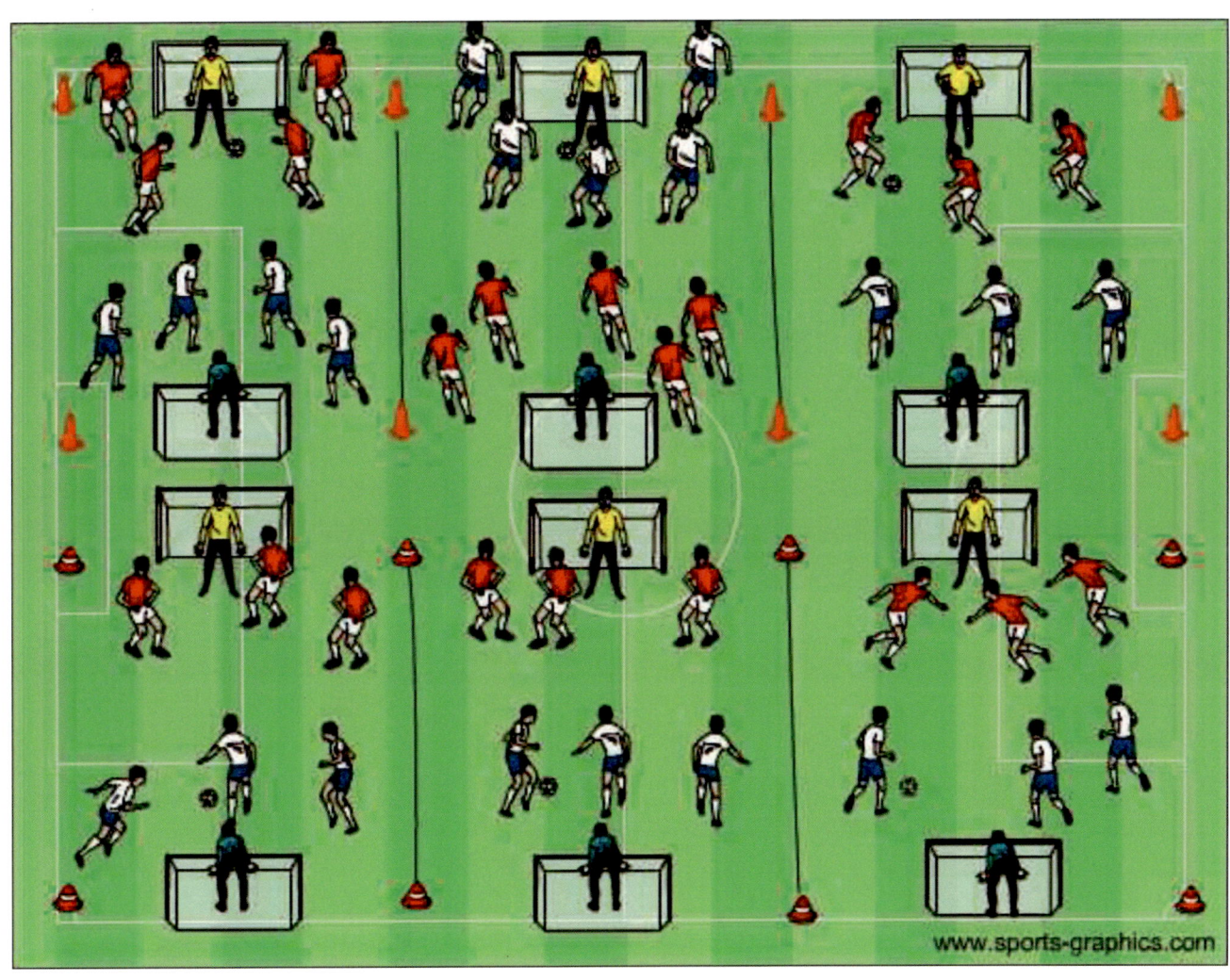

Tuesday Morning:

6.15-7.00 am

Soccer Aerobic if it is indoor, or fitness and technical sessions

Start the morning session:

8.45-9.00 Group warmups funny warmups make the kids ready for the focus on the sessions
9.00-11.30am start main training session

Technical station; 30 min. Passing, Receiving, control

1. Players working- being up couple of minutes with the ball three ways stepovers turns.

2. The players pick up the ball in the hand. Kick the ball over your head with the shoeless and then control the ball Receive the ball with the inside foot .coaches have to pay attention this very important the most rate for the kids and explain the ball have to touch the ground first **and that moment when the ball start coming up that moment you cover the ball with your inside foot**. So, the ball goanna stays with you on the ground - right away you can start dribbling or any other movement.

3. Same be that number 2 the players kicking the ball up in the air over your head and controlling receiving the ball with the outside food coaches have to pay attention that moment when the ball coming up from the ground that moment have to cover the ball with your outside foot. same way like with the inside foot the ball stayed with the player and right away can answer it dribbling turning with an excellent control.

4.

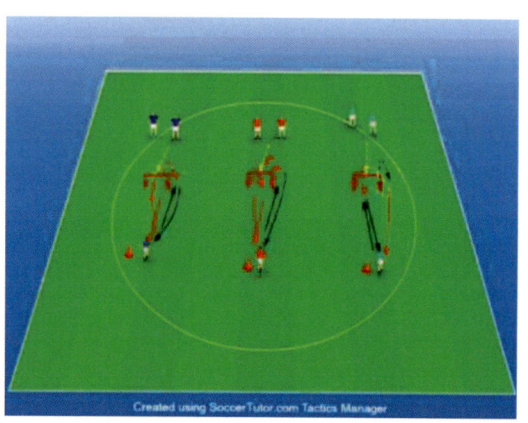

Player without the ball run forward jump over the small gate pass the ball back to the player then jump sideways left over the gate passing the ball back again then jump over right the gate and push the ball back over then switching position

Mark a rectangle with cone. The corners in the rectangle must be occupied by two players. If the number of players is higher, the exercise is easier because there is more time to think. There is one ball in two groups. The groups with ball must stand diagonally to each other. There is one player on each of the two long stretches of the rectangle. The ball owners fit on the opposite long track and then run to the long-distance position, which is located right next to the passers-by. Players on the long side of the rectangle control the ball and pass diagonally further into the next corner. They also do not follow their passport but run diagonally to the position from which they received the pass. Now the same process starts from the other side.

Tactical Station: 30 min. Topic is 2 v 2, 3 v 2 and give and go

1. Players warming up with 2 V 1 and 2 V 2 passing exercise

2. Teaching give and go – or wall passing

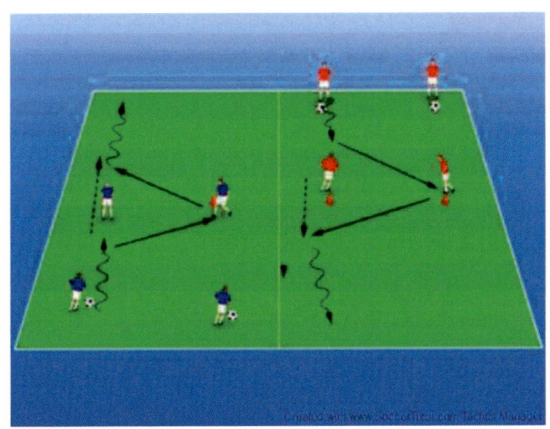

Players dribbling with the ball Direct to the defender then make a diagonal pass to the partner who giving a direct pass behind the defender to the space and the player running to the ball and Received the ball in the space then dribble until the end of the field.

3. Basic give and go game.

Two teams playing four players red and blue and two defenders the game is going with giving go, the two defenders on top the balls and the players can play for red or can play for blue team. Player who has the Ball can dribble and passing the ball but the player who receiving the ball must play direct pass back

Dribbling Station; 30 min

1. Individual dribbling in the circle form

Player start Dribbling individual and the direction turning stop the ball start again 3 minutes. The key points the players cannot hit each other ball, they cannot hit each other body, must go away from each other and heads up by the dribbling.

2 Players are circular. Markings are not strictly necessary, but they make orientation easier. The dribbler always moves into the rectangle and leaves the rectangle on any side. He dribbles to the teammate at the edge of the circle and hands over the ball there. So, the exercise goes on and on.

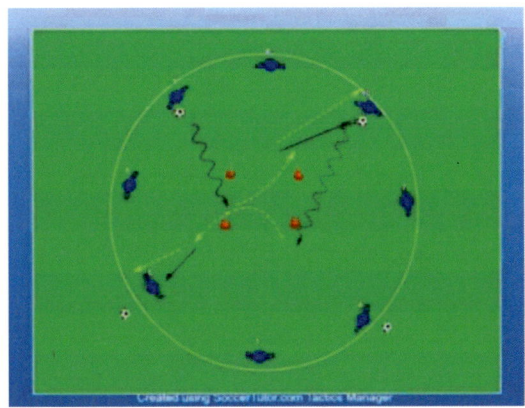

3. Double technical training with passing

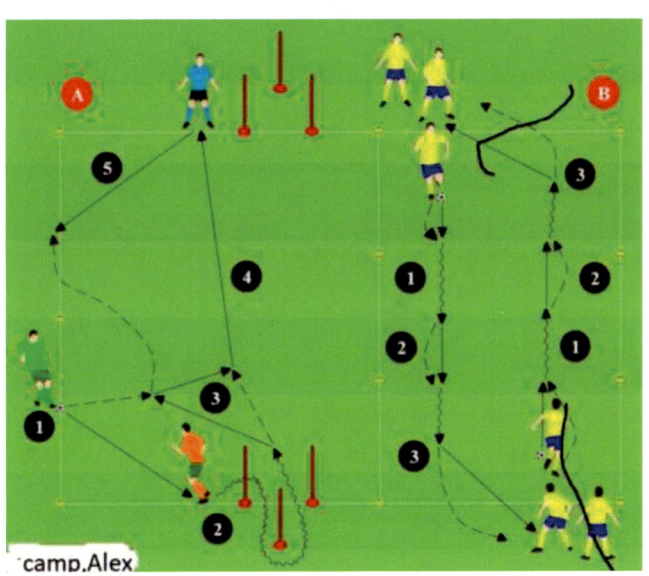

In this double technical game form, two processes are executed simultaneously, of course each can also be offered in isolation. With two processes, a lot of variety is created by the group changes. The technical game form Double passes, dribbling, offering and pass into the depths On field A, the players should fit, skillfully dribble and a player is always offering himself to double pass play. He constantly runs a diagonal run, which is required by a pass into the depth. For players green the process is very intense and there is the possibility to fill this position twice. However, to keep the exercise in the "river" it is recommended to leave it with three players. If the forms A and B are executed at the time, player changes can take place again and again, so the technical training becomes varied.

11.00 am Shooting finishing.

Players going to the evening coach and starting the shooting 30 minutes

first simple shooting and finishing from the ground when the players ready for the next combination shooting then we can start the following exercise.

replace-we-the-dummy's

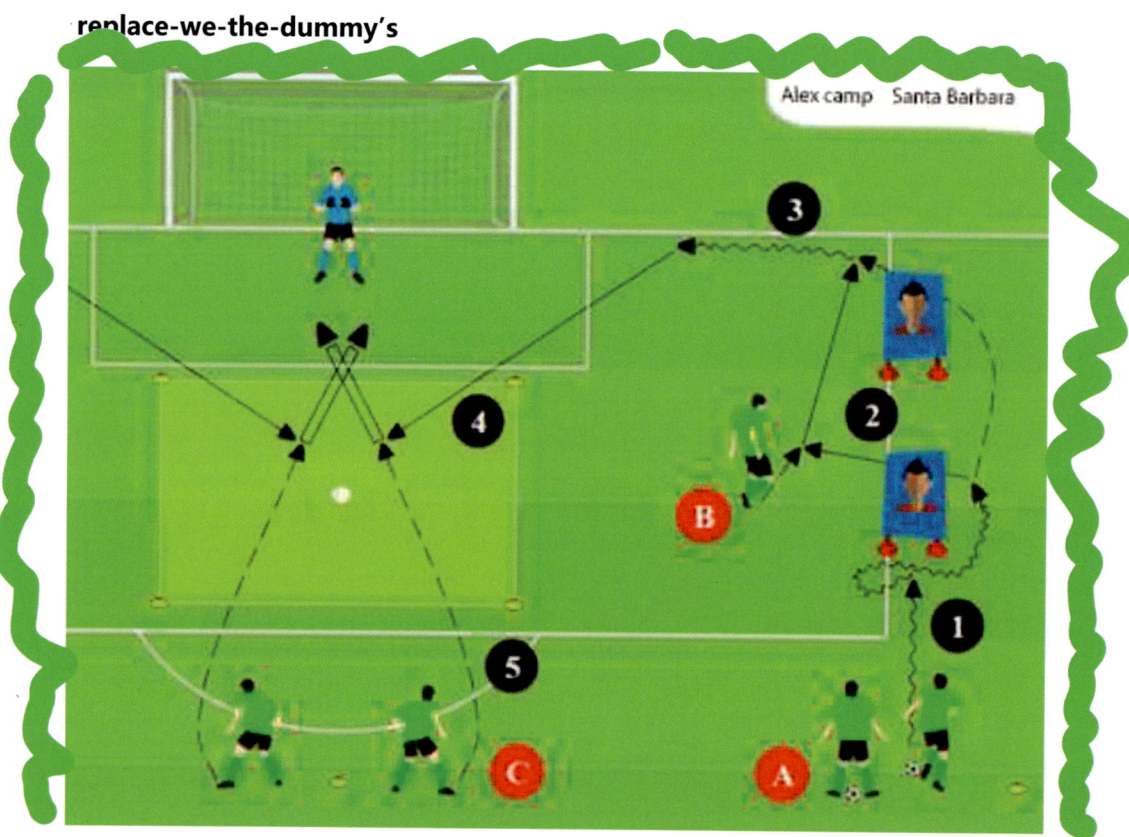

Fake TRAINING, Hiding AND PASS IN THE BACKS OF THE DEFENSE This is about fast and fin-rich dribbling over the wings. The starting player deliberately moves to the sideline, so he lures the opponent to the side. The interplay between A and B takes place as a wall game, with emotional ball-passing past the dummies. When dribbling at the baseline, the ball is always guided very tightly and controlled. The pass to the back-room field takes place only at the last moment and can also be executed as a no-look pass

11.30 Go Lunch

Tuesday afternoon session.

1.45-2.00 pm Group volume up for the volume up make the kids ready for the main session

2.00-4.30pm Start the main training session

Technical station; 30 min.

1.Technical exercise in Group 3 ball control 15 min

Players throwing the ball for each other the receiving player finish first with the foot control the ball then pick it up and throw it to the next player. receiving the ball with inside food outside foot with thigh. Then going to the chest and with the head.

2. **TECHNICAL WORK:** *Opening to Receive, Speed of Play -15 minutes*

- Divide players into 3 training groups
- Flat cone in the middle of the exercise
- Emphasis on speed of play, body position to turn quickly and cleanly, communication
- Add a layoff from middleman
- Add a wall-pass combination on the flanks

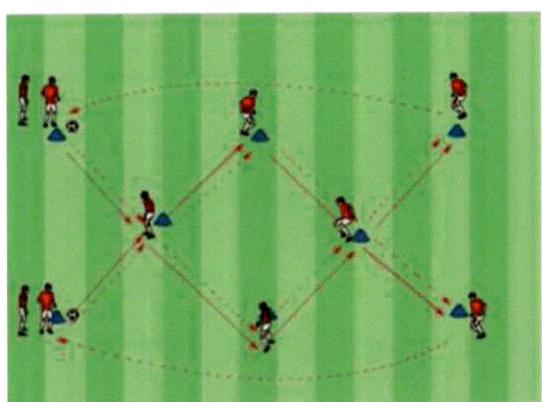

Tactical station: l topic is Take Over-Triangle - and 2 v2 3 versus 2 and 3 versus 3

Repeating give and go and shielding.

1. Take over 10 minutes

play us creating a four groups posizione Two groups has a ball first start one group trebling in the middle the opposite side the player coming without the ball and ask for take over -they can say I got it -I take it -let it go -give it to me -important the dribbler does not possible just going to leave it another player just goanna take it and accelerate.

2. Triangle; 10 minutes

Players going to four groups 3 Offensive player and one difference in player. play Ed who has the ball need help under pressure right side and the left side on open player. defensive player giving the pressure then the player passes the ball to one of the offensive partners. The other offensive player moved to the next corner -get open.

3. 3v3 Basic Game

Bunch ball is a constant problem in youth soccer. This results from the players inability to maintain their shape. The distance and angles between the players are lost and, as a team, they are not able to work together efficiently. Since three players make the smallest shape, a triangle, **3v3 games in modified forms** are an excellent way to introduce this concept. There are still lots of 1v1 opportunities and the

basic lessons from 2v2 can be expanded and built on. 3v3 also guarantees that there is open space somewhere on the field.

dribbling station; 30 minutes

player start warming up with the ball through blink three direction turns stop the ball start.

then start repeating the fake number one #2 and #3

Next the coach introduced a fake #4 fake number 5 and the fake #6

-Fake #4.

-Players Dribbling with the ball with the outside foot start cutting the ball with outside foot turning away from the body 270 degrees then accelerate. When you are turning with the right outside foot after the 270 degree, finishing to the left hand accelerate. especially important between the turning is noticeably short and incredibly soft touches with outside food and very quick skipping happy feet. the not turning foot following the turning food very quick short steps.

-Fake #5.

It's a simple fake Dribbling with outside foot right foot take a dummy step with the left foot away from the ball left shoulder go down then take the ball with the right outside foot to the right hand diagonal- accelerate.

Fake #6.

Trebling with the right foot outside foot fake step with the left foot away from the ball then the right foot outside foot go around the ball very quick then with the left Outside foot direction to the left hand take the ball diagonal and accelerate this is the Caesar.

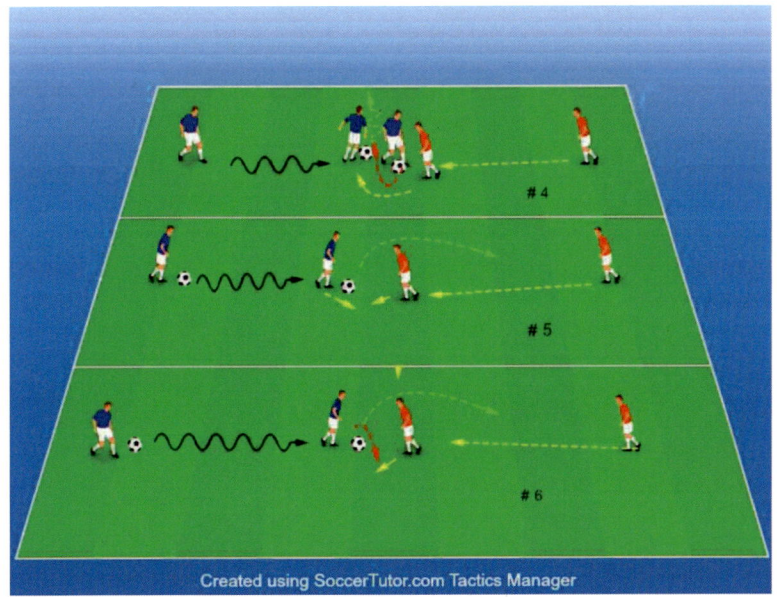

4.00-4.30 pm Shooting finishing

5 six-minute player shooting from the hand warm up for the finishing exercise

1. need a hat gate some distance from the gate. There, a ball distributor is posted, which controls the second pass, pulls through the hat gate, and lays down to the shot. In the starting group, each player has a ball. If the first pass to the player goes to the right side, he runs past the small goal on the left and receives the ball to the goal shot from the ball distributor.

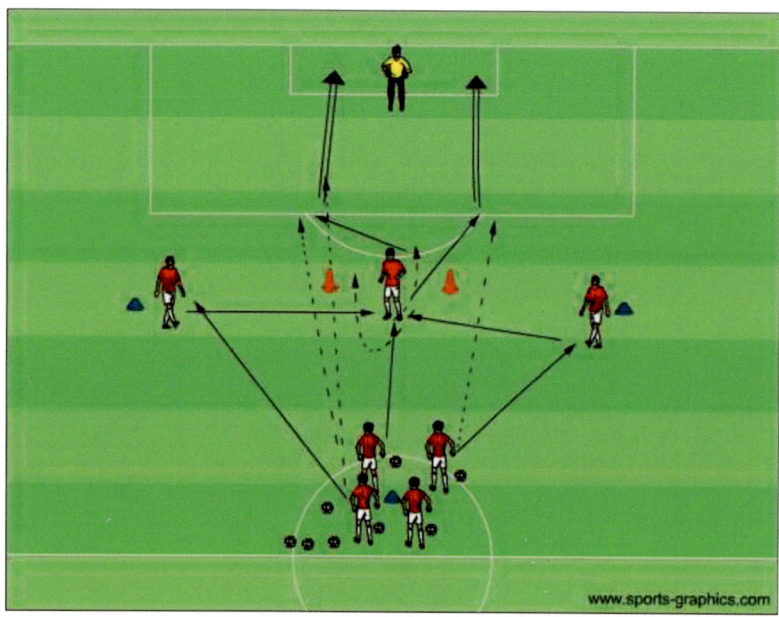

2. shooting 2 times with gates

The starter on the right side of the goal runs towards the ball distributor, receives the

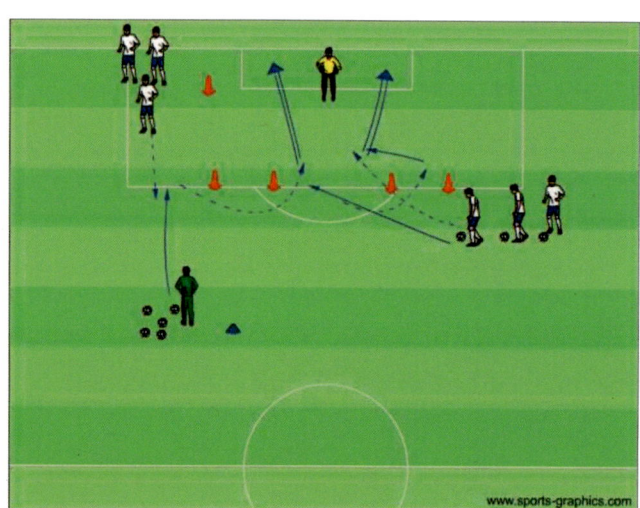

pass, dribbles immediately in the direction of the goal, and executes a shot at goal. He then runs to the first hat on the right. There he gets an accurate play from the second group, in which each player has a ball. The passer runs past the pass receiver, receives the back pass, and immediately moves in the direction of the goal to shoot. After the promotion, players swap groups

4.30 finish training go to Dinner

Tuesday evening session.

6.45 -7.00 pm warm up

7.00-7.30 pm Shooting finishing

7.30-8.30pm

play yes going to the team coaches, shooting Finishing and then small side games

4 v 4; 5 v 5; 6 v 6; 7 v 7

The evening games must have a lot of fun and try everything what you did learn the morning and afternoon sessions.

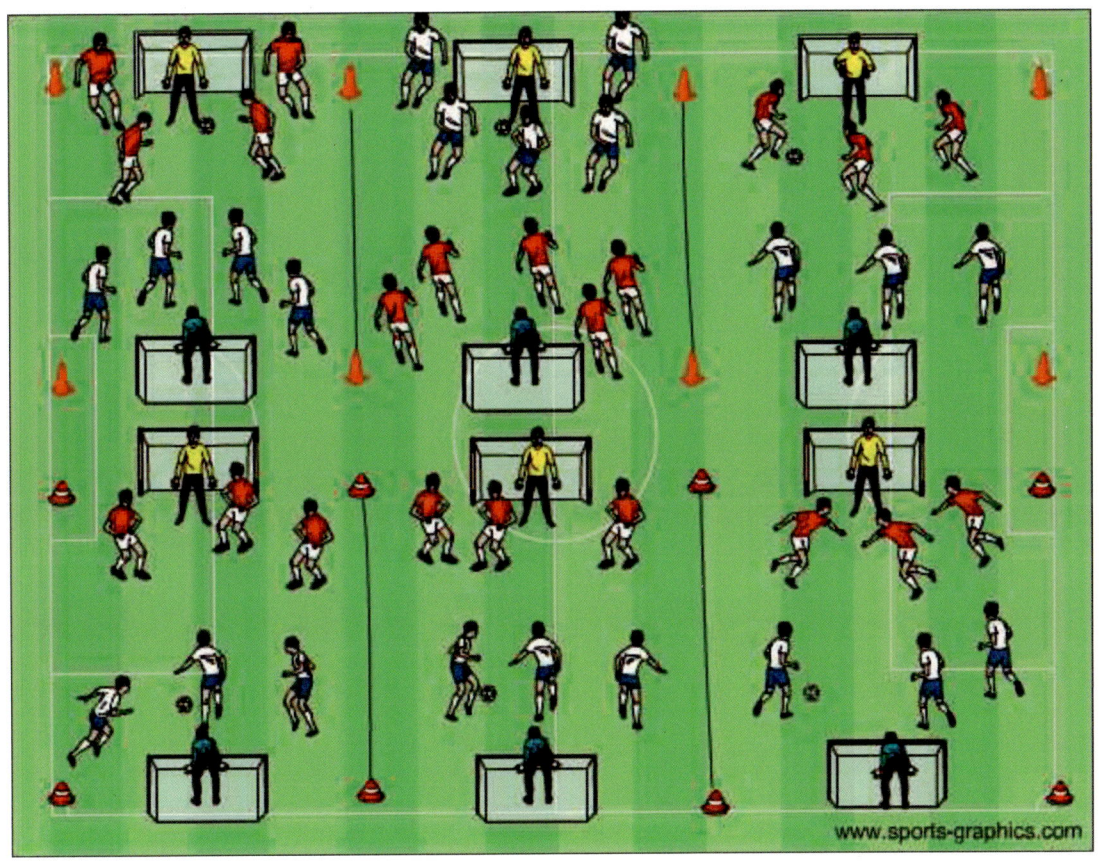

In the evening games the players must try to make what they learned in the morning take over giving goals and try to do the fake sin again this is a life practice.

Wednesday Morning:

6.15-7.00 am

Soccer Aerobic if it is indoor, or fitness and technical sessions outdoor

Start the morning session:

8.45-9.00 Group warmups funny warmups make the kids ready for the focus on the sessions
9.00-11.30am start main training session

Technical Station; 30 min. warming up 2 players passing the ball in motion.

1, Players go in group 3 first with 2 balls. 15 min.

The players in Group 3 one player has the ball in the hand and going to Throw it to right and left player, his left hand sided player kicking the ball with the left foot and his right hand sided Player Kicking The ball back with the right foot .The coaches call for the changing position two or three minutes. Important players who kicking the ball must keep the ball back from the heap swing from the heap.

2. same in group 3 on the same field. 15 min.

-Drew are throwing the ball to the player the player who kicking the ball back receiving it with the thigh and kicking the ball back in the air without bouncing

-Next throwing the ball to the chest, Player receiving it with the chest and kicking the ball back in the air to the thrower without bouncing.

-Next throwing to the head, player receiving it with the head and kicking the ball back in the air to the thrower without bouncing. **Coach can put in more touches before kicking the ball back!**

Tactical Station: 30 min. Topic is Overlap

1. Overlap outside line-open the space to the partner- 15 min

Red player passing the ball to the partner, partner dribbling inside filled taking the defender with him partner running into the open space and receiving the ball by the outside line on the service of helping. **Important players must dribble very intensive inside to the center field because the defender must go with him and open the space clearly for the partner.**

2. Overlap with crosses; 15 min

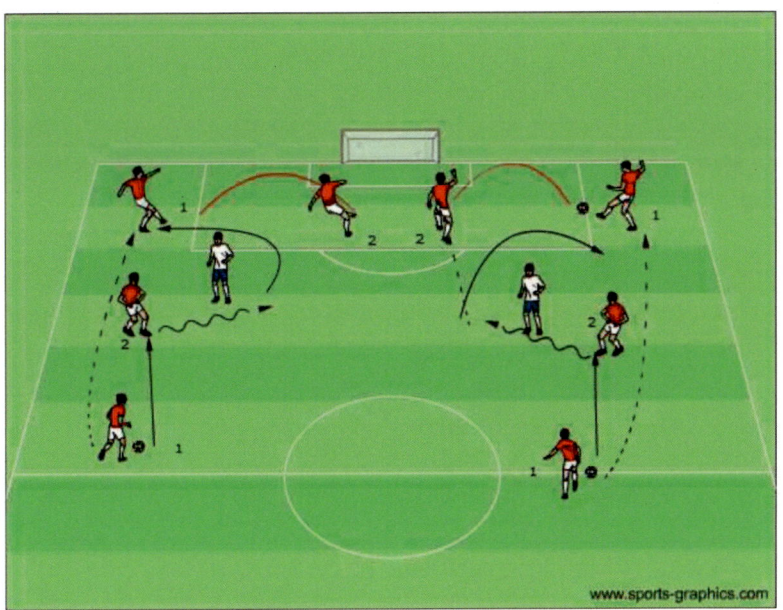

Play album pushing the ball two player 2 player 2 trebling insight in the center taking the defender with him player one overlap player 2 running into the space receiving the pass from player 2 looking up between player to have to run in a center player 1 going to crush the ball into the center and player to finish. **The defender must follow player two by the dribbling because he cannot let the player to dribble to the goal and take a shot.**

Dribbling Station: 30 min.

go with dribbling changing directions 3 minutes

Players going to repeat and practice the fake from Number one until #6

Coach going to explain and teach fake #7 fake #8 and week number 9.

fake #7.

Player dribbling with outside foot Then with the right outside foot do the outside Caesar-, the next with the left foot do a half outside Caesar. The left hand stretched forward do not let the defender come close to you buddy, then behind the left Hill with the right foot inside parts kicking the ball left by the defender diagonal forward, then pas the defender. Enormously powerful fake if you do it right practice it enough that is going to work every time in the game.

Fake #8.

Dribbling with the outside foot, Next with the soil of your right foot roll the ball outside from your body then with the inside toes kick it cross your body to the left side and take the ball with the left outside foot and the accelerate pass the defender.

When you are rolling the ball with the right foot outside from your body make a little hop forward just make it easier to finish in the second part from the fake.

Fake number 9.

dribbling with speed always outside foot dribbling, Then jump front of the ball stop the ball with the outside foot make a half turn in the air then take the ball with the right outside foot the opposite direction where you were dribbling.

Important you jump and fly and turn half turn in the air this is not the card you going to stop the ball with your outside foot the other foot landed on the ground to.

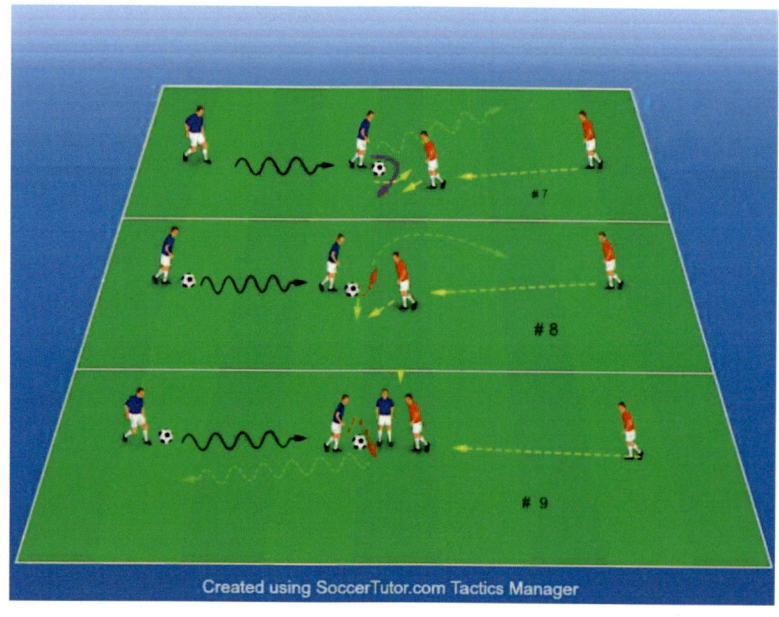

11.00 am Players going to the evening game coach and 30 minutes shooting finishing.

The players can start shooting simple on the ground because the coach is knowing the players today can make it really difficult finishing against goalkeeper put the defender in or just try to shoot throwing the ball hitting in the air make it more fun for the kids .

11.30 Lunch

Wednesday Afternoon Sessions:

1.45-2.00 pm Group volume up for the volume up make the kids ready for the main session

2.00-4.30pm Start the main training session

Technical Station: 30 min.

Players start warming up 3 minutes between 2 three players passing the ball receiving turning important the process using inside food using outside foot, away from the body crossing the body

1, We need a field width of half a penalty area (large field about 20 meters) and a field height of also about 20 meters. The practice field is marked with 4 hats. For the sequence of both at the same time, two more hats are set up analogously at the other end of the penalty area. There is also a goal with a goalkeeper. In the starting group (A) there are several players with ball. In the other positions (B and C) one player without a ball is enough, better two.

Expiration:

From the starting group (A) the ball is matched the player (B). The passer immediately offers itself sideways. B plays back and offers itself to the wall game with C. A fits diagonally to C and then assumes the position of B. C fits across to B and sprints to the hat in the penalty area. B plays in the run of C and then takes over the position of C. C controls the ball briefly. C finishes with a shot on goal, picks up the ball and moves into the starting group.

Variations

Two practice fields (see chart). The teams compete against each other. Which team scores the most goals in each time? The square sizes are constantly changing, so players must adjust to new distances again and again. The starting group is posted on the con on the other side (center). Accordingly, the pass and walkways change. Insert running fins/body illusions. Tips Demand accurate pass play. The last pass must be tuned so that the scorer can control the ball without losing pace.

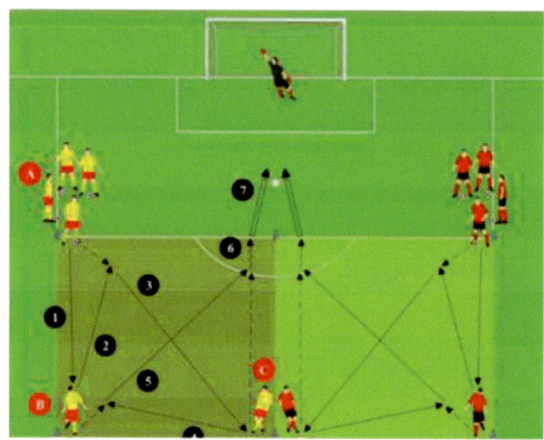

2. SPRINT CONNECTION ACTIONS - TECHNIQUE AND COGNITION

We increase the pressure through competitions and thus achieve a higher motivation in the process. The technical elements require correct execution under competitive conditions close to the game. The setup is simple, the explanation is done quickly. The challenge for the players is not the right practice run, but the technical elements contained therein. All descriptions that are needed for the practice run can also be found in the attached PDF, incl. graphic. Two sequences were shown in the graphic. It is recommended to demand identical content on both sides and to run competitions in the second step

Organization: So that we can hold competitions, we build two practice fields side by side. We need two mini-gates (big gates, bar gates). Enough balls are available. In addition, there are 2 starting marks, 2x4 different colored cons and two target cons in front of the gates. A square is about 3x3 meters in size, at each corner there is a con with a different color. The distances correspond to the performance of the team, which we divide into two groups. The starting players are in the center of the square without the ball. Procedure A = One ball is dropped at the target con, further balls are ready at the trainer. Procedure B = The balls are in the starting group.

Procedure A: The trainer calls two to four con colors; these must be completed exactly in this order. The player in the center orbits (sprints) the called cons in the correct order. The player then starts to the target con and shoots at the goal. Procedure B: The trainer calls two to four hat colors; these must be completed exactly in this order. The player in the center orbits (sprints) the called cons in the correct order and returns to the square. There he expects a play from the player from the starting group. He turns up and dribbles towards the target con. In front of the goal con, he executes a predetermined trick and then shoots at the goal. to A: The coach does not call colors, but club

names, for example "Dortmund" for teams. The cons are assigned a number from 1 to 4. For example, if the trainer calls "1,4,2", the player is started in the order 1-4-2. The colors are changed, yellow means orange, orange means red, etc. Competition: Players can score one point each for the team. Who hits the gate first? for B: See Variants for A. Competition: In the case of goal success, there is only one point for previous, technically correct execution. It is not fit into the square, the ball is thrown high, half-high. Tips Ball acceptance inside the square! The ball must not jump off the foot! Fast second contact! Flat precise play to the player in the square. Quick response and run the colors in the correct order.

3. Tiki-Taka passing "A"; 15 min

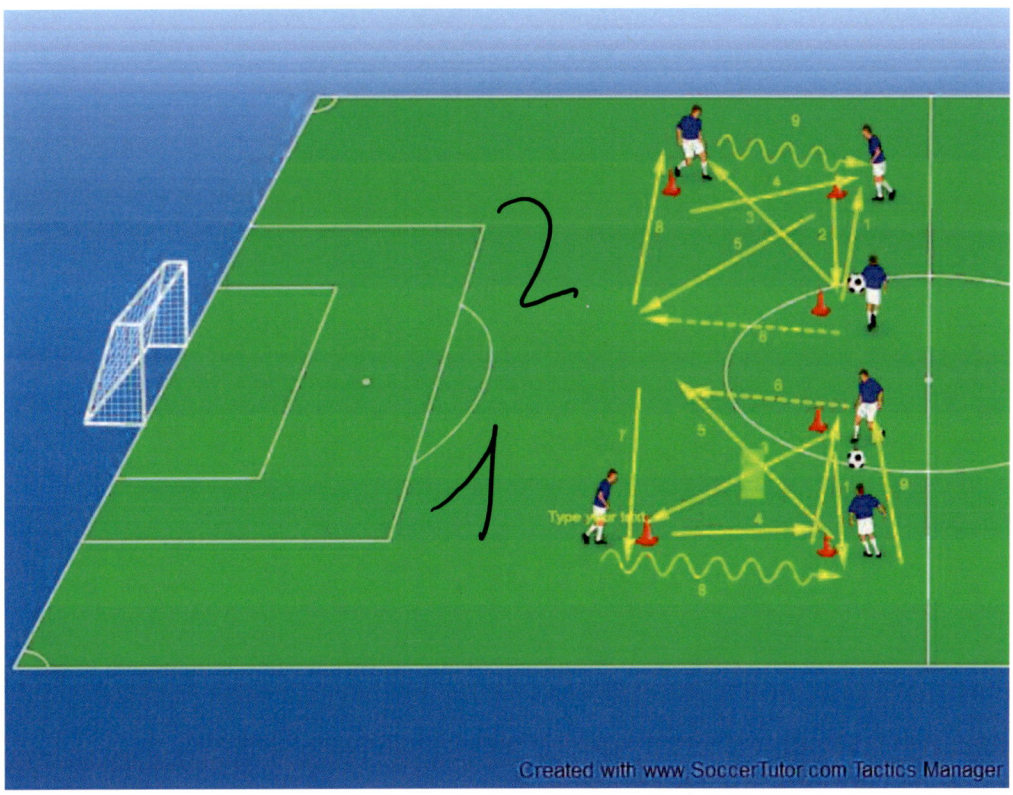

Fallow with the passes the numbers and the players move where the pass go. Group one move with the clock, group two move opposite way the clock

4. Passing Tiki-Taka then finishing 15 min

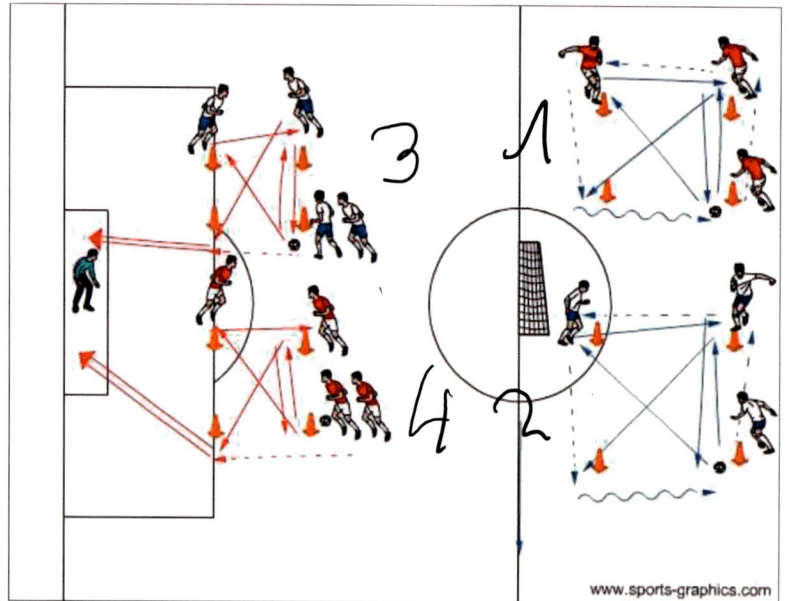

The number 1 and #2 exercise the players passing the ball Same way then the exercise before, the 3rd and 4th exercise going the same way but the last player does not Dribble back to the start position so just going and shooting finishing.

Tactical Station: 30 min. Topic is overlap and take over-defense and offense

1. Overlap in Group with passing movement trebling communication most nice teamwork. 15-20 min

Especially important the communication heads up players must understand each other movement have to be serious organized then the guys goanna have a fun.

2. Simple overlap passing end movement. 10 min

Player passing the ball to the center the center process to the other side to the center player then the possible running overlap receiving the ball from the second passes then play forward to the ball To the other side and he moved there too

3. Take over against defender and finishing .15 min.

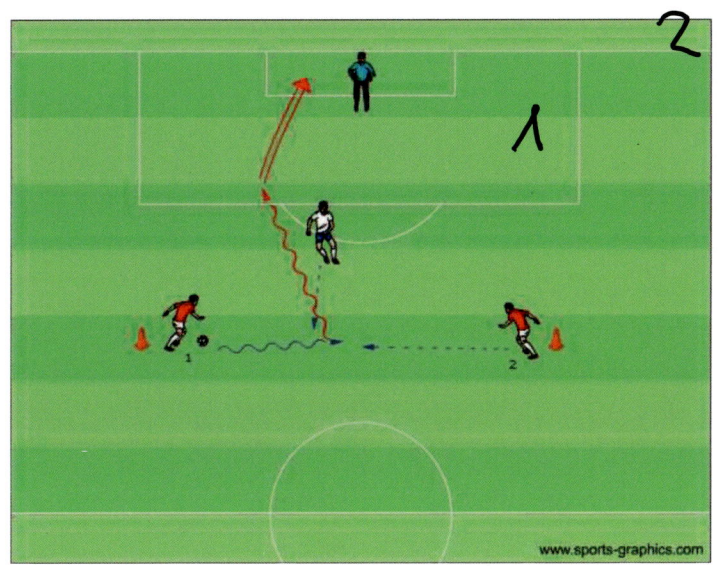

player number one triple with the ball into the field ,player 2 coming towards him the defender try to stop the Dribbler the Dribbler fake a movement then the number 2 taking the ball over Dribble to the goal and shoot ,

Dribble station: 30 minutes repeat all 9 fakes and practice it individual

Fake number one:

Dribbling with the outside foot, then stop the ball with the right foot jump over the ball forward, in the air you do a half turn left hand, then take the ball with the left outside foot, accelerate.

Do it both ways.

Fake number two:

Dribbling with the outside food ,then speed it up ,the next do a fake kick with the right foot, roll the ball back, between you do a half turn Coming up in the air ,and the rolling foot taking the ball and accelerate .Is very important to sell the fake Kick and you're doing everything with one foot.

Fake number three:

Dribbling with the outside food then, right footstep to the ball from the left site, then left foot go inside Caesar around the ball, then turn and take the ball with the right inside foot then accelerate.

-Fake #4.

-Players Dribbling with the ball with the outside foot start cutting the ball with outside foot turning away from the body 270 degrees then accelerate. When you are turning with the right outside foot after the 270 degrees, finishing to the left hand accelerate. particularly important between the turning is truly short and incredibly soft touches with outside food and very quick skipping happy feet. Did not turning foot following the turning food very quick my every step.

-Fake #5.

It's a simple fake Dribbling with outside foot right foot take a dummy step with the left foot away from the ball left shoulder go down then take the ball with the right outside foot to the right hand diagonal- accelerate.

Fake #6.

Trebling with the right foot outside foot fake step with the left foot away from the ball then the right foot outside foot go around the ball very quick then with the left Outside foot direction to the left hand take the ball diagonal and accelerate this is the Caesar.

fake #7.

Player dribbling with outside foot Then with the right outside foot do the Caesar- outside Caesar, the next with the left foot do a half outside scissor. then behind the left Hill with the right foot inside parts kicking the ball diagonal forward.

Enormously powerful fake if you do it right practice it enough that is going to work every time in the game.

Fake #8.

Dribbling with the outside foot, Next with the soil of your right foot roll the ball outside from your body then with the inside toes kick it cross your body to the left side and take the bar with the left outside foot and the accelerate.

When you are rolling the ball with the right foot outside from your body make a little hop forward just make it easier to finish in the second part from the fake.

Fake number 9.

dribbling with speed always outside foot dribbling, Then jump front of the ball stop the ball with the outside foot make a half turn in the air then take the ball with the right outside foot the opposite direction where you were dribbling.

Important you jump and fly and turn half turn in the air this is not the card you going to stop the ball with your outside foot the other foot landed on the ground to.

Coach must make sure the kids learning everything correctly and fix every mistake right away!

4.00 pm Wednesday if need it- we can keep the shooting session give a little rest for the players.

Wednesday Evening Session.

6.45 -7.00 pm warm up

7.00-7.30 pm Shooting finishing

7.30-8.30pm evening small sided games; 4 v 4; 5 v 5; 6 v 6; 7 v 7.

The evening games must have a lot of fun and try everything what you did learn the morning and afternoon sessions.

evening is very good idea to keep the half team with you and with the other half team go to the another coach ,play against other opponent is good to communicate with the coaches to know, how strong they are players and you send to the more advanced players in one group and the less advanced players to On other group to play as guest .

Thursday Morning:

6.15-7.00 am

Soccer Aerobic if it is indoor, or fitness and technical sessions

Start the morning session:

8.45-9.00 Group warmups funny warmups make the kids ready for the focus on the sessions 9.00-11.30am start main training session

Technical Station: 30 Min.

1. Using our body to handle the ball.

Using the chest: 10 min

Controlling the ball with the chest is technically difficult and is used in play when there is enough room for secure control.

Anxiety is often associated with this technique and soccer players sometimes have problems with it at first that are fully unfounded. Whether male or female, introduce your players carefully to this technique. It is like with headers: if there is pain on the first attempts, a block can develop. Therefore, it is advisable to use lighter balls or even foam balls for the first attempts, you can then build it up.

When learning the technique, the players should approach the balls themselves by throwing them slightly in the air, then increase the height of throw and continue to ball thrown from various heights. In the next phase, the ball is hit as a pass and controlled with the chest after a jump. Combine the execution of the technique with taking possession of the ball for a shot on goal or for dribbling

BODY Position + BALL CONTROL:

- A. Rest your eyes on the ball
- B. Adopt the correct position towards the Ball, easy walking stance, knee bent slightly.
- C. Arms angled slightly, lifted somewhat to one side.
- D. Shoulders back -this increases the chest area.
- E. The chest is in a slight/medium angle under the ball
- F. If the ball bounces on the chest, then move back in a flexible manner and let the ball drop down.
- G. Now the ball is controlled on the pitch.

Using the head; 20 min

n soccer training headers are often neglected, though it is an important part of every soccer match. In both the defensive and the offensive position, the header is the only possibility to pass on high balls precisely. We know that many young talents were struggling with the header technique. This has not been changed over the years.

Header training shall avoid health damages. This means a range of appropriate balls, the creation of the basics of the header training. If there is any pain in the training, it will be difficult to get a certain enthusiasm for heading in the future. Headers are then performed hesitantly and fearfully.

There are different types of header techniques. With every technique the ball can be directed by body turn

The header from a standing position is technically the easiest type but provides you with the most important basics of all header types.
- Watch the trajectory (Arch) of the ball.
- Right position to the ball.
- Gain momentum by tightening the upper part of your body backwards.
- The eyes are open.
- Fix your neck.
- Press the chin on your chest.
- Jump ahead with your body. Hit the ball with the right timing, not too far in front or in the back of the upper part of the body.
- Hit the ball with the whole forehead.
- If you want to change the direction of the ball, change the upper part of the body in the respective direction before heading.

2. Header after jumping with both feet

This type is technically much more challenging than the header from a standing position. Especially the right timing is often a problem. It can be performed by using the following motion sequence:
- Watch the trajectory 9 Arch) of the ball.
- Right position to the ball.
- Jump dynamically.
- Gaining momentum for the jump is supported by using both arms.
- The jump goes upwards and not forward.

- The upper part of the body and the lower leg are tightened backwards (bow tension).
- The eyes are open.
- Fix your neck.
- Press the chin on your chest.
- Hit the ball on the highest point.
- Hit the ball with the whole forehead.
- If you want to change the direction of the ball, change the upper part of the body in the respective direction before heading. The turn can also be done whilst jumping, but also in the air

Heading game only with the head you can score you can pass the ball with the head.

3. Heading after jumping with one foot

The performance of a header after jumping using just one foot is always done out of running motion. It is difficult and requires a lot of drill to control your body in the air.

Furthermore, the right timing is not as easy to implement as by jumping with both feet. The header after jumping with just one foot can be performed much more dynamically. The player reaches a much higher jumping height and therefore gets much more pressure behind the ball.

- Watch the trajectory (Arch) of the ball.
- Run dynamically towards the ball.
- Jump with one foot.
- Support the jumping foot by slightly bending the playing foot.
- Support the jump by using both arms.
- Try to jump extremely high and not too far forward.
- Gain more momentum by tightening the upper part of your body backwards.
- The eyes are open.
- Fix your neck.

- Press the chin on your chest.
- Jump ahead with your body.
- Hit the ball on the highest point.
- Hit the ball with the whole forehead.
- If you want to change the direction of the ball, change the upper part of the body dynamically in the respective direction before heading. Support the direction change by a respective motion of your head.

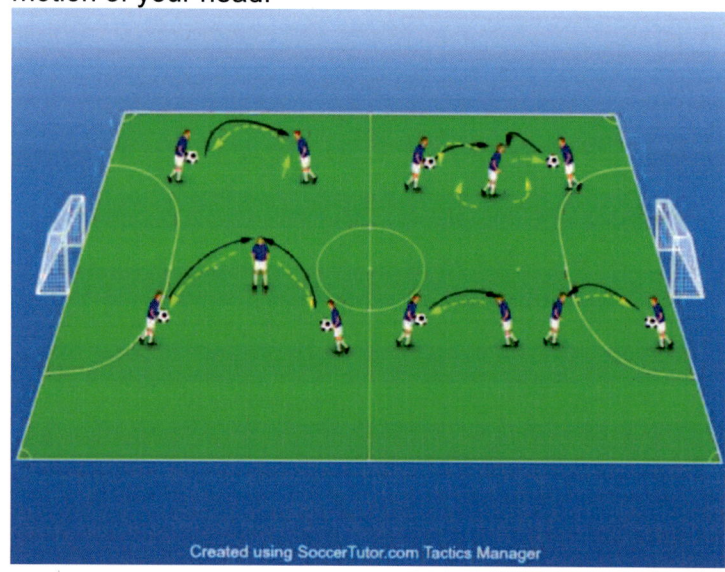

4. Diving Header

The diving header is a dramatic action in a soccer match and therefore extremely popular. After controlling the basics of the header technique, the execution is relatively easy. All you need is a little bit of courage to let yourself drop from large height. The diving header can be performed from a standing position and out of a running motion. The use of the diving header makes sense, if a match situation needs to be clarified (goal, heading the ball out of the danger zone). Attention: Injuries are possible if there are other opponent players around.

Watch the trajectory of the ball.
- Run dynamically towards the ball.
- Jump with both feet.
- Fix your neck.
- Stretch your neck upwards.
- Hit the ball with the whole forehead.
- Catch your body with your hands.
- If you want to change the direction of the ball, change the upper part of the body dynamically in the respective direction before heading. Support the direction change by a respective motion of your head. The result is some kind of "snake motion" in the air.

Dribbling Station: 30 min

Players Dribbling around outside food inside food how will it do in turns vitamin golf with the ball.

1. Dribbling-fakes-and shoot

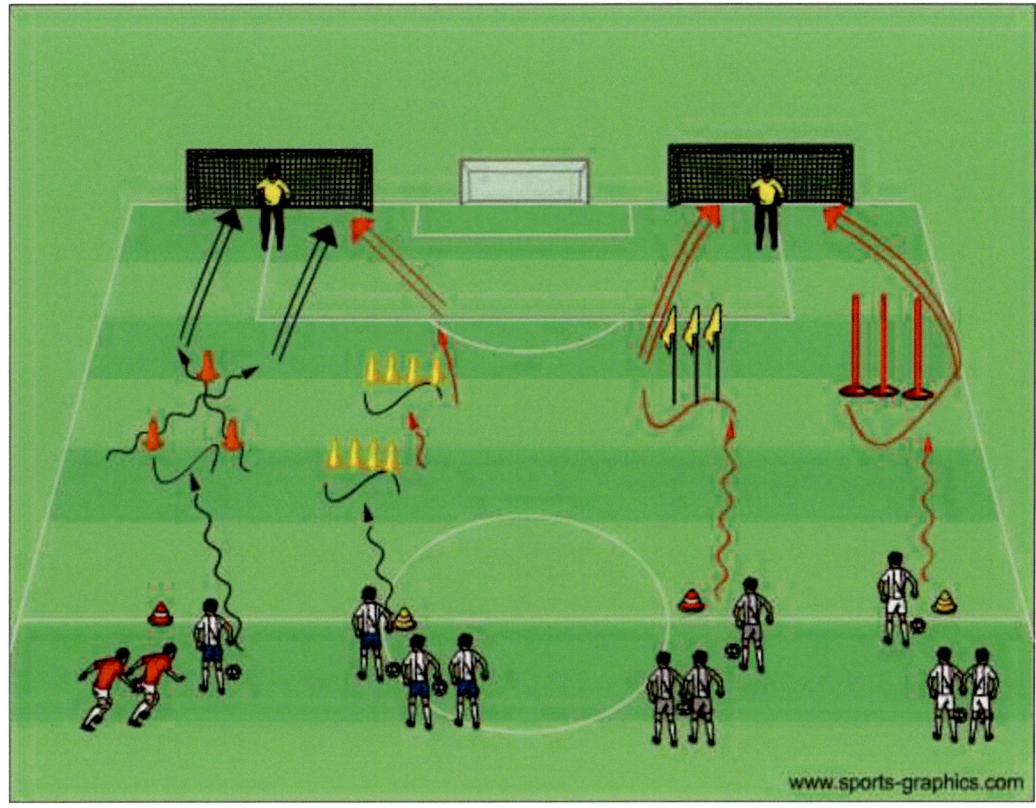

Players dribbling doing the fakes and shooting the players have to use all learned 9 fakes or they can use any other fakes but they have to use simple and **different position** different cones different fakes it's no defender there right now later we going to do the same with defenders .

Coaches must pay attention if kids have a different problem doing this exercise then the taking them separately and making the shooting quite simple and teaching the technique show displayers goodnight finishing and shooting.

Tactical Station; 30 Min; 3 v 3; 6 v3; 6 v 5 in defense and offense

1. 3 v 3 position

So, we have three zones: defensive zone, midfield (central zone), attack zone. these three zones are divided into a left, middle, and right playing field
Explain this classification to your team so that all players on the field know each other. A coach board is ideal for this purpose. 10 minutes and the matter are done.

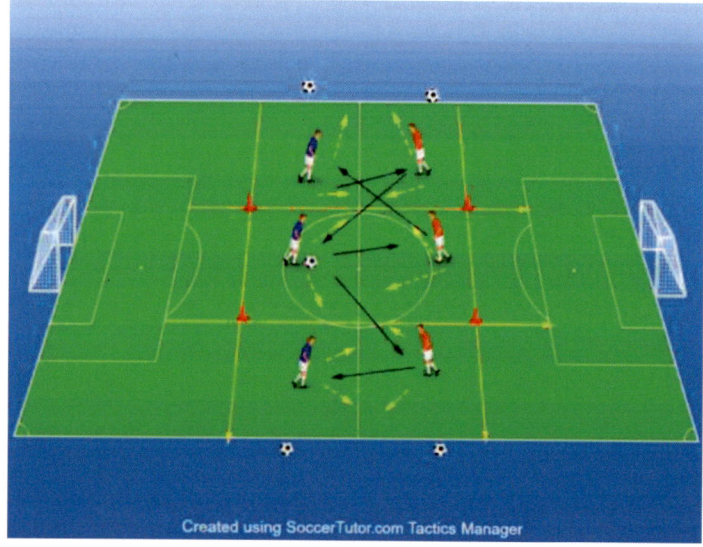

first

As the next explanation you can have balls pass through the zones

Second

The six players each occupy one field. When changing places, players always run into a field that is not occupied. Two teams can also perform these exercises simultaneously with one ball each.

Third:

shows the execution of the previous exercise form without a trainer. For this, three players fit a ball, the defense shifts accordingly. The defense is passive. Principle: The further away an attacker is from the ball, the less important it becomes. The orientation is always in the direction of the ball.

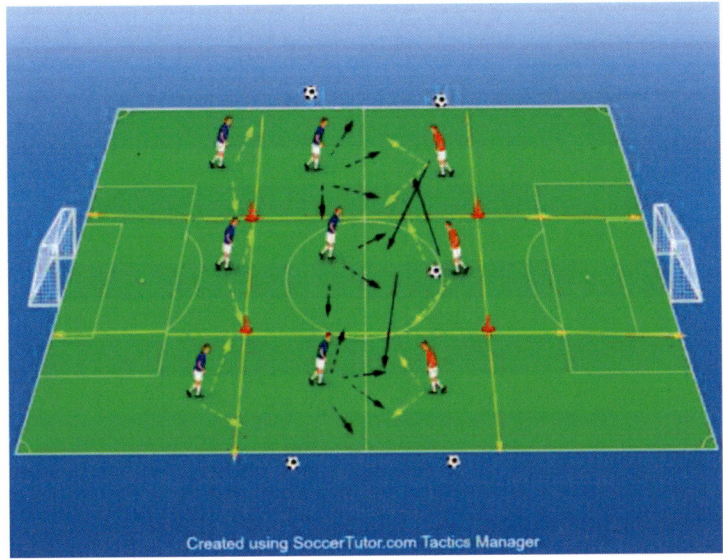

Fourth:

In the next step, three attackers attempt to enter the defense zones to score a goal. Make a game out of it. Always three attackers against six defenders. Very unfair, but great success experiences for the defensive. But there is also a huge advantage for the attackers: the defenders are not allowed to leave the fields assigned to them. Then increase the number of attackers to five small game snippets). Graphics too offensive? Sometimes I tend to exaggerate! Again, and again the move to the ball takes place. This exercise also becomes interesting when you remove the goal and the attackers try to get over the baseline with the ball.

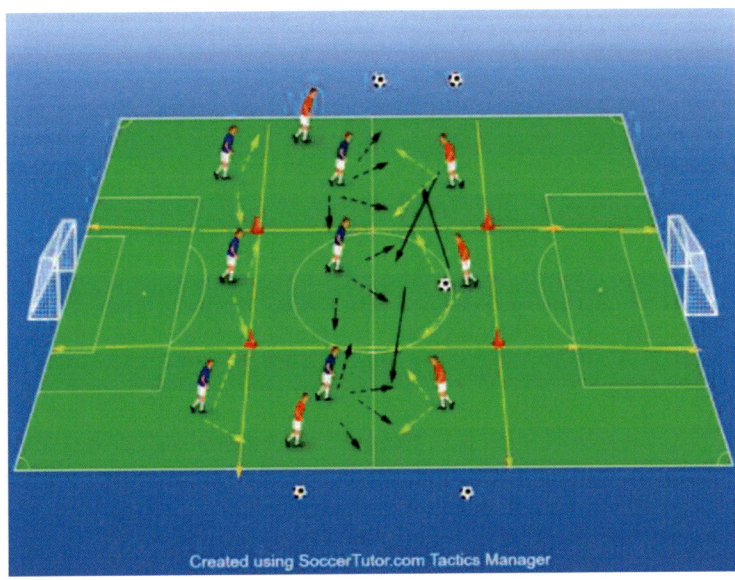

11.00 – 11.30 am shooting finishing

1. sshooting finishing with 3 targets

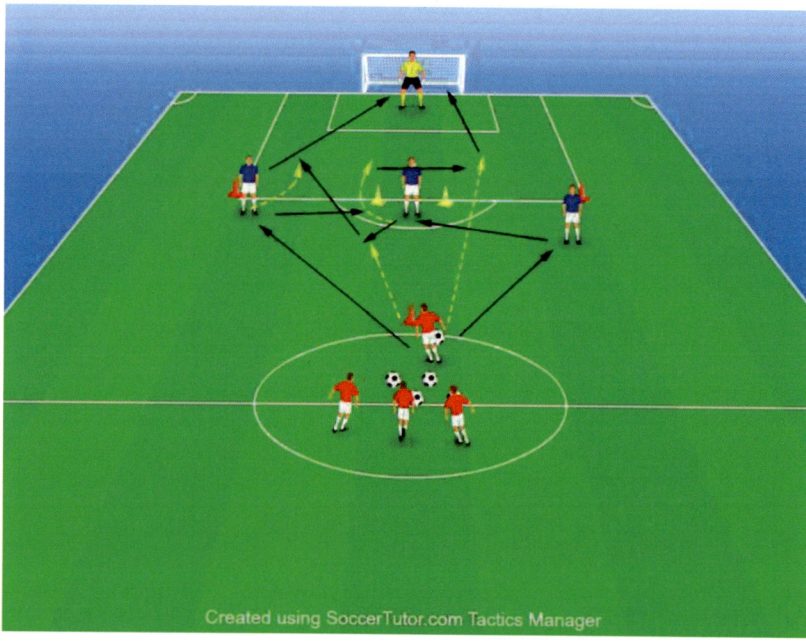

the red player passing the ball to the right or left outside player then run into the space-the outside player pass to the center and the center player turn and pass into the space to the red player who finishing

net pass to the left he pass to the center player pass a short ball to the red player who did pass to him, then the red player passes to the into the space to the left player who finishing

3. Pass combination from double direction

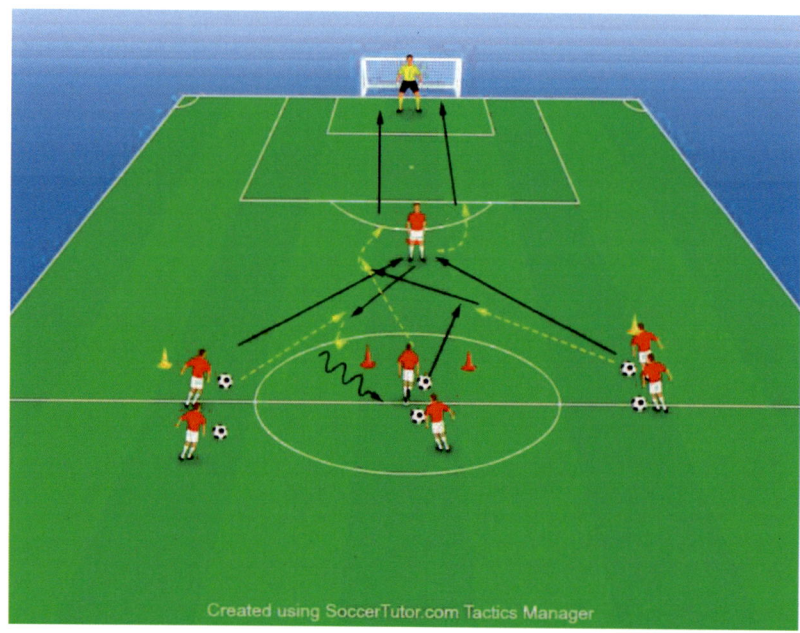

A pass combination with a total of 2 shots on goal in one action is something special. The central player in the process, the player is in the top. He is not only a ball distributor, but also a scorer.

Wir benötigen zum Start einen Spieler in der Spitze und drei weitere Gruppen, dort hat jeder Spieler einen Ball zur Verfügung. Der erste Pass erfolgt von der linken Übungsseite in die Spitze, Rückpass und dann bietet sich der Passgeber auf der rechten Übungsseite an. Genaues Zuspiel und dann folgt der Torschuss. Der letzte Passgeber übernimmt anschließend die Position in der Spitze. Jetzt ist der Startspieler in der zentralen Gruppe gefordert. Er passt in die Spitze, folgt seinem Pass, erhält den Rückpass und schießt aufs Tor. Damit ist die Aktion abgeschlossen und der Ablauf startet erneut.

11.30; Lunch

Thursday afternoon session.

1.45-2.00 pm Group volume up for the volume up make the kids ready for the main session

2.00-4.30pm Start the main training session

Technical Station: 30 min

Players start warming up with the ball two players one ball passing receiving turning double passes 5 minutes.

1. Tiki-Taka passing – players follow the are passes 15 min

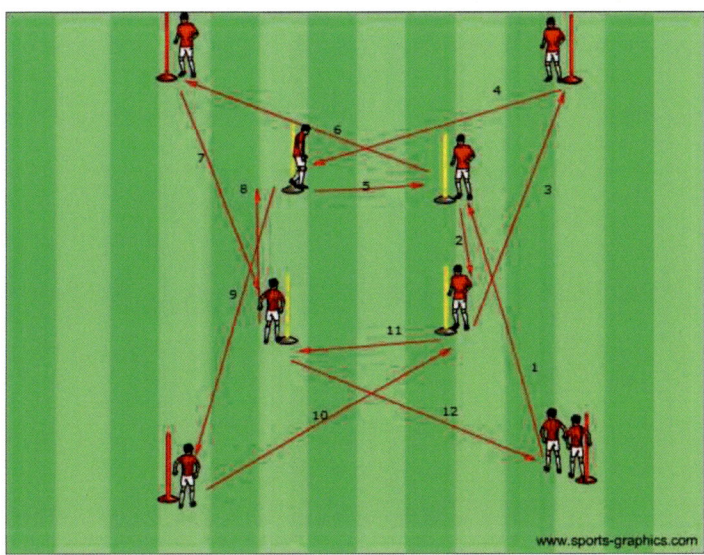

Set up the exercise with eight flags proximately 10 to 15 yards from each other every flags going one player except the stock position is a group

Players passing the ball and after the bus following exactly the position where they did pass the ball you can see the numbers that direction they have to follow important if the players can use one touch -first time passing - high level technique. First the players cannot pass the ball first time then let them receive the ball and often the receiving one or two touches pass the ball.

2.Double pass which small goal target. 15 min

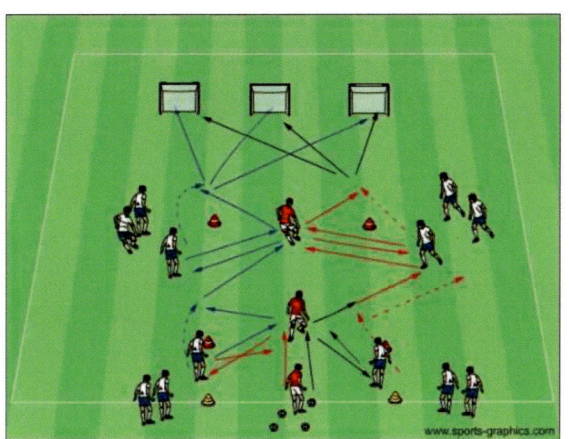

. This exercise requires a starter, two center players, and four groups. The groups are located to the left and right of the starter and on both sides of the practice field at the level of the second central player. The starter fits the first player in the center who moves to a practice side. The pass receiver plays the ball to the started player of this field side. This immediately fits back, bypasses the hat, and then receives the return pass. He controls the ball and fits the back-center player, who fits the next player started from the side. Then again double pass around the hat with final shot on goal. The two lateral players exchange the groups, the center players

Tactical Station. 30 min – 4 v 2; 4 v 3.

1. First introduce The Ford versus 2 diamond position explain the penetration process and hold the defense can protect themselves against the penetration buses.

Very important two defender have to run pressure the other have to cover don't open the split too much becausr the troopers penetration posts is the killer bus for defenders.in offense the four players have to move communicate quick passes and force with the position change and the passing speed make a mistake from the defenders and open the split bus and the penetration pass. The offensive group with the movement can create the diamond form.

2.For Mrs 3 small games the offensive players must create penetration passing against the three defenders. Here we ought to goal and goalkeepers.

You need to split your players into two attacking teams of four players, three defenders and two goalkeepers. The three defenders stand in the center and defend both goals in turn. The attackers stand one team at each end. The game starts with the goalkeeper opposite one of the teams passing the length of the pitch to the attackers who then go 4v3 against the defenders. If the defenders win the ball, they can attack the goal opposite but when the ball goes dead an attack is started at the other end with the second goalkeeper passing long. Switch the defenders every three attacks

Game style

Teams linking up and reacting to the 4v3 overload. Passing, receiving, vision and shooting are all relevant

1. The game starts with one goalkeeper passing the length of the pitch to the attackers opposite, or the own GK pass the ball to the center player.

2. The attacking team must now use the ball like they would in a phase of transition

3. Here the team moves the ball until space opens and the attackers can get behind the defense

4. The defender is caught between covering the wide player and watching the inside forward who could advance into the penalty area

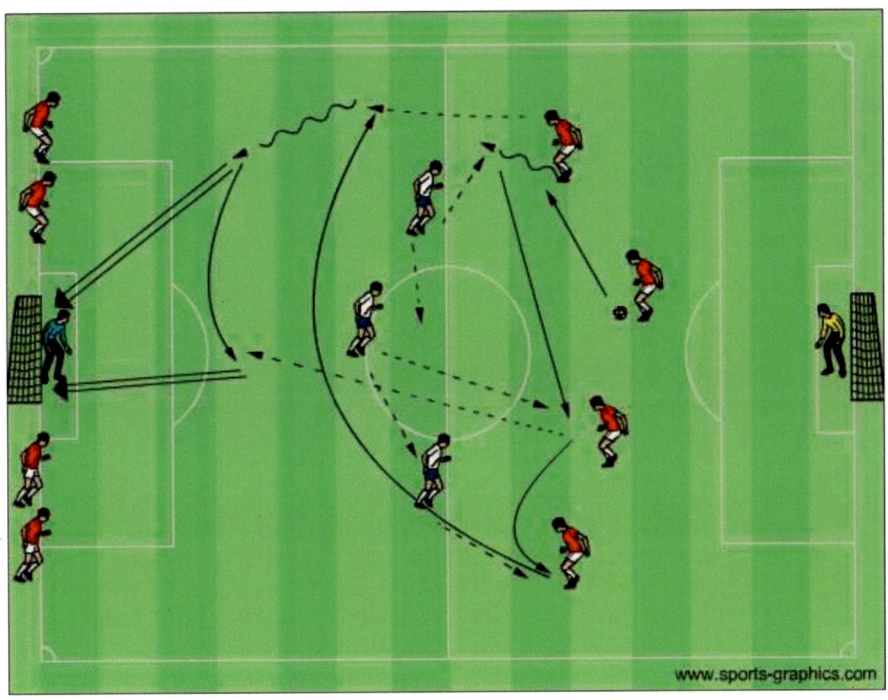

Important in offense quick position switch move the ball very quick deep and with, pushing the ball dribbling the ball very quick communication important forced the defense line opened the split to the true plus penetration plus move the difference one side then you can switch position like in a build and you behind the defense line then you have a chance to score .

Dribbling station; 30 minutes

Coaches demonstrate and teach the fake number 10 numbered 11 #12

Fake number 10.

dribbling with speed always outside foot dribbling, Then jump front of the ball stop the ball with the outside foot make a half turn in the air then take the ball with the with the right inside foot forward continuing the same direction. By switching direction important quick feet, short steps and accelerate.

Fake number 11

Dribble with the right outside food with speed then left foot step by the left side from the ball make a fake cake with the right foot and with the right inside food master ball back behind your left foot hills, Then with the left outside for accelerate.

Fake number 12

Dribbling with the outside food towards to the defender, Close to the defender proximately 1 one 1/2 yard open you heap the right side with the right foot rolled about cross over your body then the left foot make an inside Caesar (Inside Caesar is when the inside would go around the ball) After the Caesar take the ball diagonal with the left outside food and excellent it -past the defender.

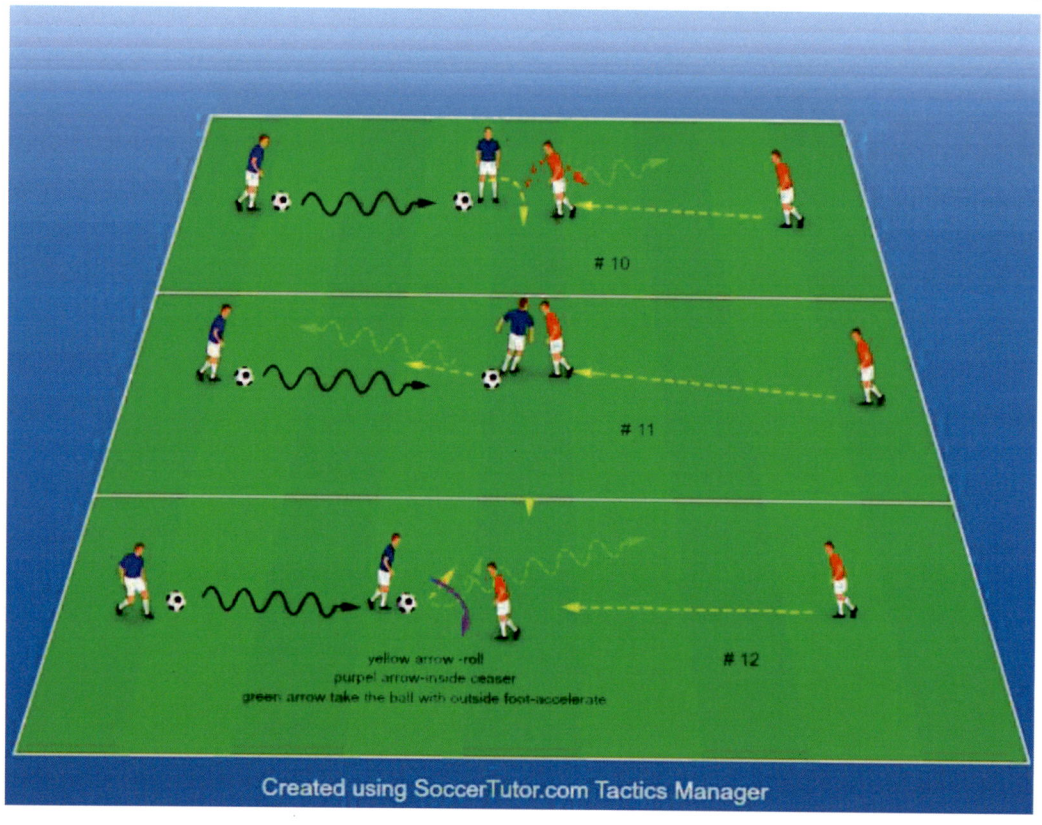

4,00-4,30 pm shooting -finishing

Combination shooting, rotation, drill

Setup

With two goals facing each other about 30 yards apart, place a goalkeeper in each goal. Set three flags at midfield on the left, center, and right sides of the field. On the left and right flags, place a cone 5 yards past the flags and set a player at each of these cones. Two players should start at the center flag, one player for each side of the drill. The remaining players should start along the end line with a ball each.

Instructions

Player 1 plays a ball into player 2. Player 2 checks to the ball and plays it back to player 1. Player 1 plays the ball into player 3. Player 3 lays off a ball to player 2. Player 2 has a timed run around the flag and shoots 1st time on goal. All players rotate forward one position (Player 1 becomes Player 2, Player 2 Becomes Player 3, Player 3 shags the ball).

Variations

Limit all passes and touches to ONE-TOUCH.

Coaching Points

- Good solid passes play in 1 touch if possible.
- Good timed movement and runs (do not get there too early).
- Player prepping the touch for the shooter should simply lay the ball off for a good 1 time shot.
- Good shooting form leaning forward through the ball and landing on the kicking foot.

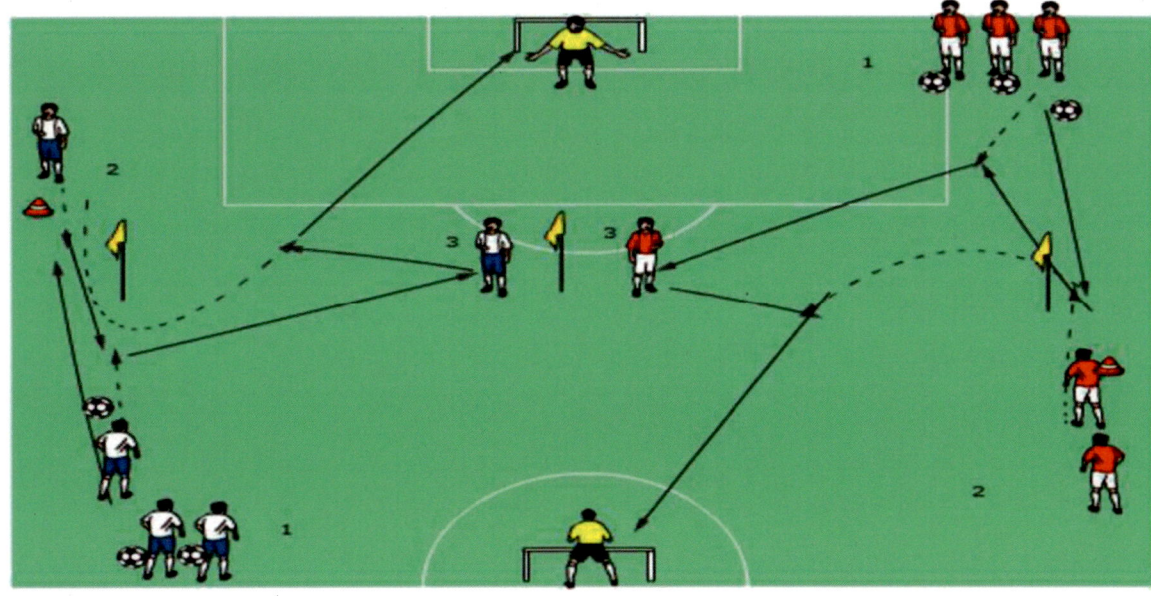

2. Shooting

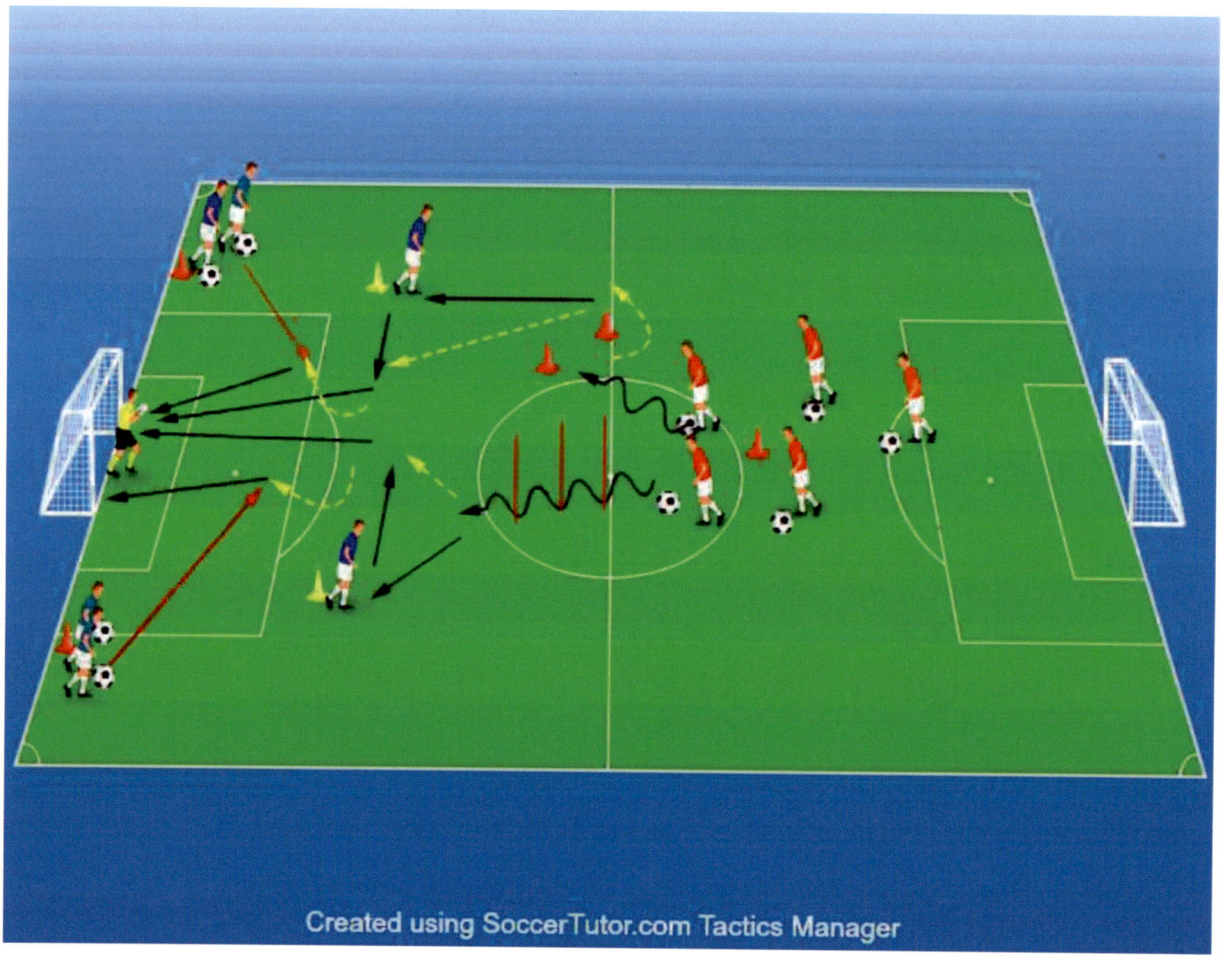

Setup; We have one goalkeeper, five groups from players, player dribbling through on the flags giving the pass the first con player in the left side he passing back to him to the center he is hooting then turning to the left side and from the goal line get the second pass and the player taking a second shut.

Coach organized which player to which group Going and taking positions.

4:30 PM finished afternoon sessions players going to dinner

Thursday evening session.

6.45 -7.00 pm warm up

7.00-7.30 pm Shooting finishing

7.30-8.30pm evening small sided games; 4 v 4; 5 v 5; 6 v 6; 7 v 7.

The evening games must have a lot of fun and try everything what you did learn the morning and afternoon sessions.

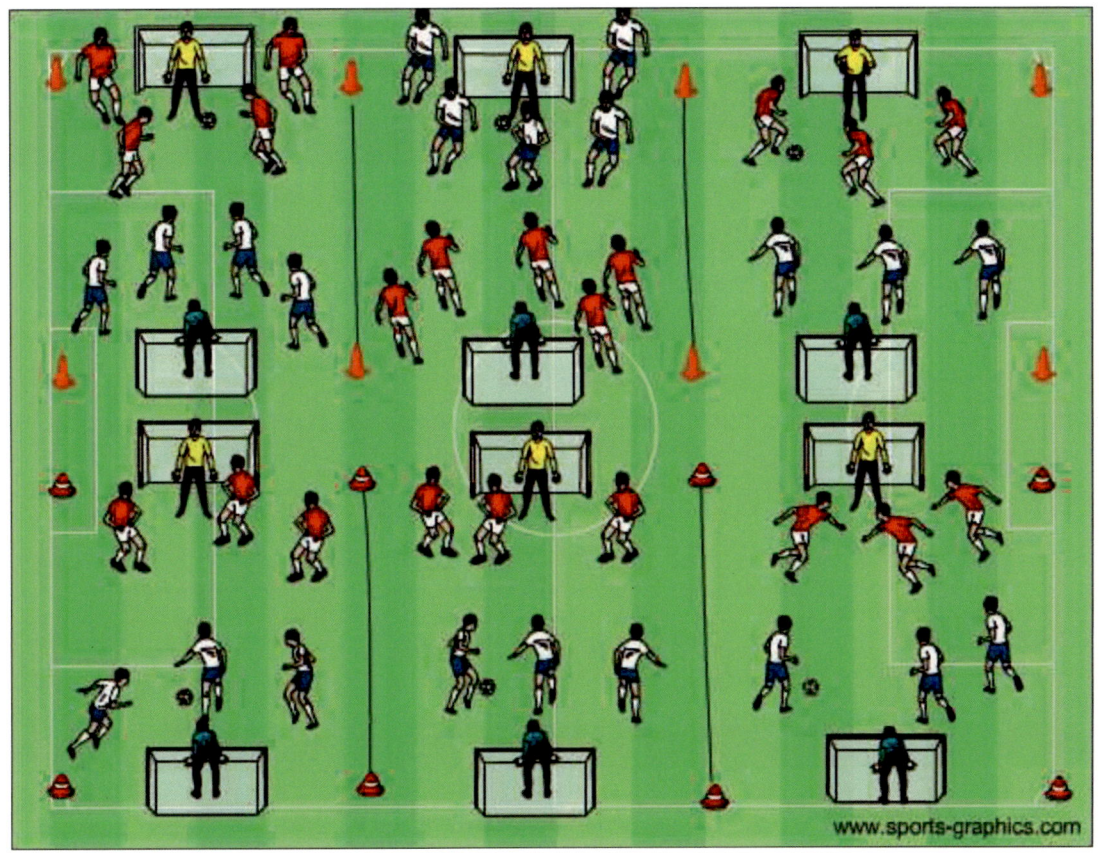

evening is very good idea to keep the half team with you and with the other half team go to the another coach ,play against other opponent is good to communicate with the coaches to know, how strong they are players and you send to the more advanced players in one group and the less advanced players to On other group to play as guest .

Friday morning.

6.15-7.00 am

Soccer Aerobic if it is indoor, or fitness and technical sessions

Start the morning session:

8.45-9.00 Group warmups funny warmups make the kids ready for the focus on the sessions 9.00-11.30am start main training session

Technical Station: 30 min. shooting technique, side volley, volley

- 1, Happy feet (Which is helping you make your body ready for shooting .and coming in the right shooting position to the ball.)
- Opposite footstep to the ball -no shooting foot- by the side from the ball away from the ball on your shoe size
- Opposite foot toes facing the target
- By the shooting foot the shoelace the Sheen and the knee facing the target facing the ball
- By the shooting foot ankle locked and the toes done
- Before you hit the ball, your hip must come up
- run to the ball and hit the ball important follow through the direction where you shoot
- After you hit the ball a little magic hope forward is optimal getting a good position after the shot
- Important head forward chest over the ball before the shot look up where you would like to hit the ball

    2. Shooting after bounce

Play a throwing the ball the other players running to the ball and shooting of the bounce, if possible first time.

3. shooting, cross, volley no where am I

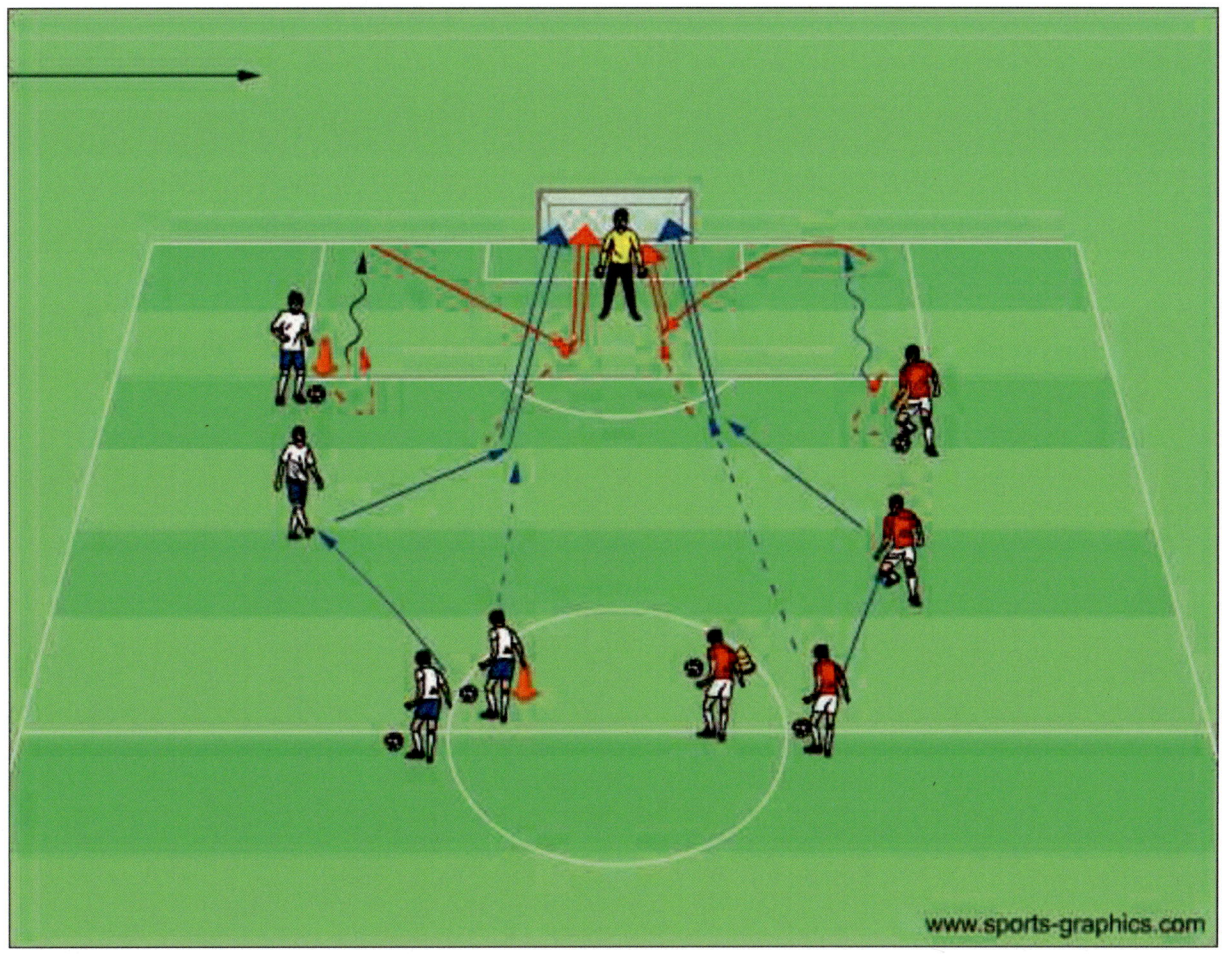

Player pass the ball to the side player he pass giving go in a center, player running to the ball shoot second side players turn around the corn dribbled onto the goal line and cross it in and the centered player shoot volley first time.

This is an extremely complicated exercise because the timing concentration communication all must work together. Because II outside player has a ball so the time is very short to the shooters to make themselves ready to finish correctly
This is excellent exercise under complicated circumstances to finish ,Pass , focus, receiving the ball develop the reaction speed.

Tactical station; 30 minutes – 6 v 2 [4 v 4; 5 v 5; 6 v 4; all with GK.

.

1, 15 min [6 v 2; 5 v 5

Important the six players very quick movement switching sides switching positions the ball must run after one or two touches we want to see very quick shots.

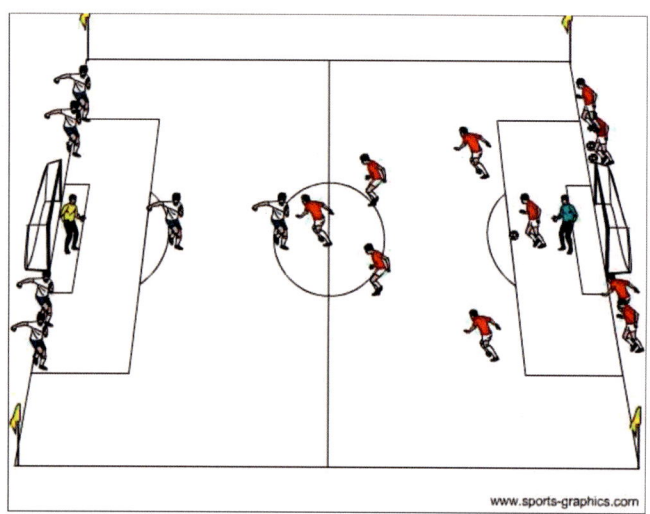

2.15 min 5 v 5; 6 v 4

put cones every goal post one yards from the goal post we creating small goals, then the left side score the teams first, then the right side goanna be the second goal to score, this meant the players first score to the left side then the next goal have to score on the right side every single time when they score is going to in to the goal is count one point if the player scored to the wrong number the wrong side goal then they have minus five point ,concentration focus communication very quick building- passing the ball back passing the ball deep crossing the ball , they can score only when every player is over the half line .

Dribbling Station: 30 min Learning the fakes number 13 #14 and #15

fake number 13.

Dribble with the outside foot very quick very fast speed toward to the defender and you arrive close to the defender you do an insight Caesar with the right foot then with the same foot outside parts from the foot take the ball diagonal forward accelerate pass the defender.

Fake #14

Dribble with high speed with the outside foot toward to the defender Close to the defender you doing a fake Kick with a Dribbling foot then with the same foot you Pull the ball back open you hip and with the inside food ,passed the ball by the defender diagonal forward then accelerate .

Fake #15

Dribbling with high speed toward to the defender when you close to the defender jump over the ball, turn In the air 180 degrees you backed to the defender when you laundered with the right foot roll The ball diagonal forward pass the defender then accelerate.

11.00 am shooting – finishing 30 min

1. shooting finishing with 3 passes and give and go

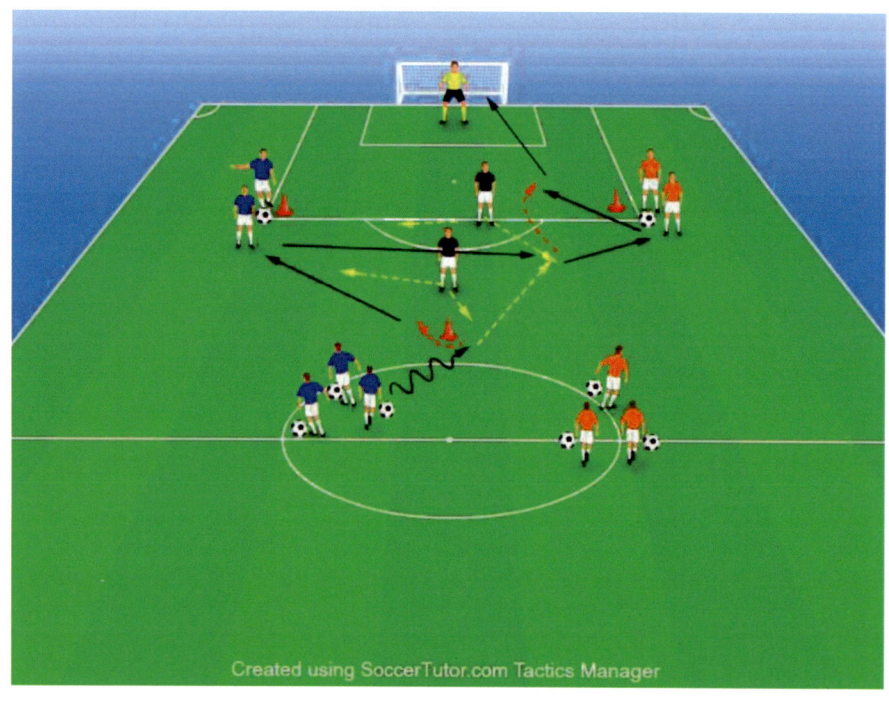

Blue players start to Dribble to the con, then fake the first defender out pass to the left side player, then right side run into the center the pass come back From the Left site. then the second defender giving the pressure, he played the ball to the right side to the red player read player pass behind the defender into the space, he ran to the ball and shoot.

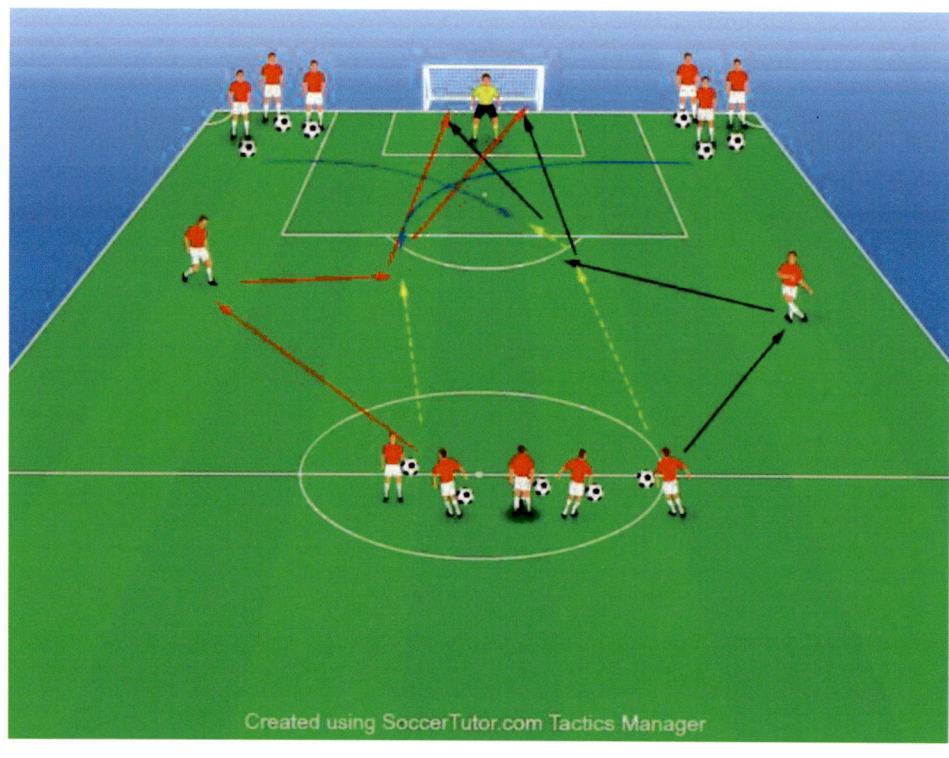

3. Post outside around forward then should and we take from the other side on the cross and finish possible first touch if not receive it control it and finish

11.30 Lunch

Friday Afternoon Session.

1.45-2.00 pm Group volume up for the volume up make the kids ready for the main session

2.00-4.30pm Start the main training session

Technical station.

1.Penetration Passing; Two players one ball 4 v 2 – 15 min

Bottoming pump for the next game the true process have to be very correct please table if you have to share the ball if you have to move without the ball give options to the player who has the ball becausr everybody who has the ball need help .

2diagonal pass-straigjht pass-overlap 15 min

One player give always straight pass the other player give diagonal pass who giving the straight past this overlap the player have to be very very quick very fast switching positions .

Dribbling station.

3 versus 3 small sided games in between practicing all fakes number one until #15

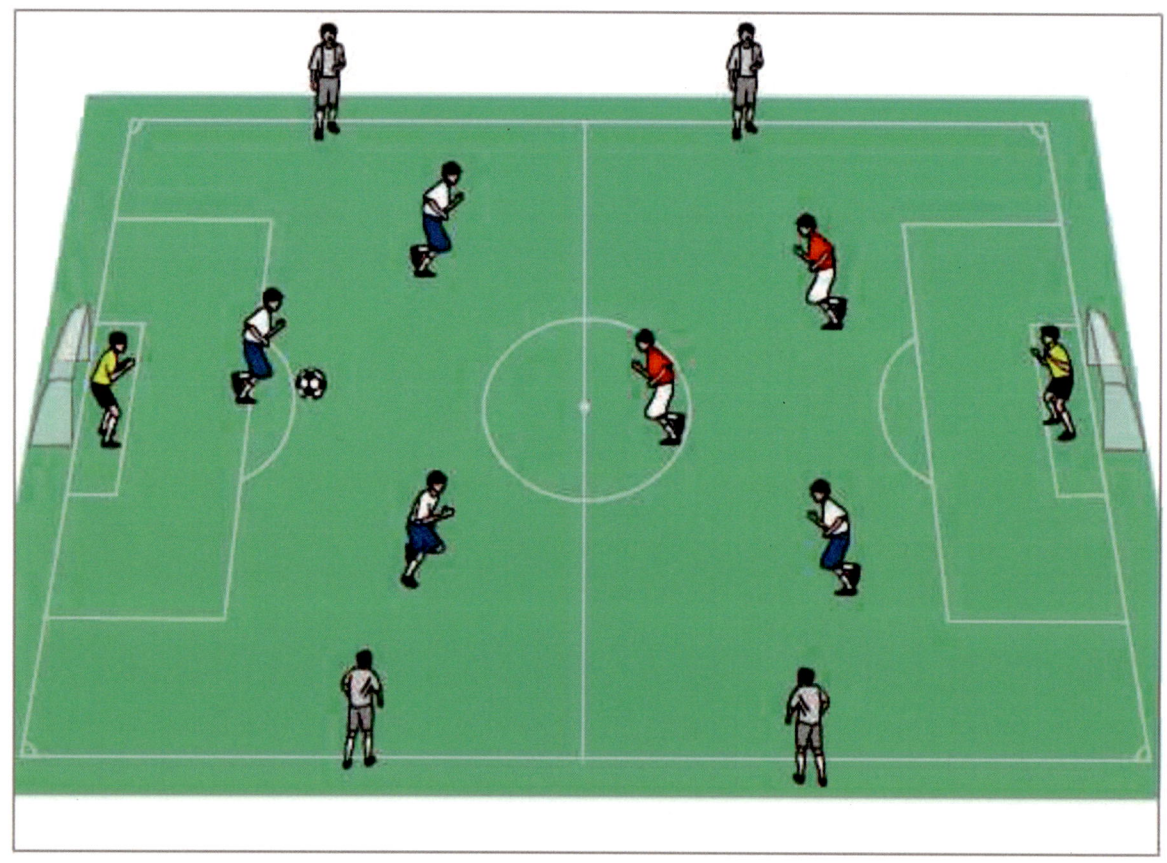

3 versus 3 game with four outside players they can help for both teams, they must pass the ball back to the team who passed the ball to them but if it is possible first touch. Goal is allowed only if you did one fake any fake is OK, but we would like to see fake what you learned in our camp.

Tactical station; 30 min – 5 v 5; 6 v 6; 7 v 7- take over-overlap-give and go.

the coaches would like to see small sided games building up attacking and defensive positions, using takeovers, overlaps and giving go's in position, we would like to see a lot of communications quick touches quick moves switching positions switching sites.

1. 6 v 6 9 4 v 4 plus 2 outside)

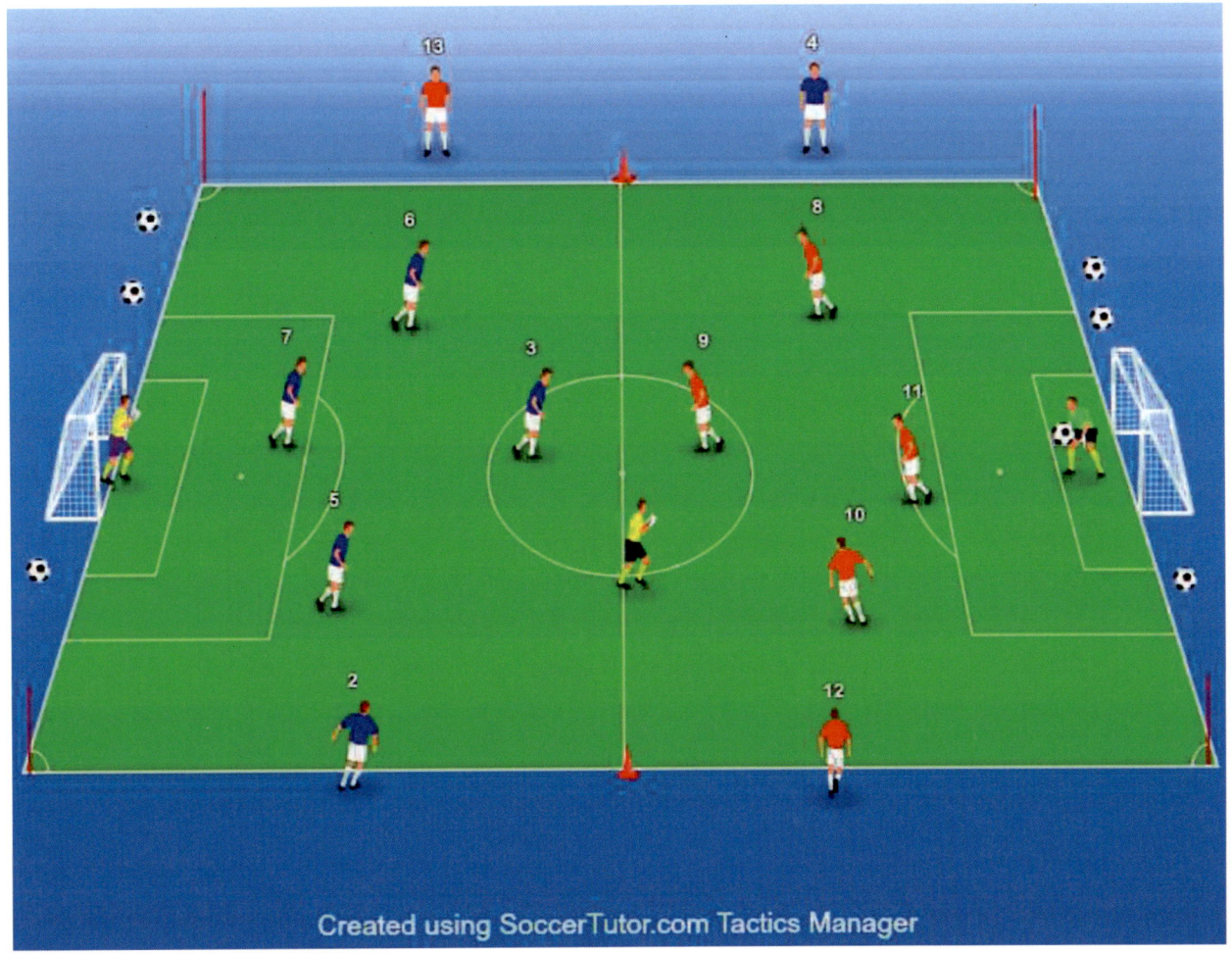

Photo with photo game these two outside players it's important to game going for goals against goalkeepers before you score you have to use both outside players .the outside biggest can move corner until the half line the ball in de zone is not out of position. They can triple and looking for a good partner open partner.

2.2nd variation the same field the same number by using the outside players the outside players who received the ball can triple in or possible into teammates then can come in you can score only if both outside players inside in a field with pass. That moment when the team lost the ball lost the position the two outside players must go off from the field right away.

Otherwise its regular game corner kick free kicks indirect free kick did not free kick

2.8 v 8

It was eight but we would like the team position is 3-3-2 plus goalkeeper.

Building up offense you seek outside players using penetration passes using long balls using short balls lot of communication and we would like to see a lot of improvisation from the players. the coach can stop the game and making explaining mistakes positions and correct and explain the right decision.

Free kicks corner kicks variations.

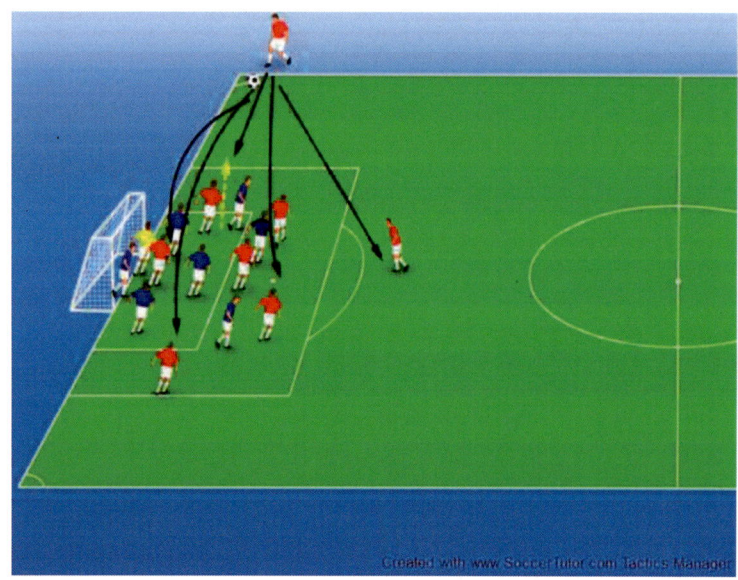 **cornel kicks**

Free kicks; # 1

One player standing in the middle close to the wall the shooter passed the ball outside by the wall into the space the player from the Center turn very quick on the wall get the ball and shoot or cross it in.

Free kick # 2

One player stand in front of the ball outside the shootist cheap to ball over the wall and outside players run to the ball and take a shot

Free kick # 3

Shooter ghostbuster ball to the left side to open player this player gross it over the wall into the space the right side and the shooter running to the ball and take a shot

Free kick # 4

One player standing front of the ball one 1/2 yards the shooter post about to the player front of the wall displayer opposing back from the lab side open player from the shooter and he'd take a shot

other Variation the shooters right away should over the wall tried to score

Shooting variations with lot of movement

4.00 pm shooting finishing; 30 min

We recommend the "Plantar Turn", but also many other turns from our "Tricks" section are suitable for this exercise. The players must focus on a lot of things again. The exact pass, the turn and then the ball should still be placed. Despite the difficulty, your players will enjoy the process. Not only the turn ensures a successful experience, but also the possible subsequent goal success ensures radiant faces. Description: After the exact pass, the pass receiver processes the ball immediately into the turn and then immediately to the shot on goal

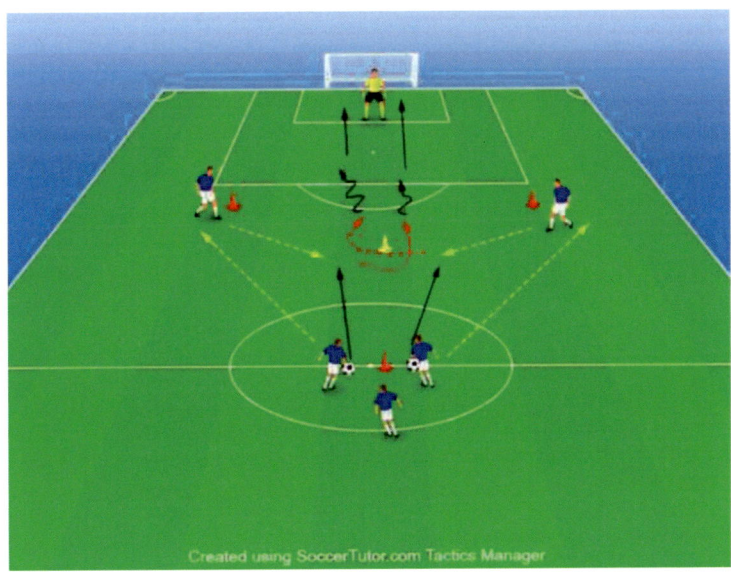

Variations with 5 passes or more.

Exactly five passes to the goal success, whereby the third, fourth and fifth passes can be beaten at different heights. As a result, the difficulty level varies in the process. Start with flat passes throughout the action, then the players quickly get used to the running and passing paths. Then increase the flow by installing half-height and high allusion. This makes it difficult to control the ball, to forward the ball and, of course, to shoot the goal. Description: We mark the starting position on the left side next to the gate. The first pass is a short pass, the mark is slightly offset to the starting mark. A third row is located far away centrally in front of the gate. This and the starting position must be filled at least twice.

The starter fits the player at the second position, who turns with ball around the mark and fits back to the first passer started. Now the first flat, half-height or high pass takes place on the third group. The first player there controls the ball or plays directly back to the player in the second position. He puts the ball back on the passer, who then shoots at the goal. After the action, players swap positions as seen in the animation.

4.30 Dinner

Friday evening session:

6.45 -7.00 pm warm up

7.00-7.30 pm Shooting finishing

7.30-8.30pm evening small sided games; 4 v 4; 5 v 5; 6 v 6; 7 v 7.

The evening games must have a lot of fun and try everything what you did learn the morning and afternoon sessions

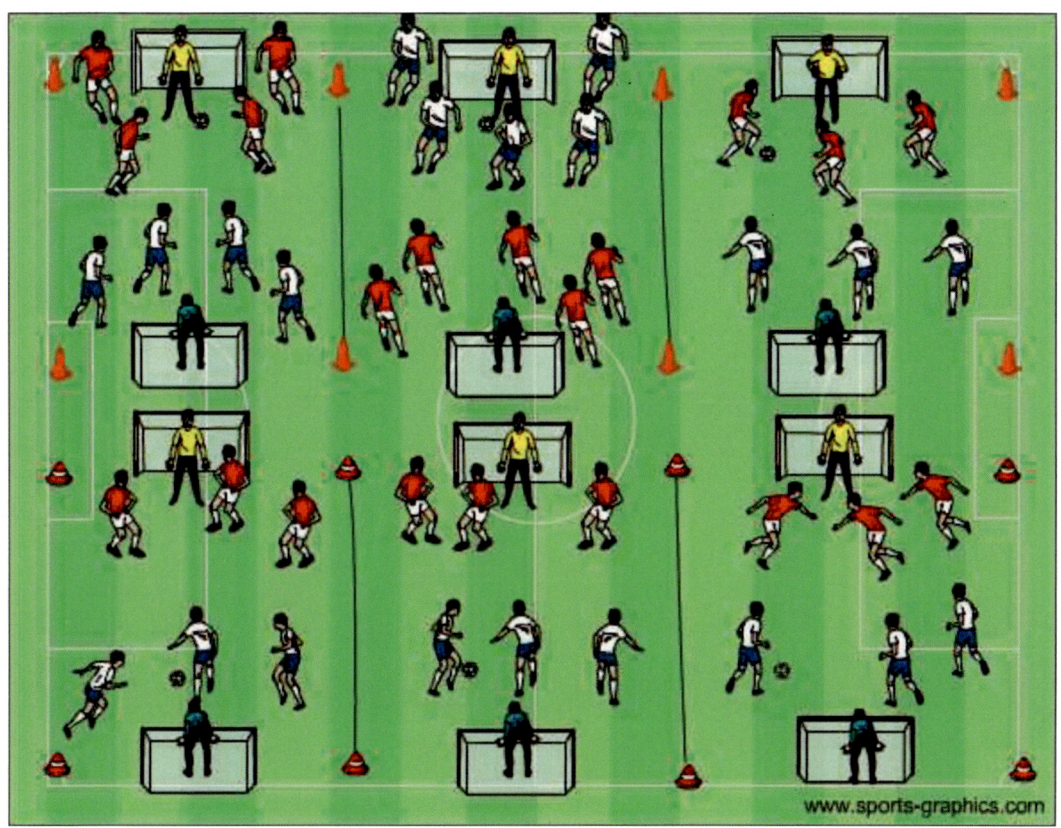

evening is very good idea to keep the half team with you and with the other half team go to the another coach ,play against other opponent is good to communicate with the coaches to know, how strong they are players and you send to the more advanced players in one group and the less advanced players to On other group to play as guest

Saturday Session.

8:45 am - Warm-ups

9:00-10:00 am Team competitions

10.00-10.30 am Final competitions

10:30 – 11.30 am games

12.00 noon Players Check-out

1.Team competitions

Teams going, they field with the evening coaches and doing the competition

1. Penalty Kicks
2. 18 yards shooting (ball must land behind the goal line in the air)
3. Heading
   Competitions 1-2-3 going for point system

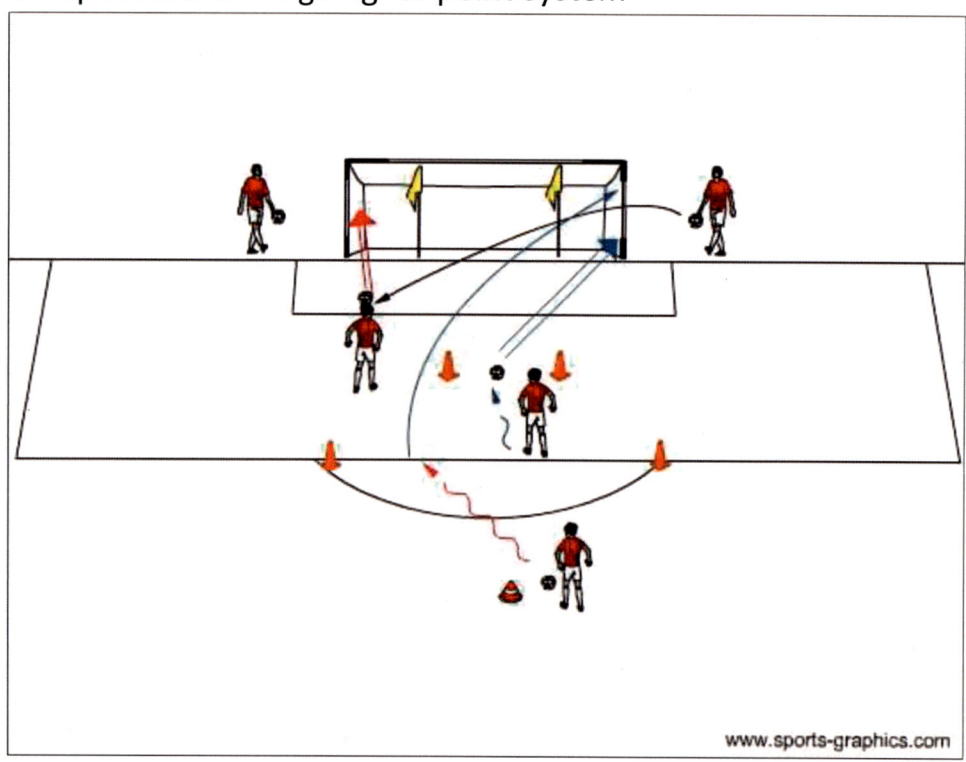

Competition 1-2-3 the ball must land behind the goal line.
In the side net is 3 point-between the flag and the post is 2 points
And in the center is 1 point

4. **King of the hill:**

Players dribbling with the ball individually and shield it because they must kick out somebody's ball. The players who is last standing in the field is the winner.
Players must move with the ball they cannot standing who does not move
Get warning second time is out from the competition.
You cannot leave your ball and kick somebody's ball out you must always in contact with your own ball.

5. **Juggling.**

Players starting in the same time and who is the last juggler is the winner. Players must keep touching the ball they cannot holding the ball on the foot or on the back. Continuing Juggling.
11.15 Price giving for the winners!!

11.30-12.00 noon Small sided games. Closing ceremony after the games

6 Coaches taking they own teams and starting very quick with the games Using small numbers (4 v 4; 5 v 5; 6 v 6) So the kids have a lot of touches and the parent's and family members can see what they kids did learned in the week.

12.oo Noon players checking out

POSITIONAL WEEK

- Positional skill, Technique and Tactic (players- stay all week with your position class) The coaches staying the whole week with the same group

Monday Morning session:

6.15-7.00 am

Soccer Aerobic if it is indoor, or fitness and technical sessions outdoor

Start the morning session:

8.45-9.00 Group warmups funny warmups make the kids ready for the focus on the sessions 9.00-11.30am start main training session

Defensive Station:

A, -. Body stance-Body position; 45 min, and 50 min number games with position.

1, Backpaddling; 30 yards, switch legs on the way back

2, Alternative legs; left leg stays at the front- then right leg stay on the front

3. Like the 1. But now with on acceleration

4. Backpuddle; inside and outside

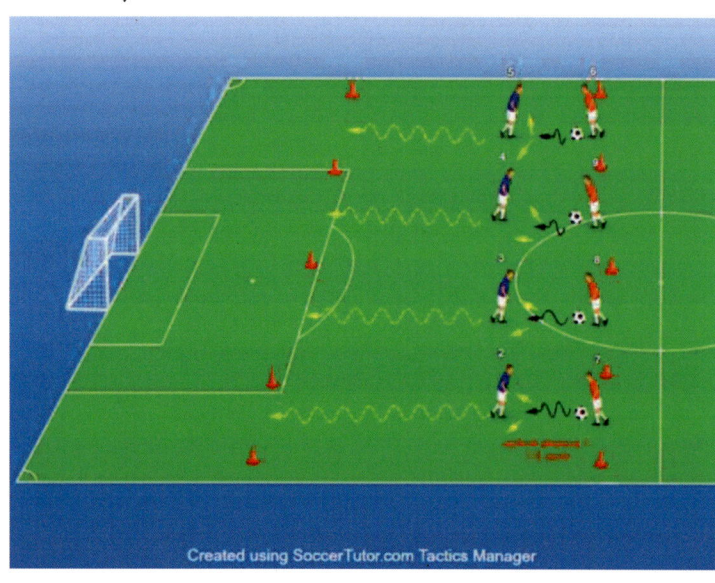

5. Black pudding: switch alternative legs- then accelerate

defender always stay with the ball, try to close the ball way going behind you, and eyes on the ball.

Forward move the ball side to side, let the Defender take the right position.

B., Number games with position-active and passive defense 1 v 1 50 min

one group playing with the GK and the keeper through the ball in the middle, coach call number – Number 1 then two players come in one of each team and play defense and offense. First must keep the exercise 1 position Without high defense, then going the game straight with full pressure. Coach timing the games and calling new numbers. Each team has the numbers for each player.

-the second field is the same way doing the defense offense but to score a small goal and shielding the ball before you score.

Important the coaches must correct the mistakes in position and give a great word if going only 1 v 1.

Play the game like 4-6 goals one game -then the losers must do some exercise and rematch the kids doing right and well. The most in these two games

11.00 am shooting finishing

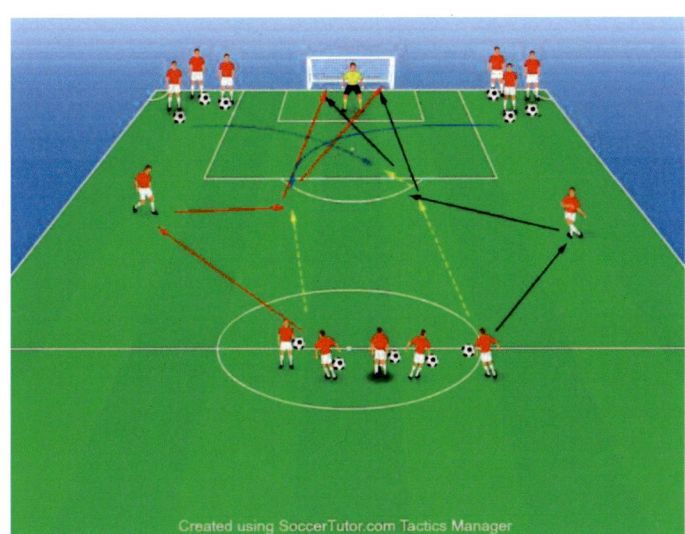

Middlefield Station:

1. **Take away; behind the defender, front of the defender and 2 Attackers and 2 defenders 35 min**

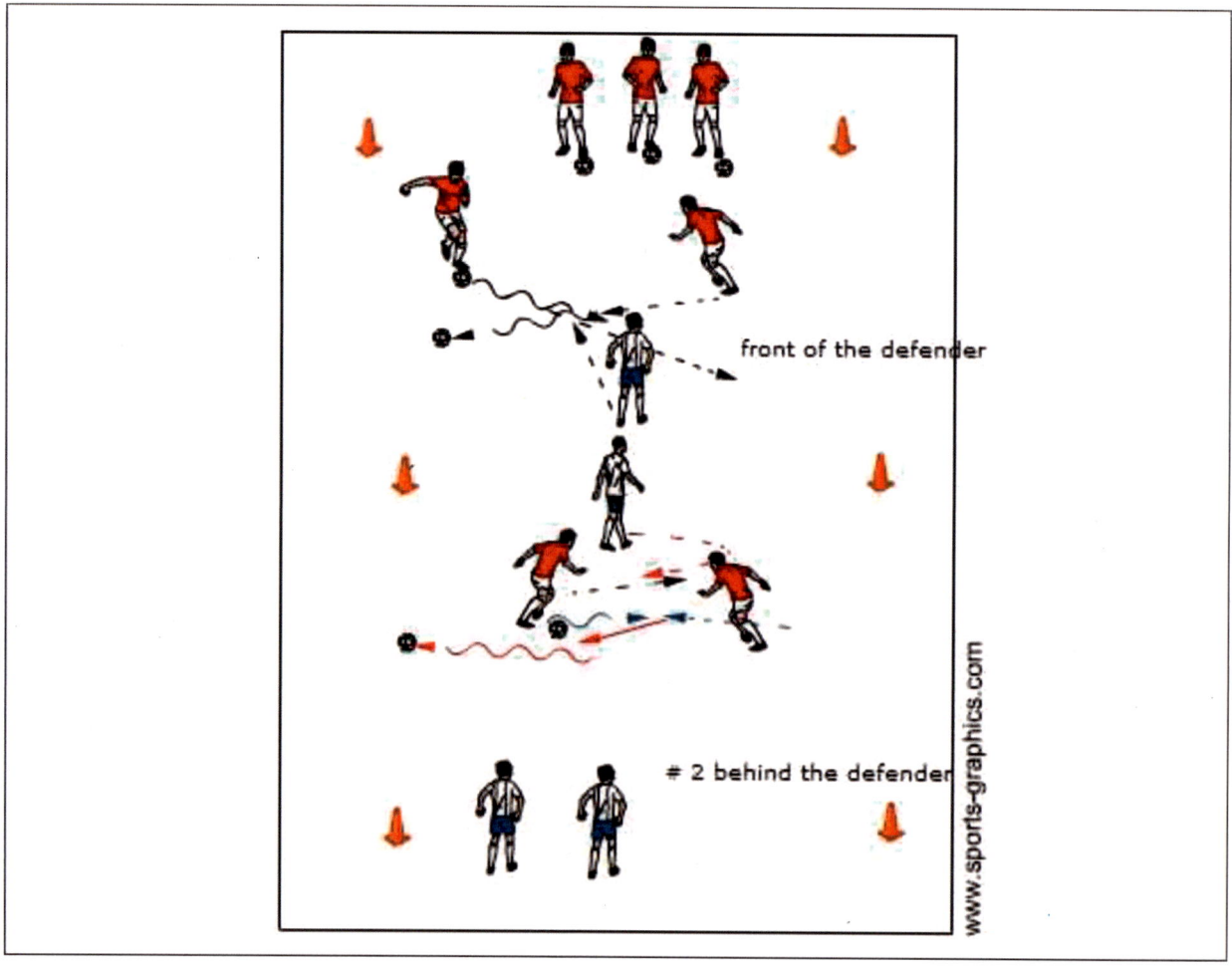

Front of the defender player dribble to the defender then partner coming and communicate then take the ball over -this player who did dribble just leave the ball, and take position between the ball and the defender, so the partner can take the ball and dribble away.

2 behind the defender- player start dribble with the ball and get the attention from the defender who turn and try to pressure and the ball, the partner run to the ball and call take over, then taking the ball and dribble away, the dribble player have to take position between the ball and the defender.

2. two attackers v 2 defender plus 1 service player 40 min

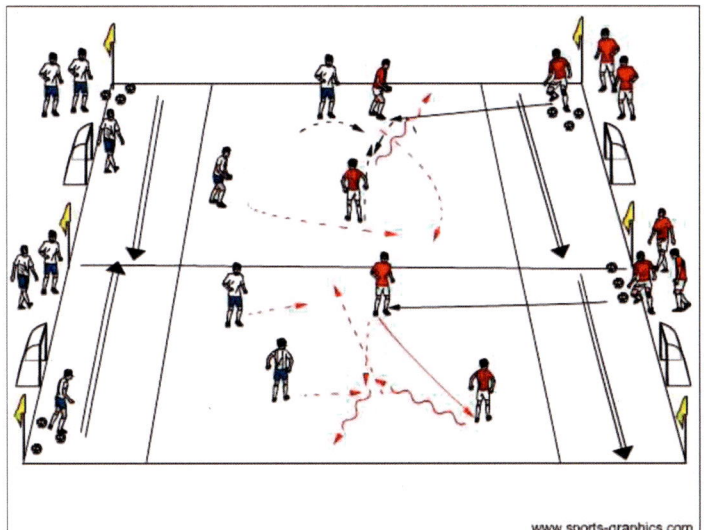

The game going 2 versus 2 with one extra service player important after The Pass receiving the ball and dribble toward to your partner get the defender on you and communicate with your partner and he going to take the ball over after start the game anytime you can use the service person in the back if you have problem to pass to you partner. After we did practice the takeover, we let the kids play 2 versus 2 plus service player and using the small sided goals side that goals to score.

3. Next game 3 v 3 positions game using small goals to finish. 40 min

Creating loud positions process communications takeovers let the kids play improvisation game, only stop the game if you can explain some great positions but there for the players, they can improvise and you want to see decisions making this is the key for that exercise. The service players going to stay and move on the sideline.

11.am shooting finishing

Offensive stations- Attackers 20 min

1. 5 versus 5 set up game players the ball in hand and can kick it in the air pass it with the foot who is receiving the ball they can't move the other players of course have to move the opponent can't give pressure who the saving the ball but can stay front of the player who has the ball in hand .we have goals we do not have goalkeepers .the kids can score after all day off their head this all two points .

2. **2 v 2, 3 v 3, 4 v 4 pressure, cover, shielding, position 30 min**

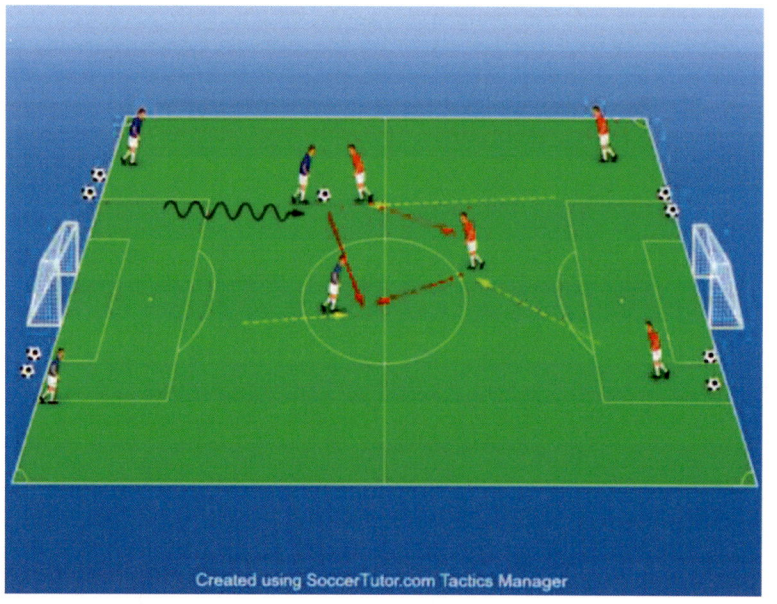

The games in the section below will help your players to improve on individual and team skills. They are simple to set up, guarantee more player participation, with more passes attempted, and more goals scored. Focus on the individual skills, pressure and cover.2 v 2 and 3 v 3 is the basic tactical exercise what the kids have to learn very well. focus on the trial angel

4 v 4 and 5 v 5 - 40 min.

Line challenge

This practice focuses on hitting wide areas with the use of group attacks and switching. We set up in a 15×35-yard area. Players must pass through the line to score, though in setting up that opportunity the idea is to pass side to side at speed to create that space for the killer through-ball. The target player must receive the ball on the other side of the line for a point to be awarded.

5 v 5 with 4 goals 40 min

1. Reds shift the ball from the right to the left
2. Forward motion from the attacking group is vital
3. Finally a diagonal forward run is made by the central blue
4. He receives the ball beyond the line to score a point

11.00 am shooting finishing
Monday Afternoon Sessions

1.45-2.00 pm Group volume up for the volume up make the kids ready for the main session

2.00-4.30pm Start the main training session

Defensive Station:

Defenders can reduce the threat on their goal by keeping the other team's forwards facing the opposite direction and moving them away from the penalty area. Use this session to enhance your defenders' skills at closing attackers and clearing the danger without necessarily making a tackle,

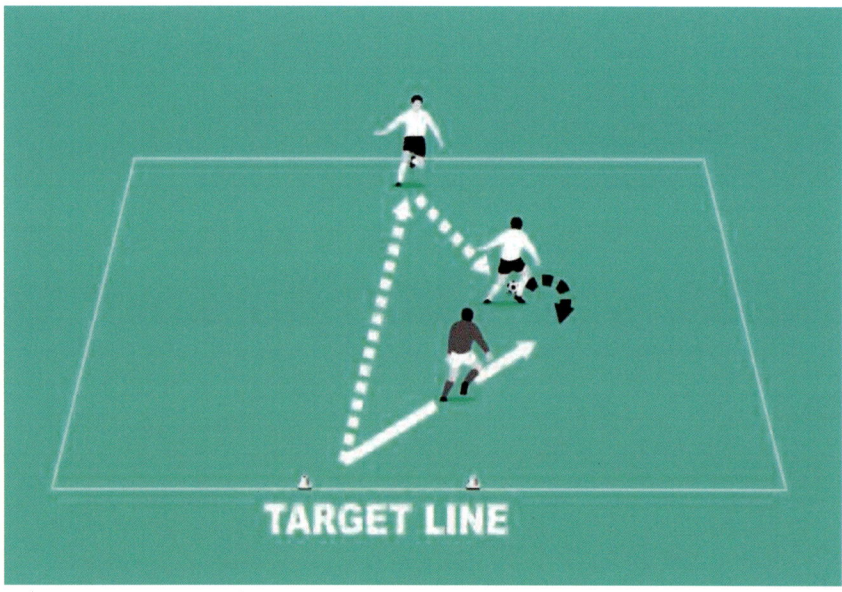

Development 30 min

When the server passes to the attacker, the defender must move to stop the attacker from turning

The most important from defender that the timing is correct, and they are not too aggressive, but the pressure must be hard. That simple exercise the coach must be incredibly careful with explaining are you timing which side you go to attack the forward. Different that have to learn read from the body position offensive player ready to turn you have to check you have to read and have to try to go challenge before the offensive player can beat you. The offensive player played the ball back to his partner that moment the defender must decide, I am talking the other player or be patient and wait what next passing let you make the right decision.

Defenders use techniques to close attackers in a 4v4 game 50 min

Play 4v4 plus two goalkeepers on a 35yards by 20 yards playing area. Set up two end zones, 20 yards from each goal line. The teams have an attacker and defender in each end zone. Ensure all players have a turn at being the defender

What to call out
- "Be patient – don't live in."
- "Watch the ball – not the fakes."
- "Win the ball if you see an opportunity."
- "Get tight, but not so you can be 'rolled'.

First contact 50 min

Not all players enjoy defending so it is essential practices are competitive, fun and give the player a reward for winning the ball (the chance to score a goal!) Encourage your defenders to make "First contact" in the bid to thwart an attack

- The practices in this session do not give players an option on whether to defend or not as the attackers are continuously working to retain the ball or score a goal. Putting your players in this environment will aid their desire to defend.
- The practices will enable you to see which players really need work on their defending skills.
- The players must see the reward of defending well and having the opportunity to attack. On winning possession, can the defender then dribble or pass forward to enable their team to become attackers?
- Then let them play four versus 2 see the defenders closing to the killer boss to the true pass and pressure and cover are especially important.

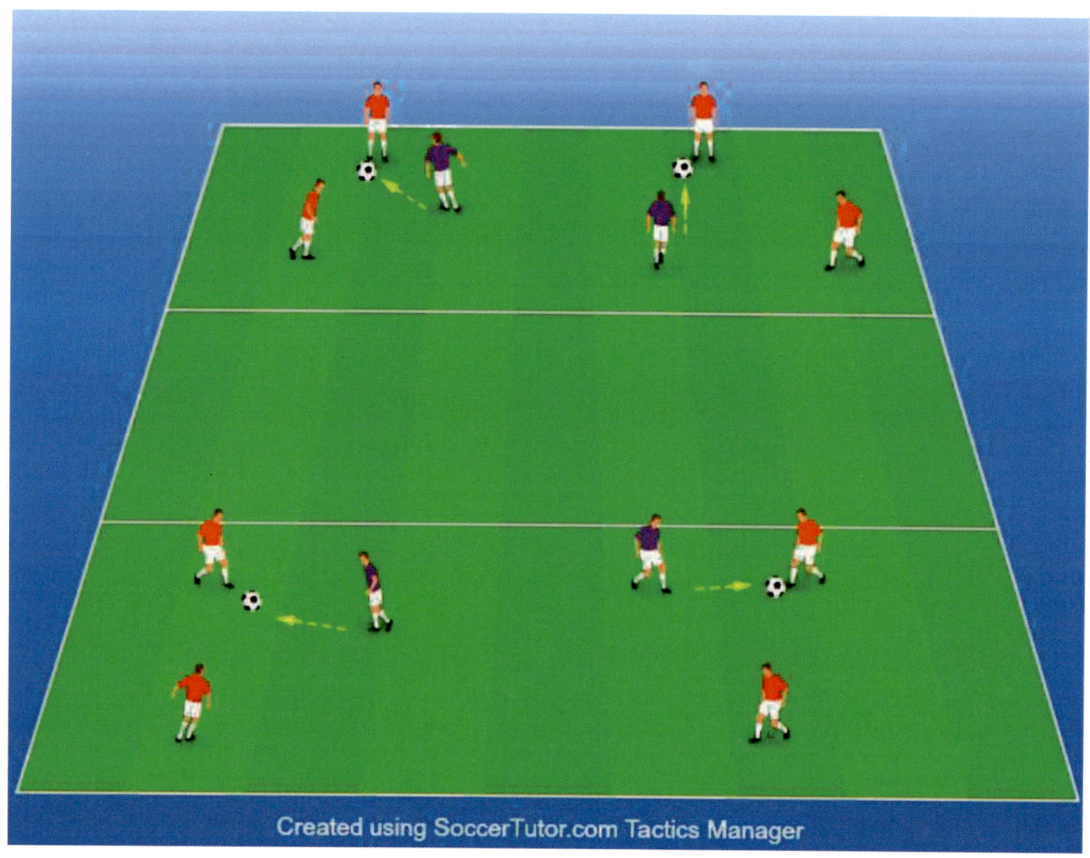

4.00 pm shooting finishing

Free exercises what the coaches thinking is good for the kids

Middlefield station.

It can be very frustrating when your midfield gets overrun by the opposition – winning the ball in these areas is key to making sure your team is not under siege from a strong opponent.

Coaching a midfield is about making sure each of your midfielders understands their role and responsibilities. With good coaching and organization your midfield should be able to support the defense and take the ball up the pitch, combining with the forwards to create and score goals. They need to have vision to see where to pass, and the skill and speed to execute their tactics

1.The midfield runner 20 min
Timing is critical

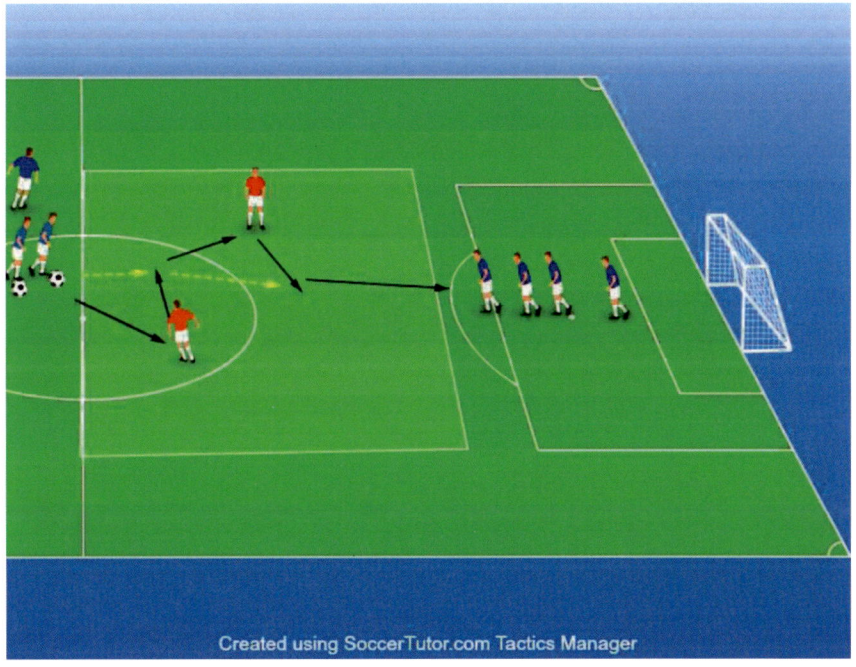

All good teams will have a top-quality, attacking midfielder. The role of this player is to get into advanced attacking positions to create and score goals. The skills required for this role include: Movement off the ball, stamina, passing, receiving, vision, shooting and combination play. Take variations maybe different angles the boss maybe more pressure can develop a little bit the timing better.

2, 3 v 3 and 4 v 4 Positioning communication and quickness 60 min

Defensively offensively the players must understand each other on the speed in the modern football is important. The players must pay deep white push the ball back then you need an open player, coach correcting and focus the positions miscommunications and first touch.

First teach the players explain offense defense and midfield zones left meter and right side. This is about creating space in midfield when build ups start from the center and the opponent center MF have possession and want to use it cleverly Create situations the players must use left right and middle area to force them two switching positions.

3.4 v 4 60 min

A key to a passing team is retaining possession in midfield. Use this session to show your players how to keep hold of the ball in the middle of the pitch. This game develops quick thinking midfielders like Players to think and so they can set up attacks by reacting quickly to moments of transition in a game, principally moving from defense to attack but first keep the ball in position.

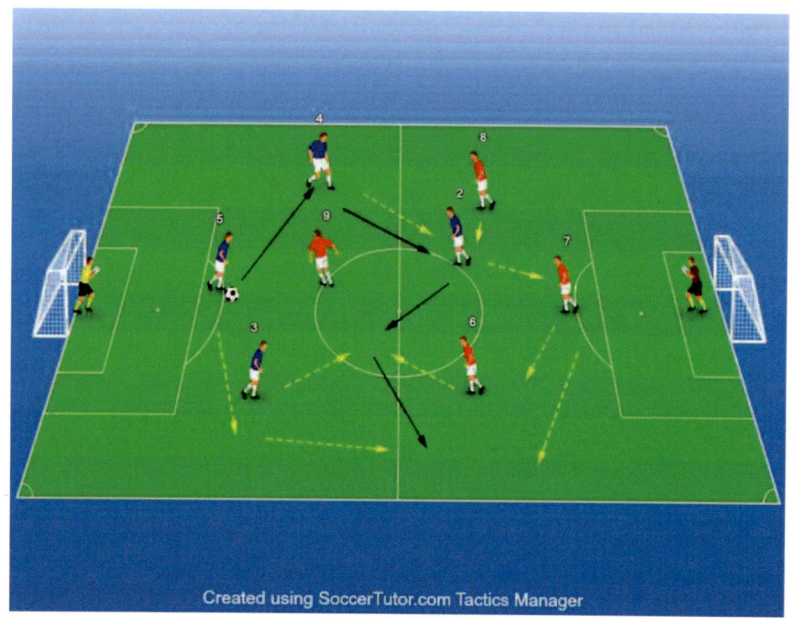

4.00 pm shooting finishing

Offensive station.

Use this session as a way of getting fast breaking teams to tear through a static defense and create lots of goalscoring chances. In this game players are working in groups to beat a defense in a transition type of situation which will happen often in matches

4 v 3 -4 v5 and variations 70 min

. The game starts with one goalkeeper passing the length of the pitch to the attackers opposite

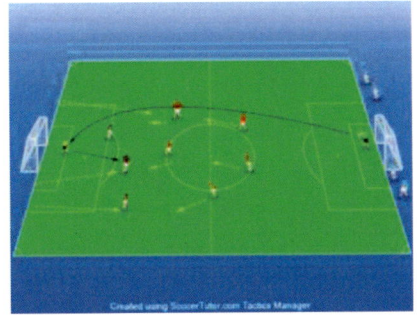

2. The attacking team must now use the ball like they would in a phase of transition

3. Here the team moves the ball until space opens and the attackers can get behind the defense

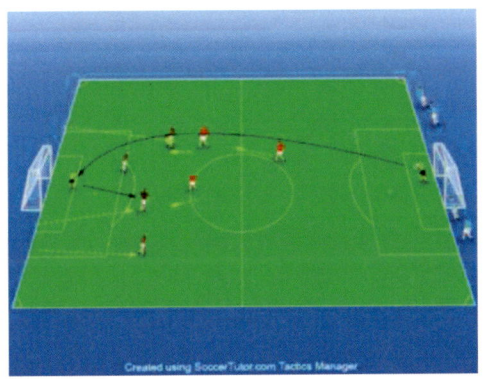

4. The defender is caught between covering the wide player and watching the inside forward who could advance into the penalty area

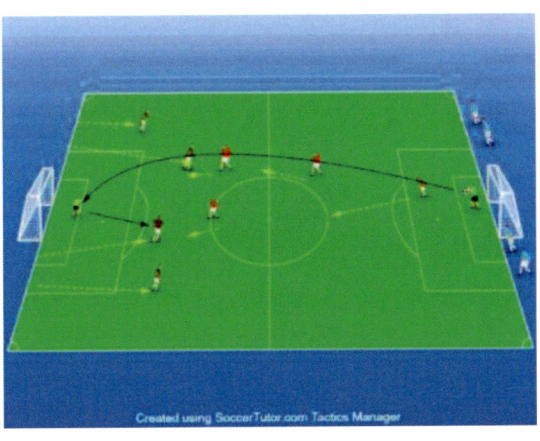

5. Once the ball goes dead the other goalkeeper passes long to the attacking team at the other end and play continues. Communicate your own weakness first touch must be very correct to play this game very quick and extremely fast and effective.

attack with take over and switch site   5 v 4 60 min

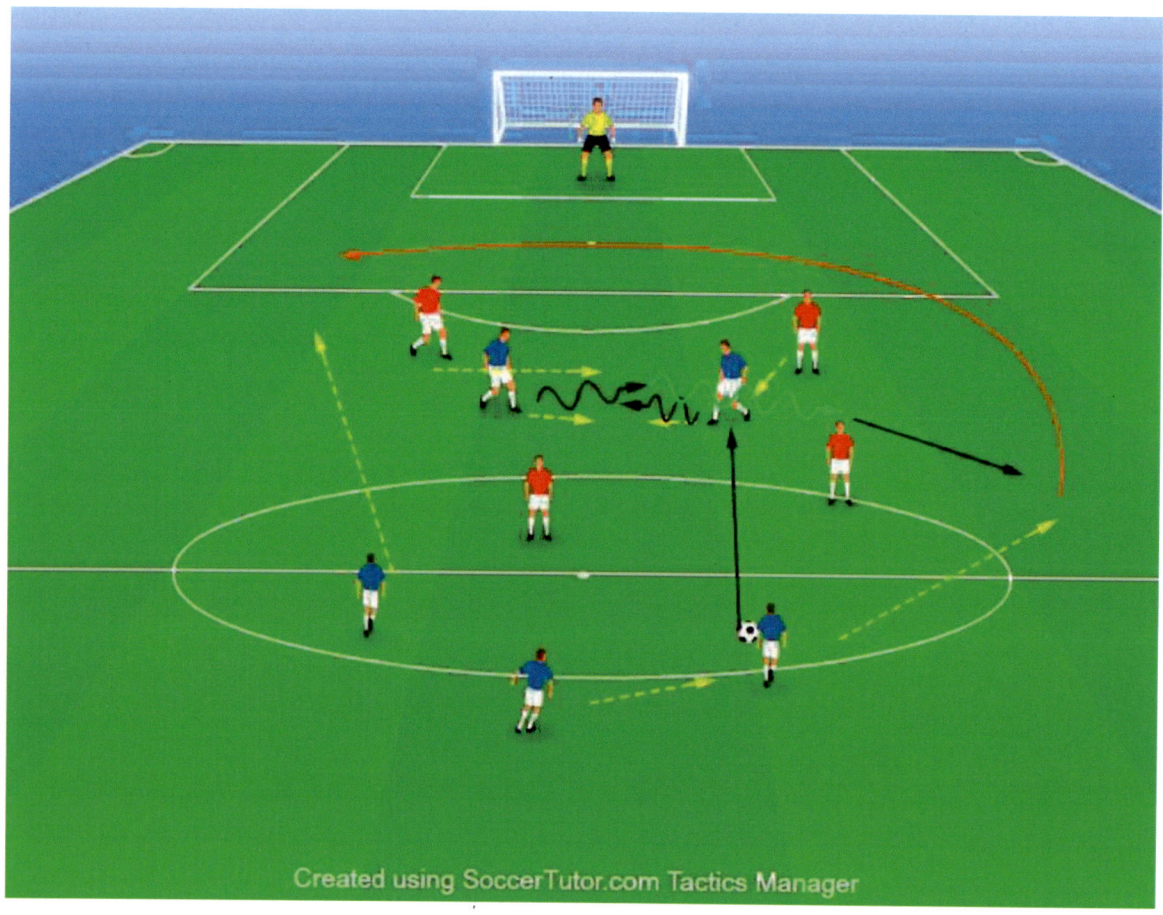

Midfield player passing the ball to the forward the two forwards making at takeover then the midfield player go wide right side ,who take the ball over that player do play the ball to the wide partner ,everybody shift in the right side open the left side for the runner, the right midfield player making a long cross to the left side. Need to focus on the movement up to follow each other, communicate, powerful offensive position.

If the difference can read the situation that moment you do not force to go through maybe losing the ball better than to play back to the last person in the midfield and start the auction again.

4.00 pm shooting finishing

Because of the focus concentration extremely hard to the shooting and finishing quite simple.

4.30 pm Dinner

Monday evening session:

6.45 -7.00 pm warm up

7.00-7.30 pm Shooting finishing

7.30-8.30pm evening small sided games; 4 v 4; 5 v 5; 6 v 6; 7 v 7;8 v 8 and 9 v 9

Could be the best if we have a team 12 players and evening, they play 6 v 6 and

Every night can switch teams and players. Monday to Wednesday then

Thursday and Friday 8 v 8 and 9 v 9 games.

The evening games must have a lot of fun and try everything what you did learn the morning and afternoon sessions

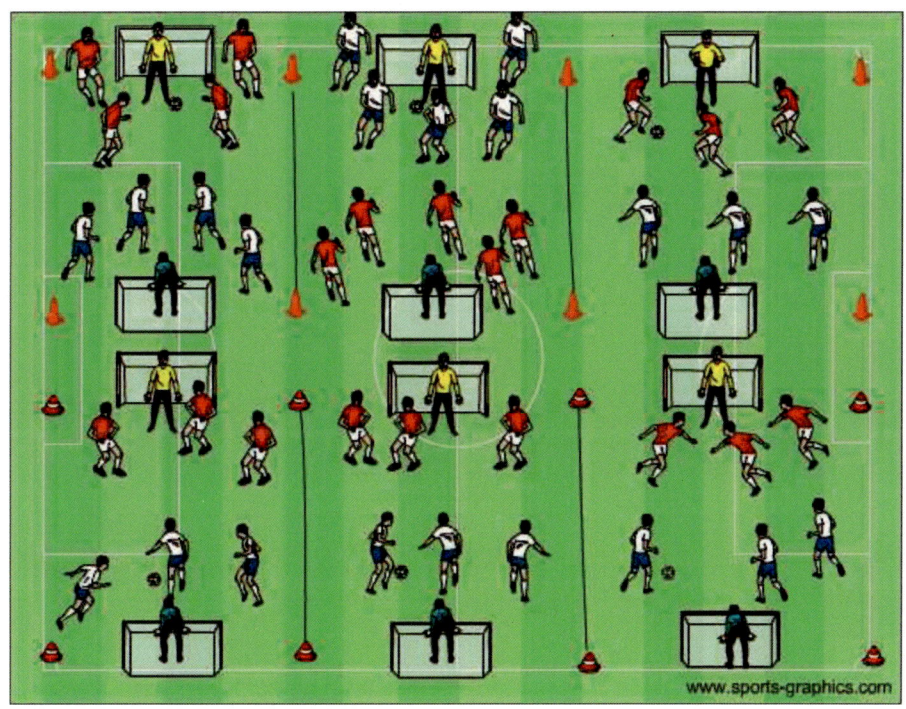

Tuesday morning session:

6.15-7.00 am

Soccer Aerobic if it is indoor, or fitness and technical sessions

Start the morning session:

8.45-9.00 Group warmups funny warmups make the kids ready for the focus on the sessions 9.00-11.30am start main training session

Defensive Station:

   1. **Center Defender Step Up; 30 min**

1,Center Forward receiving the ball in that moment one of the center defender Step up ,giving high pressure the rest defenders left right defense and the second center defender shifting inside in the middle closing out the true pass the killer pass, penetration pass.

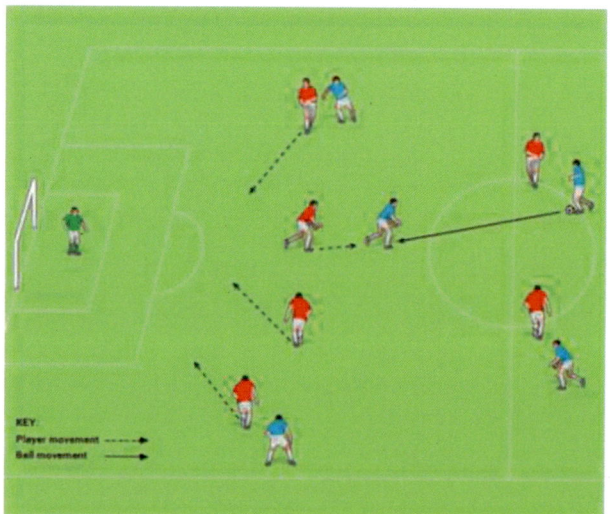

The two holding midfielder pay attention to the two offensive with runners is this possible they have to model them tight.

2.Cooper has the ball the different colors and the midfielders getting open give me an option for the keeper. 40 min

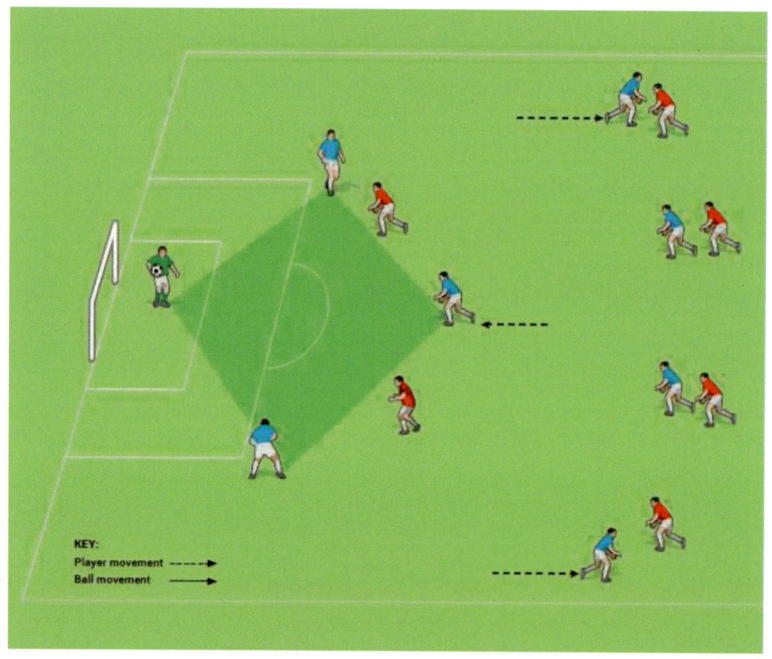

Keeper is looking for help right and left defender go white give options, the center defender checking back in the middle, right and left offensive midfielders going up ,and the two center defender trying to get attention from the keeper, they have a space to receiving the ball.The dark green marked area you can see how the defenders taking position could be an option to the goalkeeper He can decide it ,which players he going to play.

3. Defenders up Taking the defense line 35 to 40 yards they from the goal. The two-holding midfielder giving card pressure do the two offers midfielders. 50 min

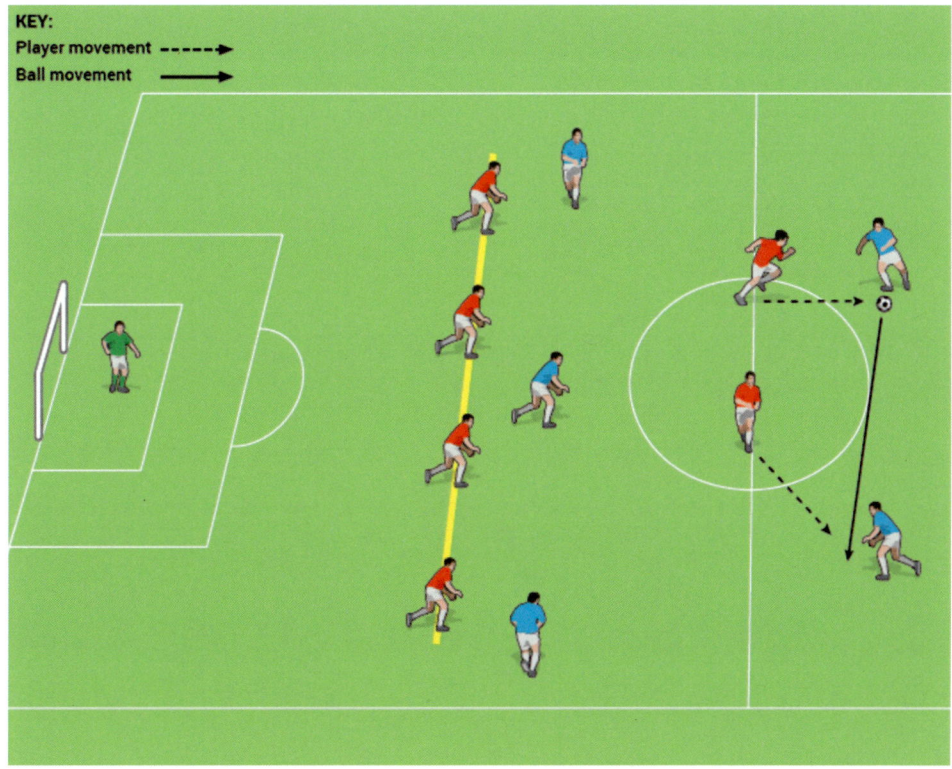

The reds form a defensive line, making it harder for attackers to stay onside when they make attacking runs

The four-defender keeping away the attacking players to making a run and stay onside, the two-holding midfielder trying to stop the two offensive players to creating attacking play.

Middlefield station.

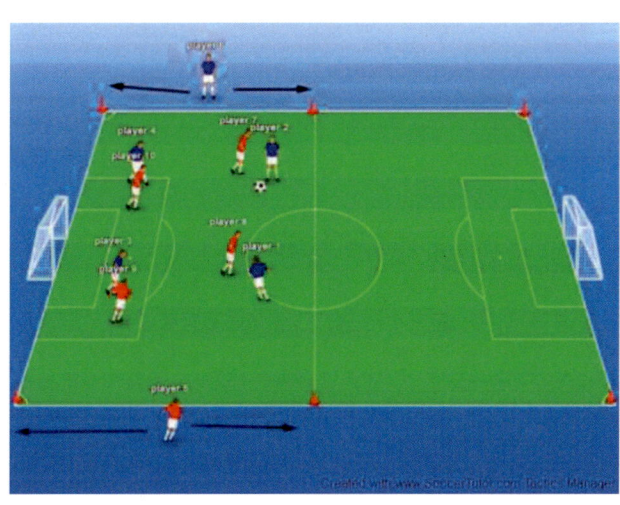

1 warming up with keep away. 4v4+2 30 min

Players with lot of movement 2 or 3 touches on the ball keeping the ball in position the two outside players anytime they can use dogs are play guys they don't have pressure that's why they have to play the ball in first touch back to the team meets.

85

2. Position in the midfield going to go through combinations and communication against an event number. 60-70 min

What they enjoy about the activity will differ.
The motivation for playing will vary among individuals.:

Emphasize the elements that appeal to the majority of participants

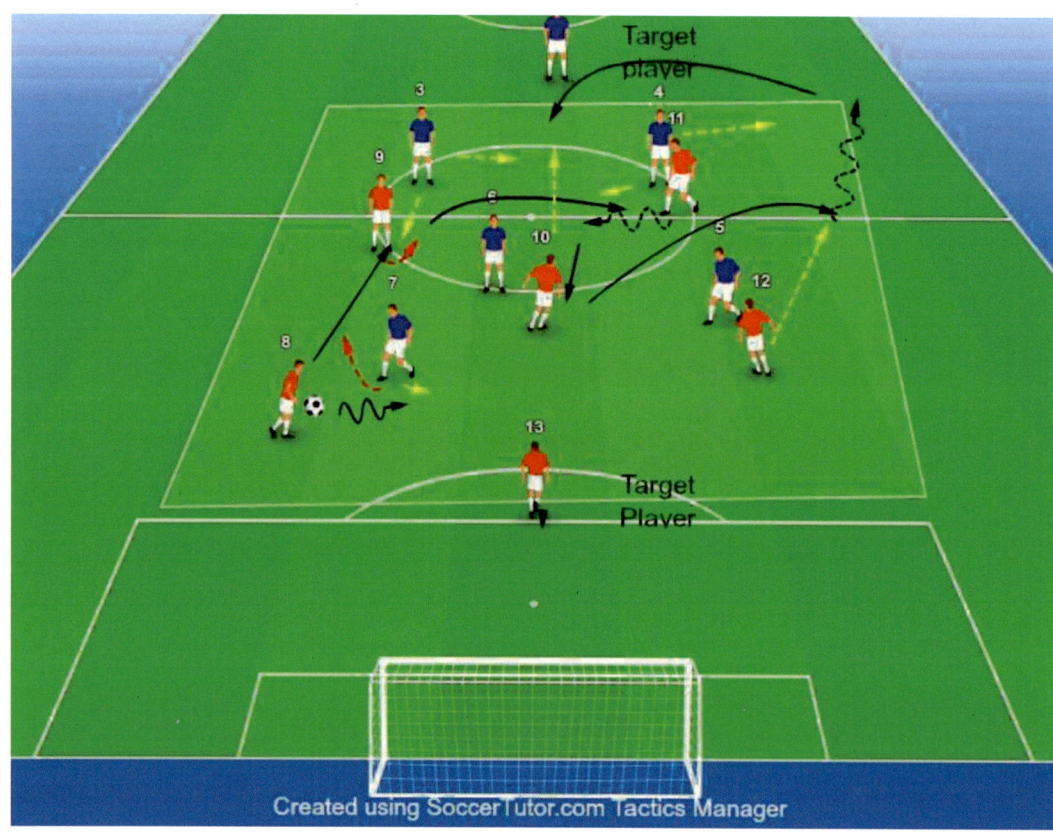

#8 Red Start dribbling inside blue 7 pressure number 8 need to return outside and pass the ball to number 9 , #3 blue giving the pressure number 9 turned inside and pass the ball to number 11, He dribble insight in the center #4 defender giving pressure ,the number 11 play the ball back to number 10. between #12 start running outside on the right side ,#10 red see this and pass the ball to him #12 dribble all away down and cross the ball in the center, numbers 10 coming in the center and pass the ball to the target player .

possible variations from the coaches with direction but let improvise the players.

blue team getting the ball take it away from the red team then the blue team same main try to play the ball to the target player victim Berg and combinations through buses white buses what option do you have.

11.00 – 11.30 am

3.4 v 4 with 2 outside players: 20 min

4 versus 4 and two outside players opportunity to score only when you used both outside players. The other opportunity to play this game you are using the two outside players and they must come into the field and be Active field players then you can score. the third variation when you pass the ball to the outside players dogs that players come in and you who passed the ball go outside become the line player.

Offensive stations.

1.2 groups of 6 player 30 min

Two groups of 6 divided of three in each side off grid one player place the ball to one of the other players on the opposite side off the grid the player who played the ball becomes the offensive team, with the player who receives the ball and they try to create 2 versus 2 the team that possessed across the line wins the point progress of three versus three and 4 versus 4

The first attacking player with the ball should dribble at the defender to make him commit the action or without it inaction of the defender should dictate which form of combination play will be used by the team of the offense.

Player must decide between situations that are most advantage to utilize the target players to get behind the oppenent using combination play .

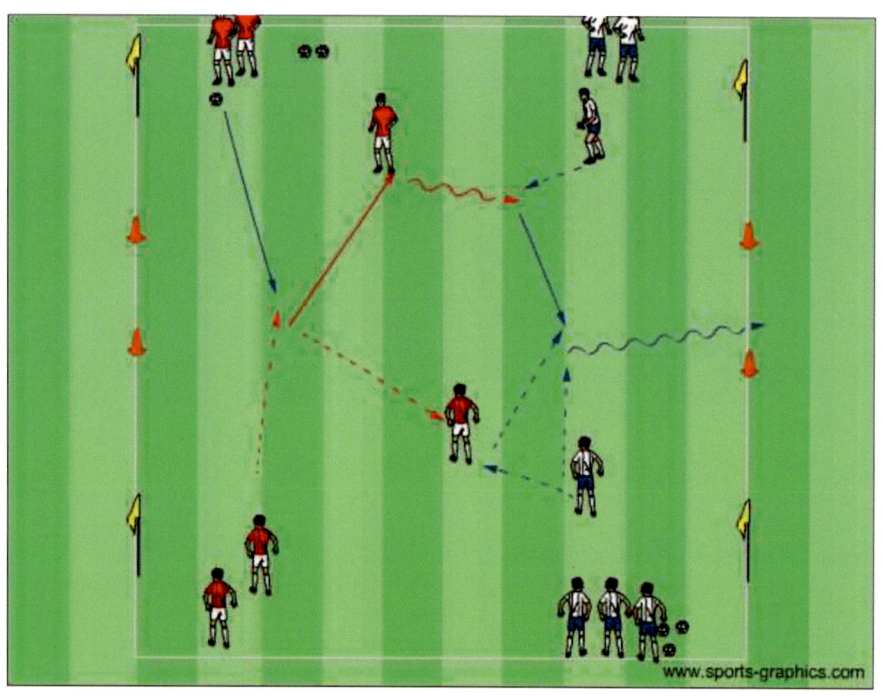

2.6 v 6 with 6 target players 50 min

Three teams with six players two teams compete inside the field why the other team play outside the field off target players. target players can use by the team in possession of the ball to help them combine to get behind the opponen,t goals are scored in a normal soccer fashion rotate the outside players of the six minutes The target players usable outside in the sideline and on the goal line too. The outside players is free they can get pressure from the inside teams.

3. 8 v 8 game combinations 30 min

Players must decide between situations that are most advantage can get out from the possessions Players need to recognize when and where to perform combinations play to get behind opponents and maintain positions .

11.00-11.30 sho0ting finishing

Simple process and crosses and finishing from both side left and right side

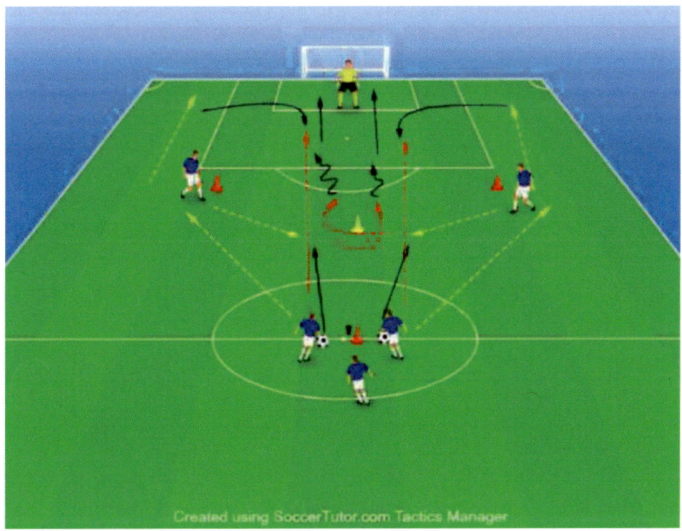

Tuesday Afternoon Session;

1.45-2.00 pm Group volume up for the volume up make the kids ready for the main session

2.00-4.30pm Start the main training session

Defensive stations ;

1.Cover shadow; 30 min

At times he is not even seen by the player controlling the ball. We wish to investigate this fact more thoroughly, in which the theoretical fundamentals are often disregarded. What does "in the shadow of a defender" mean?

To this effect, look at illustration. The ball player is situated directly in front of the defender. We have created the shadow of the defender in graphic form. In this shadow, the attacker can pass the ball only with high risk, because the defender blocks the path into the shadow area. This imaginary shadow is called "cover shadow" in many types of sports.
**it can be clearly recognized that the cover shadow changed in size if the ball carrier is in proximity of the defender. The closer the ball carrier to the defender, the larger the cover shadow gets.
What do we learn from this?**

2. General ideas about tackling   60min

An old word of soccer wisdom: winning a tackle means winning the game. Soccer is not that easy and that is a good thing. The importance of tackling increased during the last decades. For defense, to prevent the game development of the opposing team at an early point and for offensive, to assert oneself successfully against an aggressive defense.

One on one change;

Description
Mark a drill rectangle. The smaller it is, the more intensive the one-on-ones will be.
We will post three players each on two sides; the players are numbered from one to three. At the beginning of the drill, one player from each group should be in the practice rectangle. One player has a ball; the other player tries to win the ball. Give the one-on-one some time and then call two numbers. The first number is represented by the black player in our animation; the second player is yellow. The player, who takes control of the ball on command, passes to the player from his team who is offering himself. The next one-on-one can then begin.
If the ball should leave the rectangle, start the drill from the beginning.

1 v 1 Tackle 60 min

by Tackle especially important the timing, the defender need to focus concentrate on the ball and then offensive player speed beach food he dribbles the ball. Face to face tackle the defender try to stay always front of the ball And when you doing the tackle you're not diving deep.by side by side with the offensive player the different there have to focus by that dribbling the ball go a little bit more forward in that moment you diving And do the tackle with the leg which is closest to the forward And the ball

When the players doing very well you can let them finish score the different there still the ball he can score too.

Midfield station ;

1. Pressing

Basic Strategies:
- How high should a team defend?
- Where should a team try to win the ball?
- Should a team show opponents inside or outside?

The displayed tactical behaviors have an impact on the entire „defensive strategy ". However, the system of play is always influenced by players, their individual characteristics as well as their strengths and weaknesses. The opponent's system of play is equally important. In which areas are opponents compact? How do players fill out their respective roles? These are deciding factors with regards to defensive strategies.

Analysis of different types of playing in relation to the ball from a team tactical perspective.

The first question is: What is the preferred strategy of a team when defending. Should the team defend to actively win the ball, or should the team be patient to wait for mistakes of the opposing team?
This is a coach's decision. This is all about actively winning the ball

Defensive pressing; 60 min

The most common type of defending is Pressing. In my opinion, this is all about defending actively to win the ball back.
This ball-winning strategy relies on creating many 2v1 situations. A team should be looking into doubling-up on opponents in this instance

The defense line giving the pressure and shifting left and right together in one the block .

2. Offense pressure; 60 min

The graphics do show High Pressure in its preparation stage and in its final stage. It also highlights the space in which High Pressure should be applied.

High Pressure is being developed through Midfield-Offense Pressing The graphics show that High Pressure is being developed through Midfield-Offense Pressing. The defending team waits for a short pass to initiate the attack by the attacking team and immediately pushes up as a team as shown it. Important very tight and aggressive pressure if your team can win the ball and the opponent defensive area then you can ride away create counterattack.

3. small sided game with pressure 30 min

Offensive station.

1. Fundamental warm-up; 30 min

Half the group with the ball in the middle of and half without ball on the outside. Players in the middle pass to the outside and perform.
A; Double pass
Dummy runs
C; Clip the ball for self-pass
Change rolls after 90 seconds

Coaching points.
Players muss check to the ball an angle
No strait runs or passes
Play to back or front foot depending on shape of the receiving players
Receiving players muss point to where they want the ball
Communication

2. Match related 1 v 1 "1 20 min

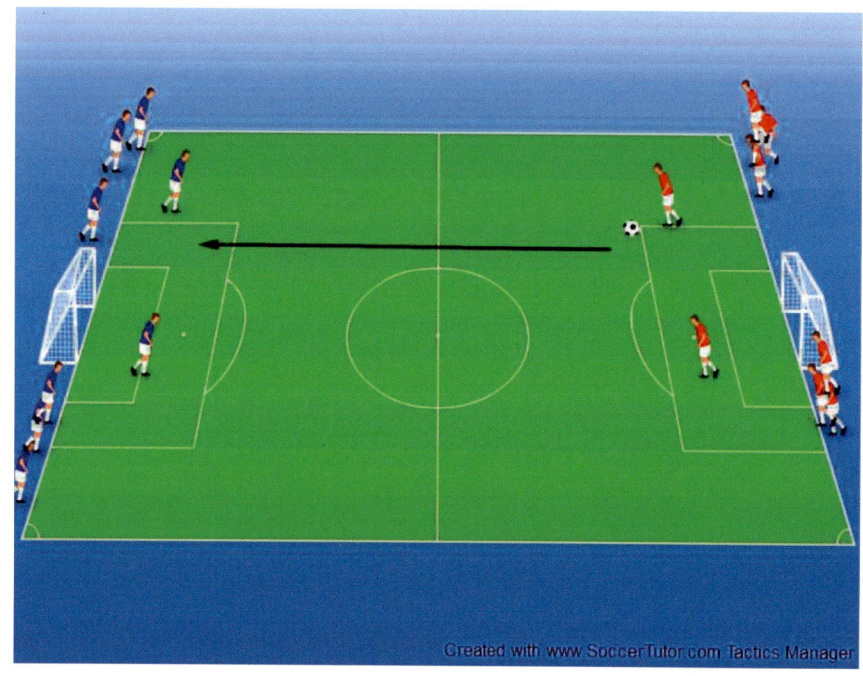

players in groups 2 players participate in 1v1 and 1 player option for the offense only support Defender still the ball he passes back to his partner who direct pass back to him the he become the offensive player.

3. Corridor soccer -Match related 4 v 4   40 min

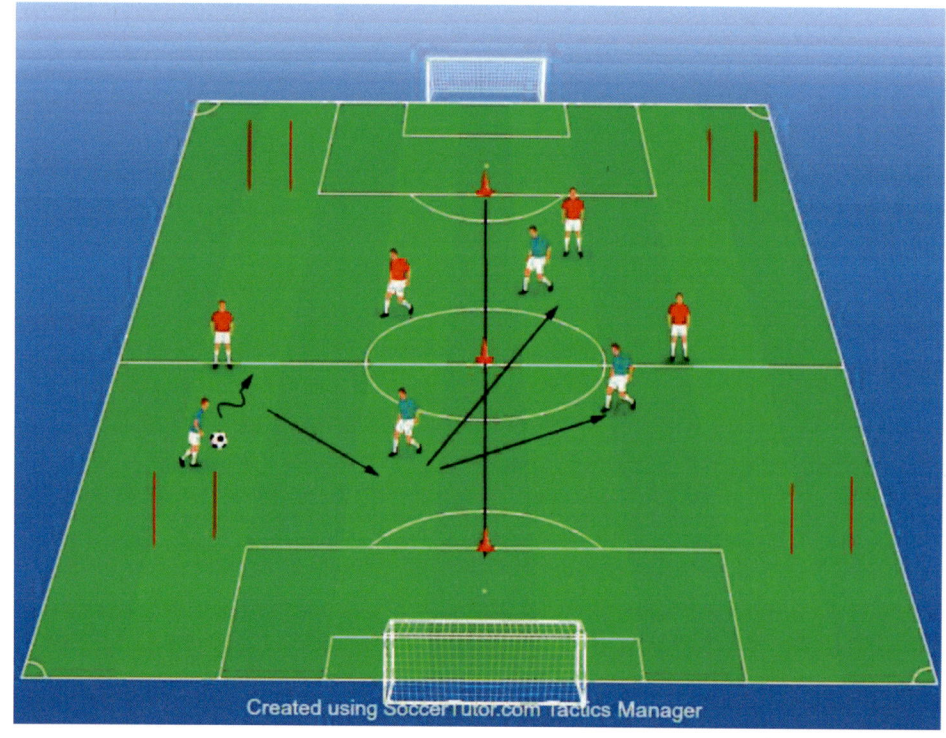

Players divded in 2 groups of 4. 2 players in the left channel and 2 players in the right channel. Players in the own chanel can,t play forward, only side or back and dribble is allowed score to the samll goals

4. Match condition; 8 v 8 you practice all above 30 min

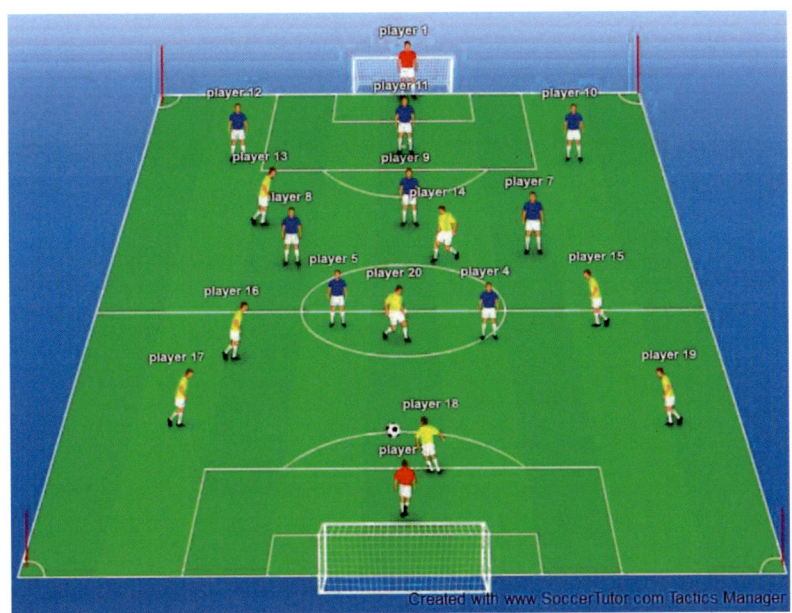

4.00-4.30 pm shooting, finishimg, crossing

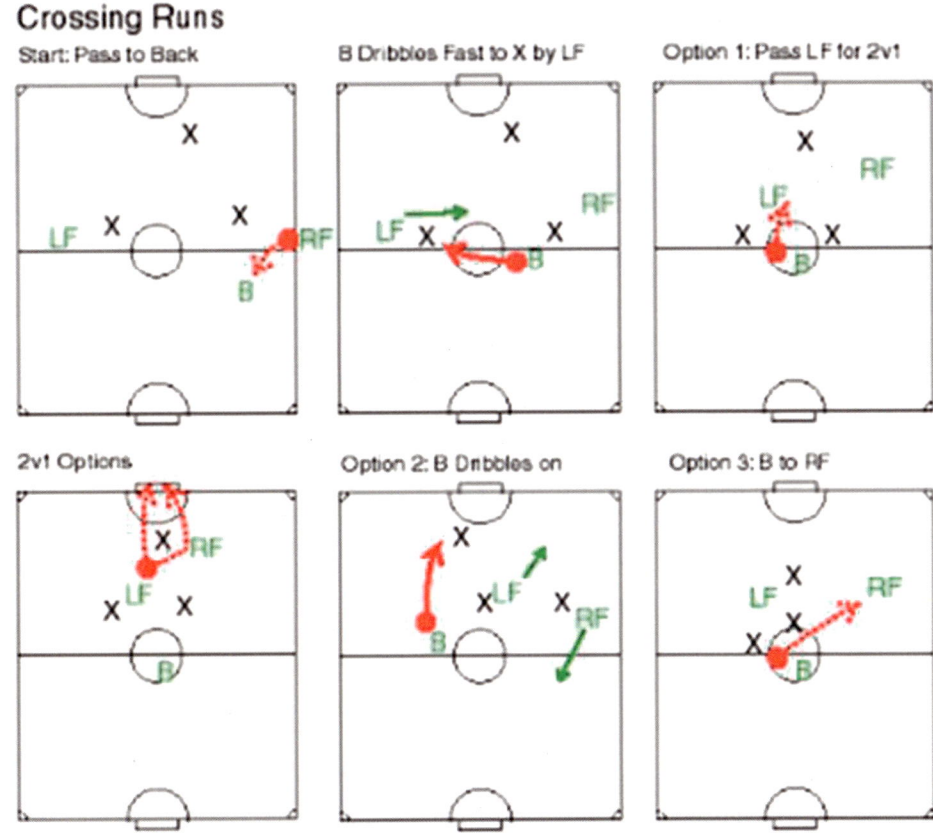

Tuesday evening session:

6.45 -7.00 pm warm up

7.00-7.30 pm Shooting finishing

7.30-8.30pm evening small sided games; 4 v 4; 5 v 5; 6 v 6; 7 v 7;8 v 8 and 9 v 9

Could be the best if we have a team 12 players and evening, they play 6 v 6 and

Every night can switch teams and players. Monday to Wednesday then

Thursday and Friday 8 v 8 and 9 v 9 games.

The evening games must have a lot of fun and try everything what you did learn the morning and afternoon sessions

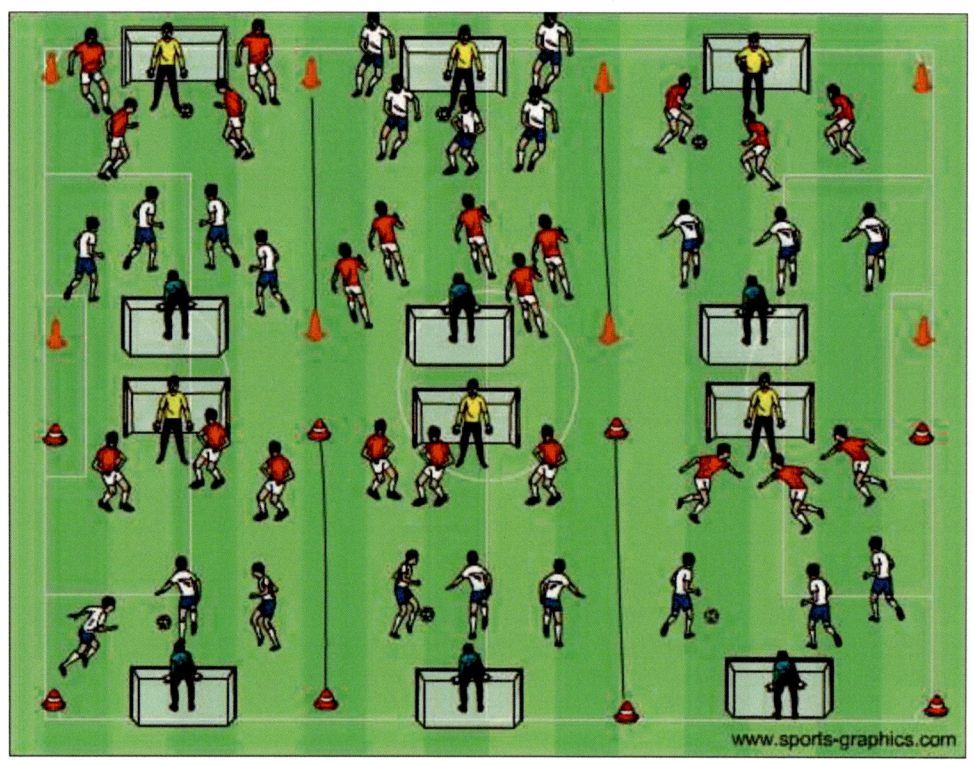

Wednesday Morning Session:

6.15-7.00 am

Soccer Aerobic if it is indoor, or fitness and technical sessions

Start the morning session:

8.45-9.00 Group warmups funny warmups make the kids ready for the focus on the sessions 9.00-11.30am start main training session

Defensive Station:

1. Great defense; 40 min

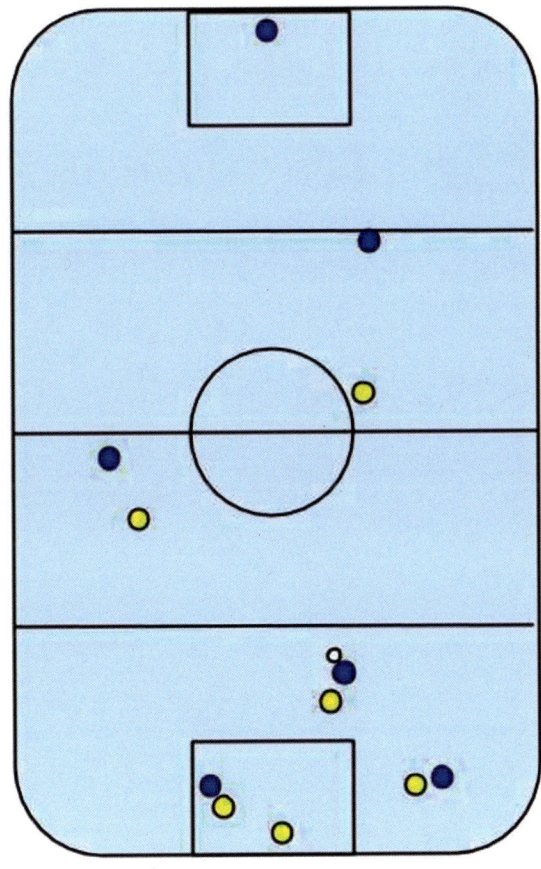

The Keys to Great Defending:

1) If you aren't marking a player, someone's open for a pass
2) Stay between the player and your own goal
3) Keep your eyes on your man and the ball (head on swivel)
4) Don't allow your man to run past you
5) The closer they get to the goal, the closer you get to them
6) Shoulder to shoulder when in your own box
7) Close down fast when the ball is in the air
8) Let your teammates know who you are marking by pointing
9) Avoid double teaming unless you have numbers
10) Don't dive in for the ball, they will easily get around you
11) Jockey with both feet well balanced under your shoulders and in line with the opponent and your goal

-VincentCollins.com

This reduces open shots on goal and causes your opponent to pass under pressure, which is where the mistakes are made.

2. Goal kick and -right left defender move up   40 min

3-5-2 atacking move after goalkick

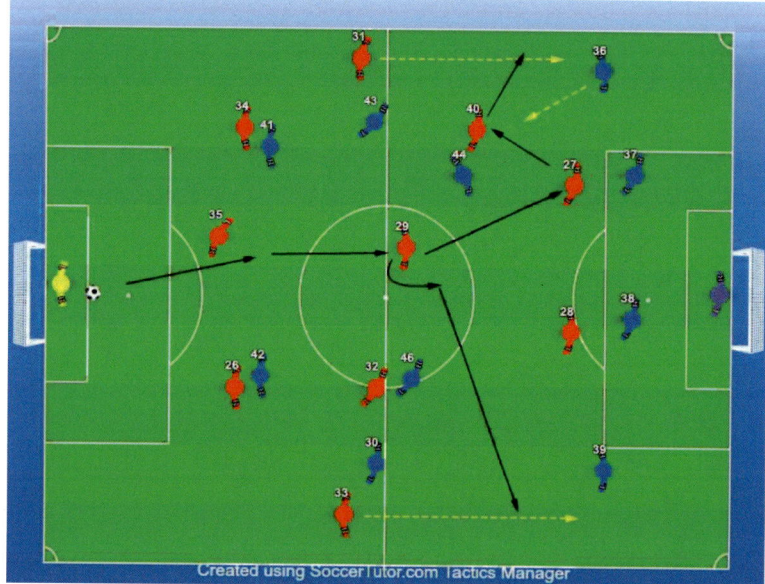

Goalkeeper pass the ball to the centre defender he pass the ball to the centre midfield who turn and making a decision pass to the left forward and going pressure on the right defender or pass the ball to the right offensive middlefielder and start trying to beat the left defender or cross the ball in the middle.In the same formation could be different way using by goal kick the right or left defender or using the left or right midfielder or the keeper can direct throw the ball to the centre midfielder.

.3. 6 v 6 game with goalkeepers. 1 goal and 2 small goals 40 min

The yellow is the offensive group the player kicked the ball direct to the goalkeeper and the keeper played the ball to the right defender after that start the game the red group is the defensive group and they score for the two small goals the yellow team score against the goalkeeper to the big goal .

Midtfield station ;

1. Marked zone. 40 min

On trainer command, everyone must immediately "freeze". Ideal time for clues, because only with a new command the game continues. Ball control: If a player controls the ball, he must not be attacked. Only a goal or pass game is prevented. Zone game: Zones are marked that are not allowed to enter or are not played. In the middle of the pitch, such an area would ensure that you have to play outside. You can play through on the market zone but you cannot go into the zone go through this room important switching sites communication very quick touches .

2. Color change and combination 50 min

team consists of 4 fielders. The 4 players of a team are marked with 2x2 different colored bodies, so we form two pairs per team. In total, we need 4x2 different colored bodies for both teams. Alternatively, the pairs of players can be marked with shirts/jerseys of the same color. of the graphic,

Team A plays against Team B. In Team A, two players wear red jerseys and two green jerseys. In Team B, two players wear blue jerseys and two orange jerseys. It is played freely, Team A against Team B. In the pass game, a color change must take place for each pass. Example: If a red player from Team A has the ball, he may only fit on one player of his team with a green jersey. Players with the green jerseys can fit only on the red players. The process at Team B is analogous to this. In the case of a "miss-color pass" there is a free kick

4 v 4 Two touches game Greek changing positions who touching the ball more times than two against that team's going to have a free kick by three free kick the other team get a penalty kick.

20 min

Offensive station;

1. Triangle passing Variations ; 20 min

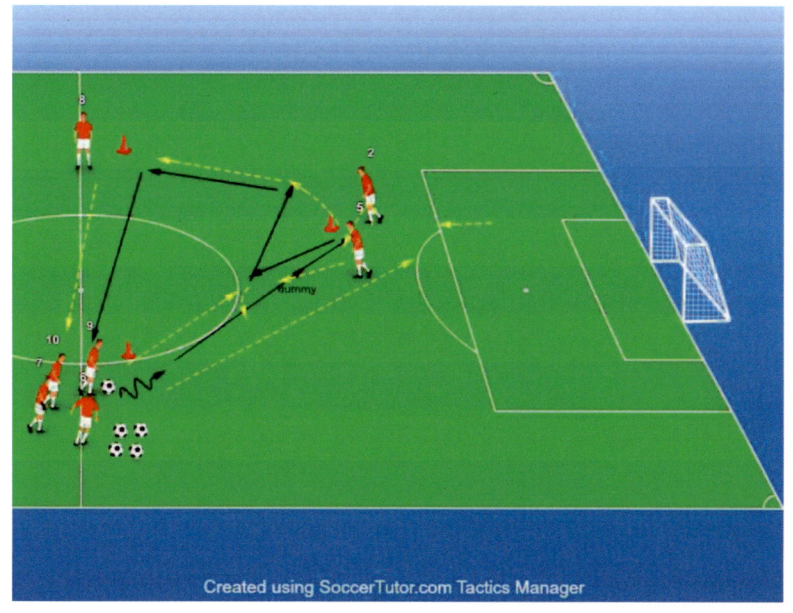

#9 starts terrible passing the ball to number 5 who do dummy #2 come to the ball the ball to number 5 who is move around the cone he possing to number 8 ,He passing the ball to number 10 then everybody move.

2. 4 group passing with 2center 20 min

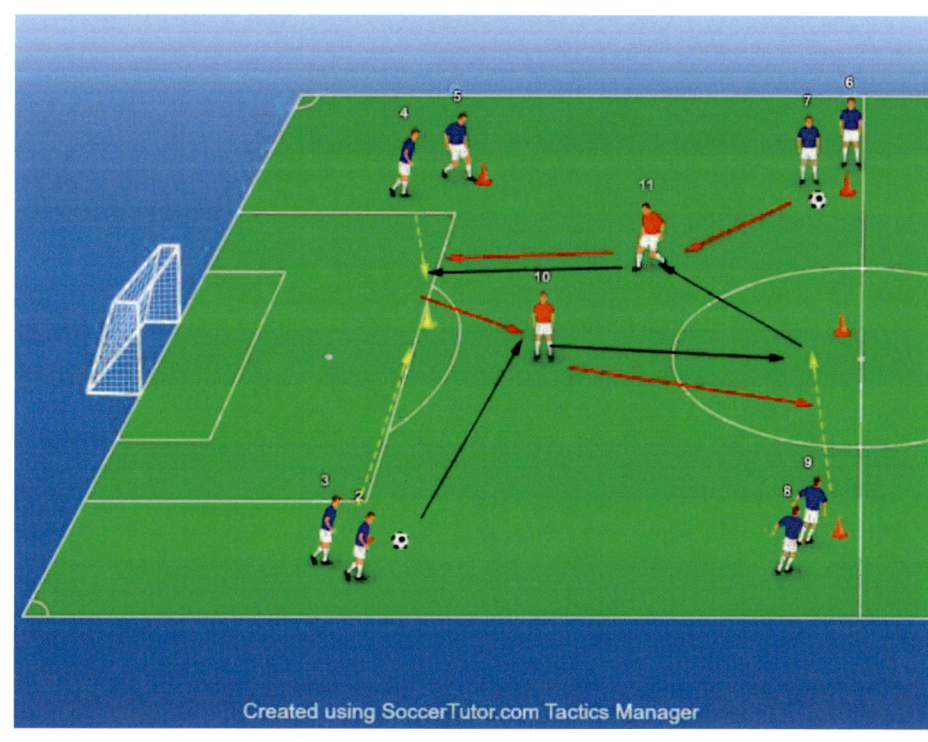

one side passing in the center and he passing the other side in the middle

and from the other side same way

3. 3 field 4 v 2 passing movements 20 min

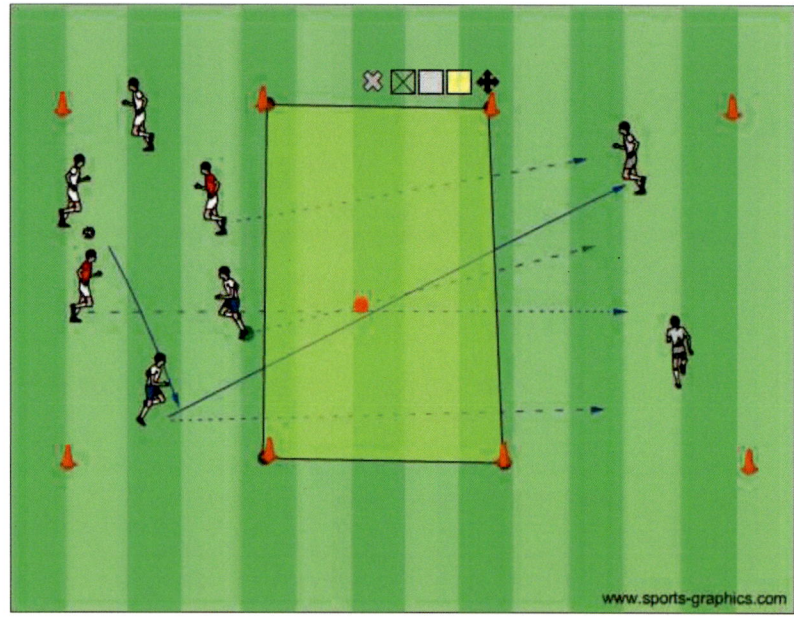

4 color teams we have 2 color play together and one color is defense

Passing 2 or 3 then must pass the others side and 2=2 players move the other field. Switching defenders coach call the color for defense.

Keep away, 4 v 2. Panetration passess, thru passes, communication.

4. passing first touches thru the gate 20 min

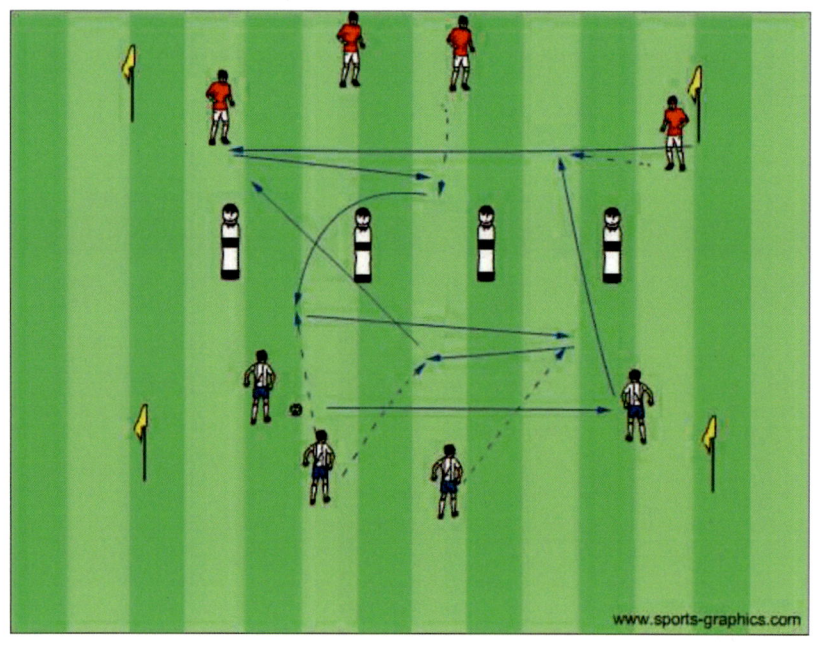

players doing a lot of movement first Touches keeping the triangle and between passing through the gate practice for penetration process practice for first touches practice for communication call for the ball talk to you partner. Focus on the first touch and the movement and keeping the triangle.

11.00-11.30 shooting finishing agains GK

Diagonal Soccer Shooting Drill

Drill Objective:

This is a simple soccer shooting drill that is great for warm-up to a shooting practice or warm-up prior to a game.

Drill Setup:

Create a 10X10 grid just beyond on the edge of the 18-yard box. Divide the team info 2 lines on the far cones facing the goal. One player from each line steps to the cone near the 18 (this player becomes the player that lays the ball off to the player on the cone farthest from

Drill Instructions:

Player 1 passes a diagonal ball to player 4, player 4 has a touch and lays the ball off into space for player 1 to run onto the ball and hit a first-time strike on goal. The shooting player (player 1) takes the place of the player that set up his shot (player 4), and player 4 shags the shot and switches lines.

Next, Player 2 passes a diagonal ball to player 3. Player 3 lays the ball off to player 2 who shoots first time on goal. Player 2 becomes the target player; the target player (player 3) shags the shot.

Make sure the players switch lines, so they shoot with both feet.

Drill Coaching Points:

- Good controlled approach on the ball
- Plant foot in good spot next to the ball
- Shoot with the appropriate foot
- Hit the ball on target

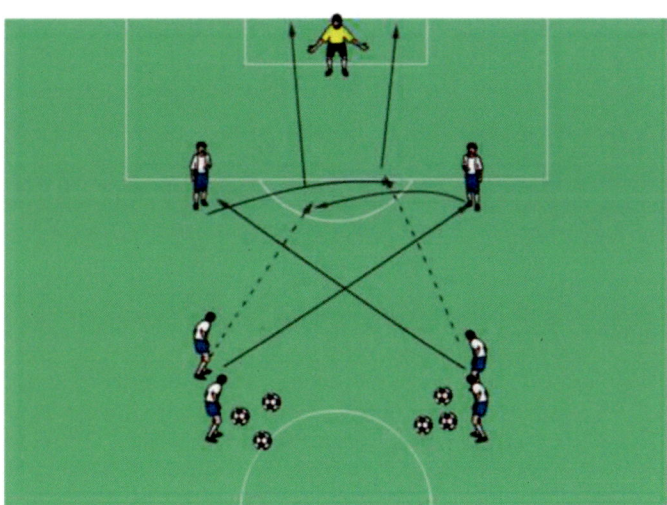

Shooting, Combo, 1v1 Shooting Drill

This is a great shooting drill that focuses on making a move before shooting, making a 1-2 combination play before shooting, then taking on a defender 1v1 before shooting.

Drill Setup:

Create 3 lines (Line 1, 2, & 3) of players about 30 yards from goal with a goalkeeper in goal. Each player in line needs a ball.

Drill Instructions:

1. Instruct line 1 to make a move and shoot before the edge of the penalty box.
2. After player 1 shoots, they need to check into player 2 for a 1-2 ball. Player 1 should lay the ball off to player 2 for a first time shot.
3. After player 2 shoots, they move to defend the player in line 3. Player 3 should beat player 2 and have a shot on goal.
4. The players should not change lines yet. Let each player work through their line 3-4 times before switching lines.

Drill Coaching Points:

- Focus on good shooting technique, landing on the kicking foot, following through onto goal, and putting the ball on target.
- Kids should pay attention and remember their next task after shooting.

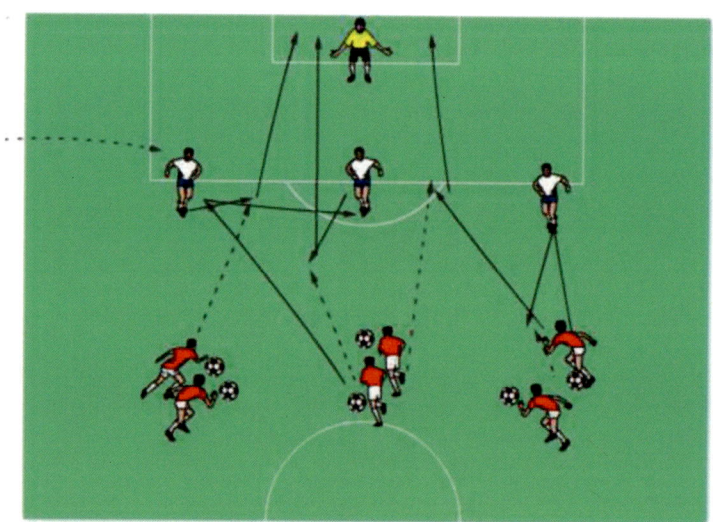

Combination shooting, rotation, drill

Setup

With two goals facing each other about 30 yards apart, place a goalkeeper in each goal. Set three flags at midfield on the left, center, and right sides of the field. On the left and right flags, place a cone 5 yards past the flags and set a player at each of these cones. Two players should start at the center flag, one player for each side of the drill. The remaining players should start along the end line with a ball each.

Instructions

Player 1 plays a ball into player 2. Player 2 checks to the ball and plays it back to player 1. Player 1 plays the ball into player 3. Player 3 lays off a ball to player 2. Player 2 has a timed run around the flag and shoots 1st time on goal. All players rotate forward one position (Player 1 becomes Player 2, Player 2 Becomes Player 3, Player 3 shags the ball).

Variations

Limit all passes and touches to ONE-TOUCH.

Coaching Points

- Good solid passes play in 1 touch if possible.
- Good timed movement and runs (do not get there too early).
- Player prepping the touch for the shooter should simply lay the ball off for a good 1 time shot.
- Good shooting form leaning forward through the ball and landing on the kicking foot.

Wednesday Afternoon Session:

1.45-2.00 pm Group volume up for the volume up make the kids ready for the main session

2.00-4.30pm Start the main training session

Defense Station:

1. 3 flatback 30 min

Blue opens up every attack from midfield Red shifts ball-oriented, tries to defend the attacks in inferior numbers and after a ball conquest by flat pass (hat gates) or diagonal flying ball (outer zones) to score a hit Duration and goal of the football training exercise: about 15 minutes Fine-tuning among the 3 defenders to move in stages Introducing a quick counter Pass security after winning the ball

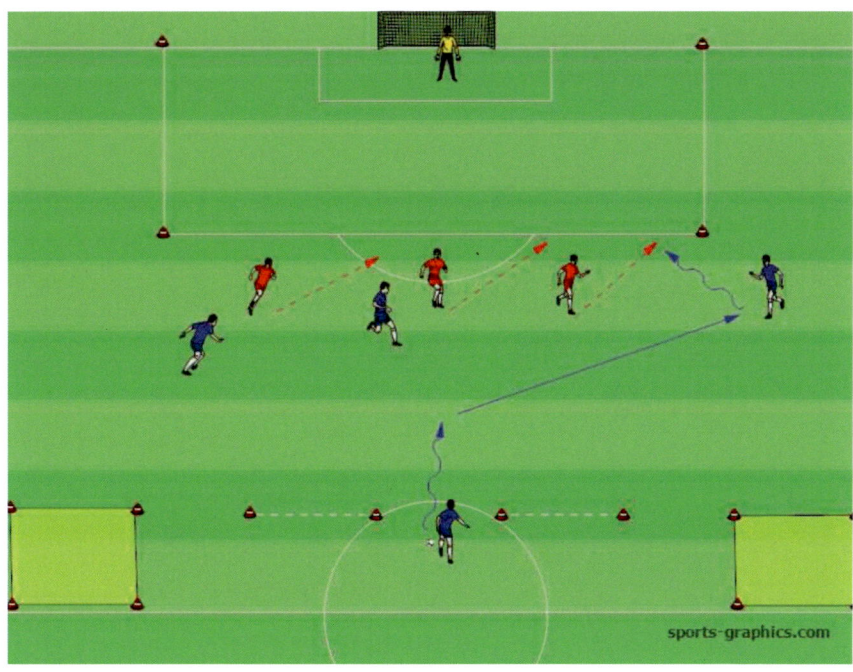

2. Flatback with miss position; 40 min

chain of four plays in the room and hands over the attackers. They move together to the near side of the ball. When a defender goes out of the chain, the other defenders must secure by entering and securing the free space. In the offensive game, one of the two external defenders intervene

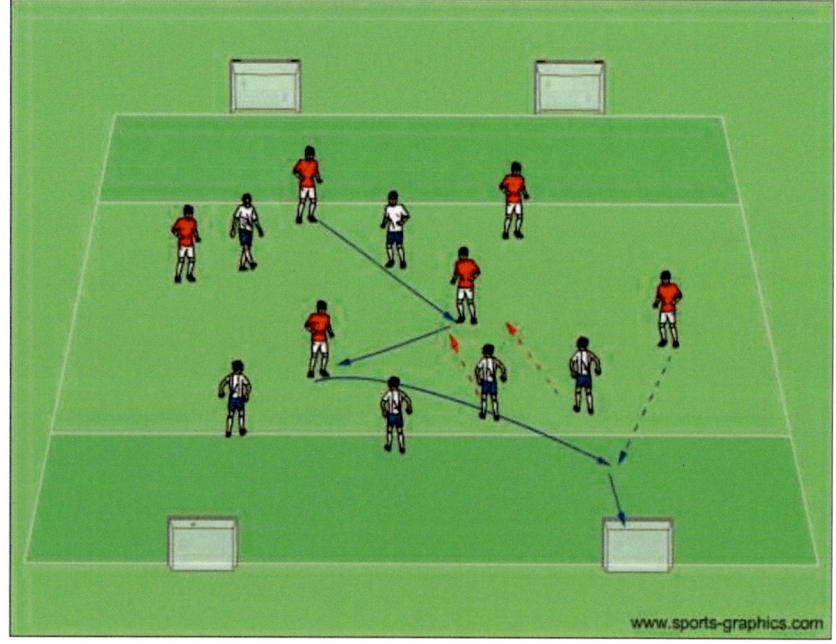

You can see in that case the second center defender and the right defender stepped up too early they won't keep the pressure on the ball open at the opportunity to the offensive team using the space behind them and they scored the goal

3. 6v5 with conter attack 50 min

The red team is in defense the offensieve team has one extra player but the two center defender give high pressure and stealing the ball and right away start a counter attack **Which is successful with finishing.**

108

Midfield station;

1. Passing warm-up 20 min

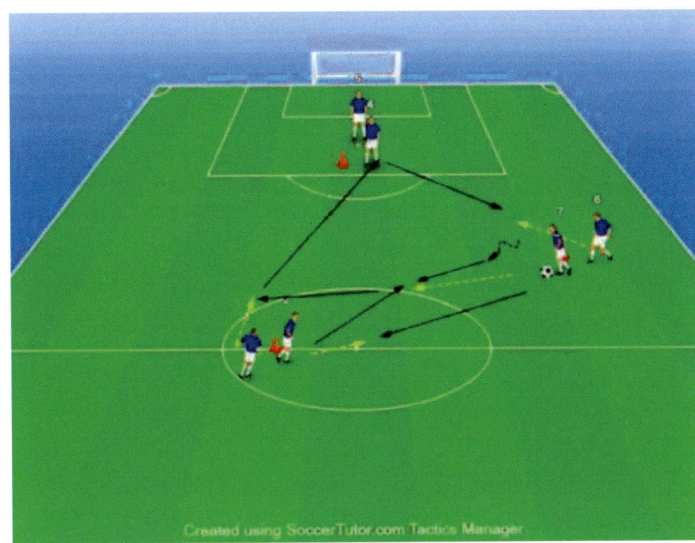

7 dribble and pass tha ball for # 2 who pass back to # 7, he pass to #3 who going behind the cone and pass to$ 4, he dribble and pass to # 6 who dribble and pass 3 4. The going to fluid. Good if the ball never stop.

2. - Switching game - Ball circulation – Possession 40 min

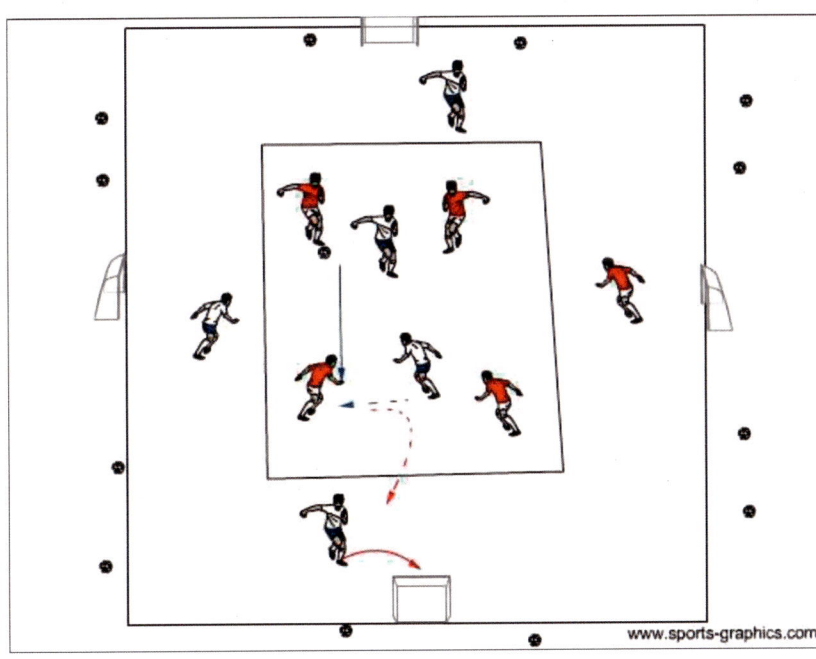

A good exercise to train the switching game and the counter-pressing. Here the ball circulation is trained, if a pass is played too short or stopped dead, the possibility arises here to actively conquer the ball and then counteract the counter-pressing by means of a deep pass or tempo dribbling.

The players outside the small field can score, red team has only one player who can help the white team has 3 players whocan score. Red team after 5 passes can play outside to score. White team can play out any time when they still the ball. Switch positions and teams.

3. 4 v 4 and 5 v 5 + 1 positioning and creating offense oportunities. 60 min

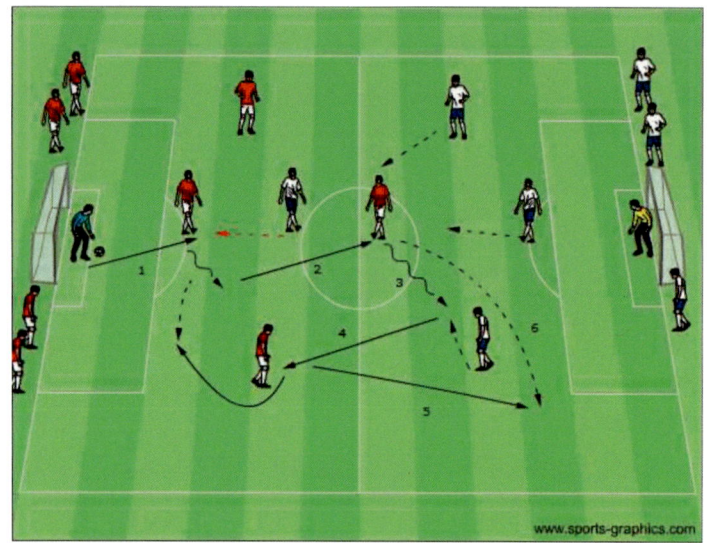

the game start 4 v 4 the players creating positins going behind the defense line , with panetrarion passes ,thru passes,switching sides and move ments faking the defense. Still the ball play back to the keeper and start the transation from the GK. Periode when the same game but by the back pass for the GK in this moment ,one extra player come in and this is 4-5.

Then play with 5 v 5 with the same ruls. 2. game 4 v 4 by ball stilling play back for the GK and new 4 v 4 players come in and the players from the field running off with sprint.

Offensive Station:

1. Cover shadow 20 min

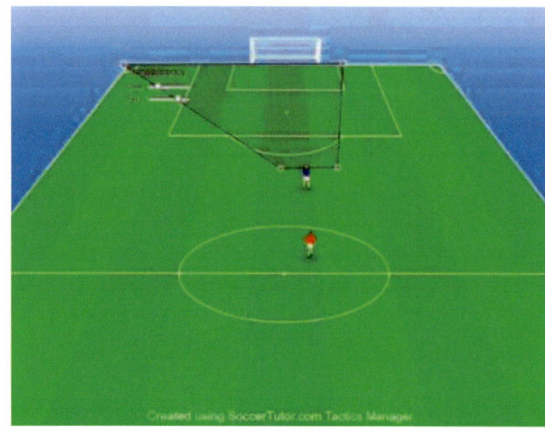

As attacker pay attention: The defender will almost always try to cover the goal with the cover shadow **(D+E)**. If you offer yourself to receive the pass think about how the cover shadow will shift within the next seconds and then be ready to receive the ball outside of that shadow.

As defender pay attention: Approach as closely as possible to the opponent in possession of the ball, so that the cover shadow is large enough. If the defense is under pressure it is essential that the spaces close to the goal be secured without cover shadow, to obstruct or forestall dangerous passes close to the goal.

Make your team aware of the theory of the „Cover Shadow ". It will be of help in the game, in defense as well as in attack.

3. Attack with 2 forwards 50 min

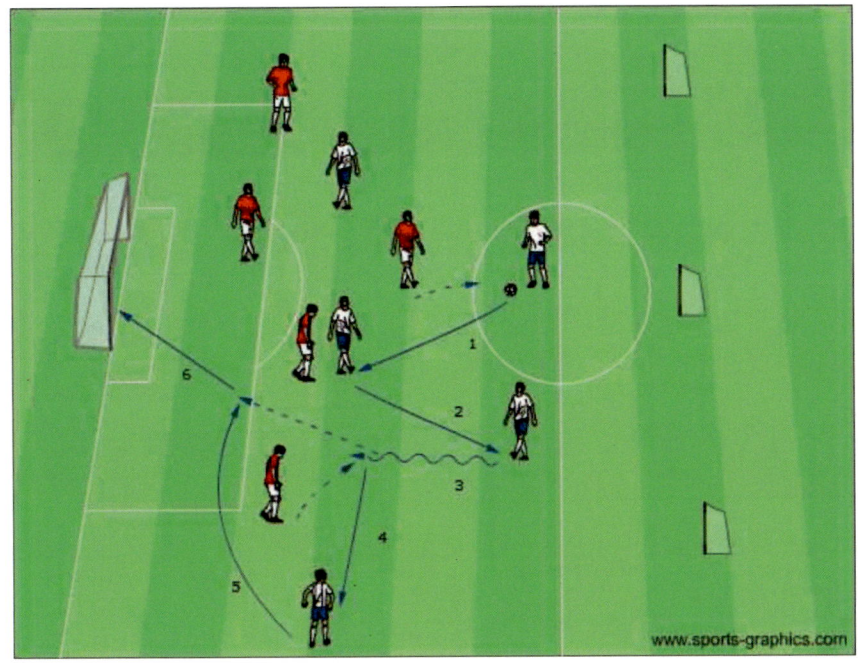

4 defense and 1 defensive MF, against 5 offense. Offense have to go first on the picture showing numbers .First ballot the forward he play back to the offensive MF, he start dribble get the defender out from the block ,then pass the ball to the left winger and after in the right time run in thru the space, the left wing curve the ball in and the MF take a shut.

Offense must develop different positions go thru and finish with shut. Could be simple and could be with more passes brack the defense.

Defender have the ball they going to take on the offense and try to go thru and score in the 3 small goals.

3. Simple curve-run and finish 50 min

offense trying to brack down the tide defense with balls behind the defense line.

With more passes and cross runs middlefilders must create a thru pass or long curves.

4.00-4.30 possible shooting – Wednesday maybe the shooting you can skip it.

Wednesday evening session;

6.45 -7.00 pm warm up

7.00-7.30 pm Shooting finishing

7.30-8.30pm evening small sided games; 4 v 4; 5 v 5; 6 v 6; 7 v 7;8 v 8 and 9 v 9

Could be the best if we have a team 12 players and evening, they play 6 v 6 and

Every night can switch teams and players. Monday to Wednesday then

Thursday and Friday 8 v 8 and 9 v 9 games.

The evening games must have a lot of fun and try everything what you did learn the morning and afternoon sessions

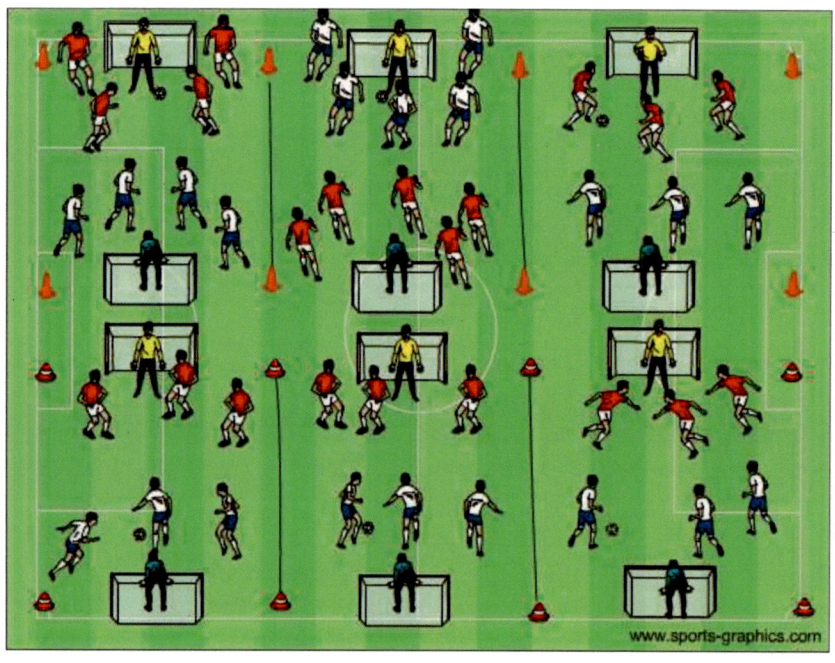

Thursday Morning Session;

6.15-7.00 am

Soccer Aerobic if it is indoor, or fitness and technical sessions

Start the morning session:

8.45-9.00 Group warmups funny warmups make the kids ready for the focus on the sessions 9.00-11.30am start main training session

Defensive Station; 40 min

Flatback shifting depense witch offense dribble and the defense give the pressure #1 -# 2 - # 3- # 4. Defenders understand the positioning then the auster forwards shifting the ball left to right right to left and we asking the defenders follow the ball position and give pressure always the right defender.

2.6 v 6 defense and offense positioning 70 min

#7 blue start dribbling then post about to ride the number 6 who trebling outside close to the line #3 blue taking a position and asking for the ball #6 post the ball to number 3 number C turn and post about the right longer behind the defender then everybody shifting difference offers offensive number for the left side making the long run for opportunity when the long cross coming he can receive it and finish it.Important all six defenders have to communicate and taking the right position to stop the blue team to score or coming two shooting position.

Defenders stealing the ball then right away combine positioning and go take the ball out from the different zone try to score to the small goals. Possible week counter attack would be very nice. Coaches need to ask more variations practice the goal kicks.

Goalkicks. 7 v 6 20 min

Go kick variation repair kick the ball to the right defender inside midfielder #8 making outside run great defender possible long behind the red number 12 #8 dribbling into the space score and a small goal. please play with the defensive group goal kicks for the Asians do the left side to the middle and from there they lose the ball try to get back the ball With high pressure

Midfield stations ;

1. 6 v 6 + GK and zone 2 times 40 min

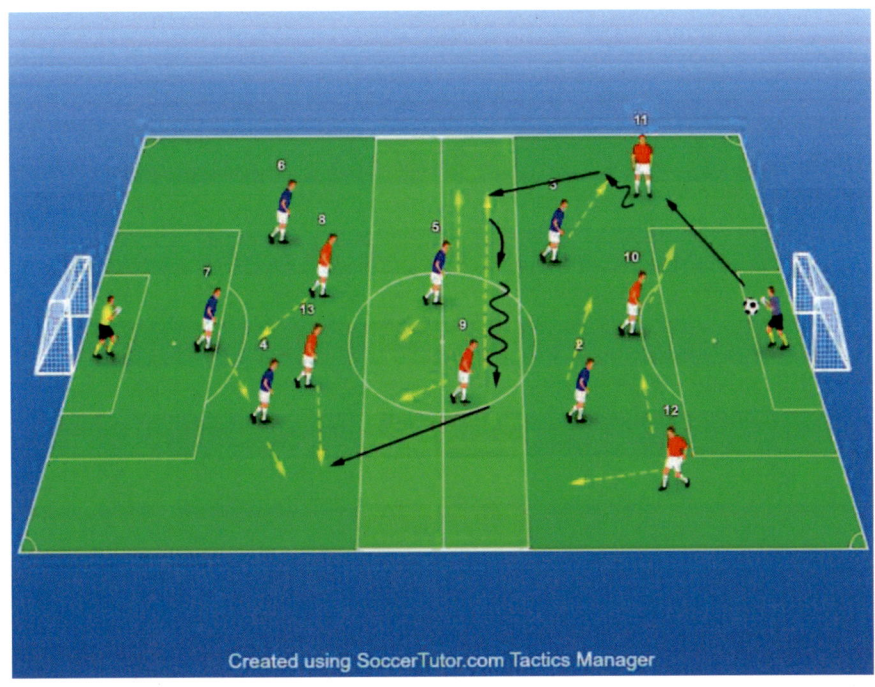

we creating three zones, defense midfield and offense. in defensive zone 3 versus 2 in the midfield zone 1 versus 1 End in offense zone 2 versus 3 .in the end zone the players can do everything but they can't leave they own Sean they have to pass the ball to the next song to create things some often save job. if they want to go forward they have to use every zone one time ,they can play back anytime. This game to play good you need a lot of movement loader positioning and good first touch Read high level communication.

The second part from that game the player example from the different zone played to the midfield zone he can follow his buses from the midfield zone you play to the offense on then you can follow too in that case the offensive zone going to 3 versus 3 game .that moment when you lost that ball everybody move back to the starting zone .

In this game we start doing corner kicks and free kicks direct and indirect free kicks. **free kicks and 30 min corner kicks**

  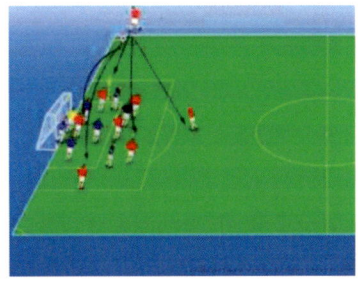

115

Offensive stations ;

1. 8 v 8 game with 3-3-2 in offense and 4-3-1 in defense 60 min

Goalkeeper throw the ball out to number 7 red he started to burn get #13 defender out from the block #13 red go wide right side #7 post about to him #3 red taking #13 position and get the boss on him #3 can decide it can push the ball in a center to number 15 post about through the right side behind the defender line #13 make their own . If defender #11 still the ball he can give right away long counterpass to #16 .Then the whole diverse line moved up very quick .leave the forwards in offside And help the number system build up the attack against the red team.

2. 8 v8 + GK Start from deep 60 min -with cornel kicks and fre kicks

Goalkeeper throw the ball to the left to number 9 #9 start dribbling get the number 15 defender attention don't post about straight forward #4 midfielder came out and receive the boss and quick play the ball forwards diagonal to number 5 between the two defender #5 tonight the way possible in the center #6 making their own true the two defender and taking a shot   **11.30 finish Lunch**

Thursday afternoon session;

1.45-2.00 pm Group volume up for the volume up make the kids ready for the main session

2.00-4.30pm Start the main training session

Defender Station;

1. Goal kick 6 v 6 , switch side then counter attack 60 min

keeper pass the ball to the right defense # 4, he start dribble after pressure pass the ball MF # 2, he turn inside and pass back to # 6, he pass to the left Defender # 7, who dribble forward get on him the red # 13, then pass inside to # 3, between # 4 right defender start runung forward into the space, # 3 see this and with a long cross switch tha ball to the right side. # 4 dribble into the space and give a long cross to the # 3 who made a nice run forward the shoot. Start more variations -keeper to the center D, then to the left D, then through it to the Midfielder. Then Long kick to the MF. Important the defenders not loosing the ball, do not force to go forward and try to beat 1 v 1 the opponent, until some partners is open you just make a pass and then move with out the ball. Get open! **Lot of positions!**

In the game with doing free kicks corner kicks. Could be direct and indirect free kicks . And thow-in variations

2. 6 v6 play back to the keeper then start again; 60 min

Defense can't go through on the offense team that's why they're not losing the ball they played the ball back to the keeper and then start again bringing the ball forward .

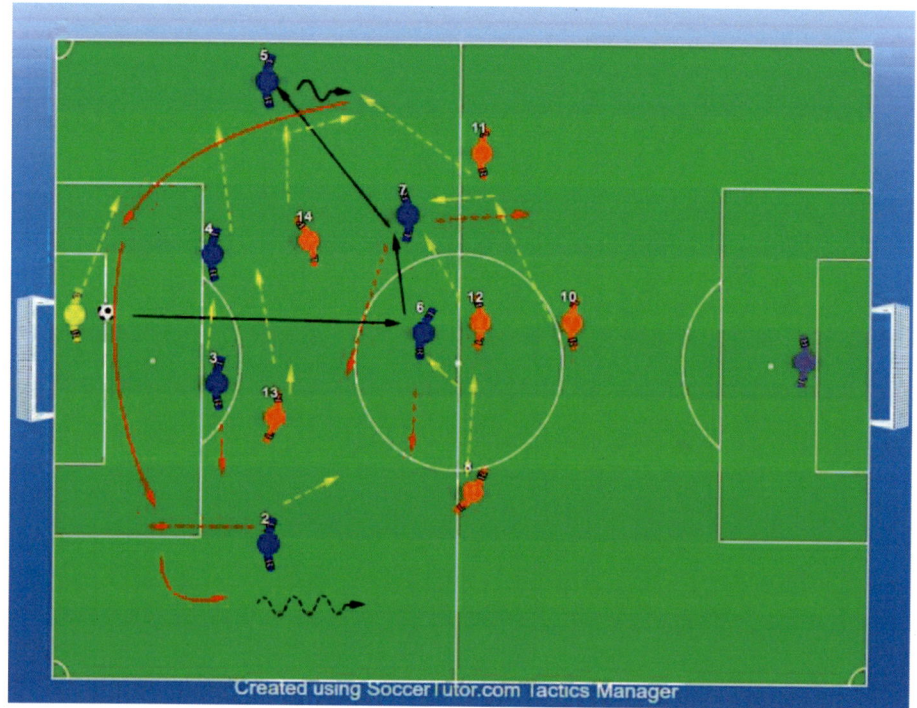

Goalkeeper kicked the ball to the number 6 long pass, he go short Pass to number 7, who turn out And play back to number 5. be'cause the pressure is to high # 5 play back to his keeper. GK turn to the other side and pass to number 2 who turn and start dribble forward. The red arraw shoing the back pass and the after moves and passes.

Next variations could be started from the keeper's hand he throwing the ball to the midfielders go through the ball to the right or left defender the keeper have to always when throwing to the right left defense coming out sideways and given options if the defender get hard pressure he can play it back to him right away.

Important not too touching the ball too many times if this possible one or two touches then play the ball quick and move they must get open very quick.

The game we using corner kicks free kicks indirect free kicks and electric kicks .

end with doing throw-in variations.

Middlefield station;

1. Warm up with keep away one outside players helping. 20 min

Position and 2-3 touches only

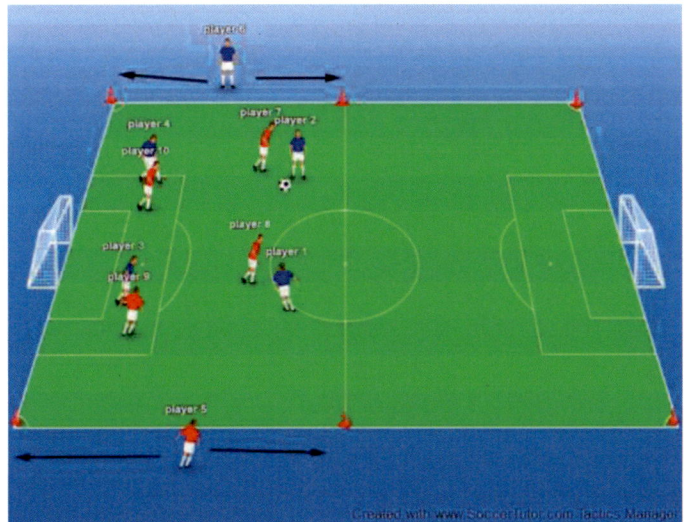

2. 7 v 7 defense offense outside attacks, 40 min

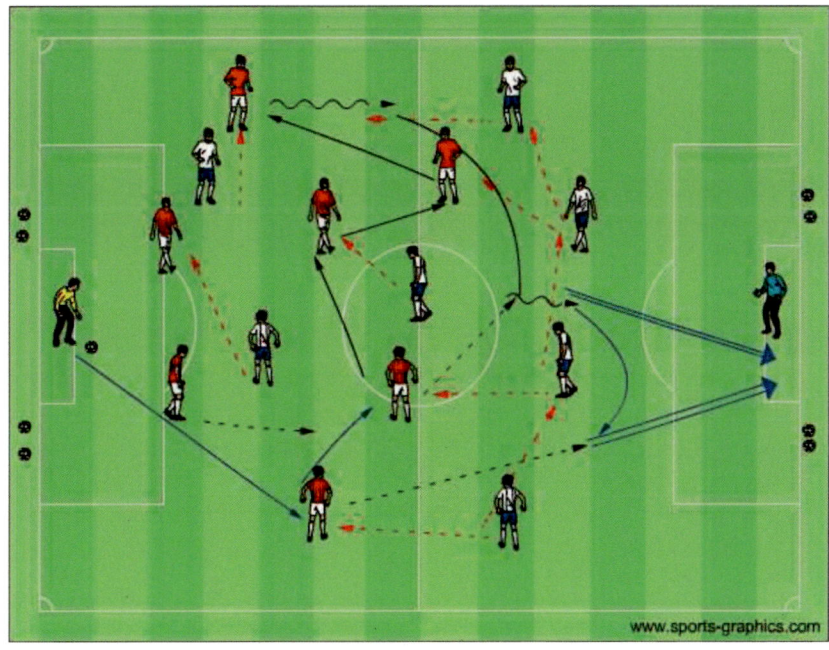

Keep it keep the ball to the outside midfielder he giving a short passing to inside to the partner who turning inside and pass the ball in the centre midfield he passing the ball to the left side inside midfield call turning back and post about back to the left defender. **he** start dribbling forward getting attention from the right defense then curved about inside from the rest of his helmet who did move in a center he can shoot right away if the pressure to close from the right defender oh center defender watch the ball right side because the right offensive midfielder moved forward and still free. corner kicks ,free kicks and throw in practice.

3. 8 v 8 free combinations game. 40 min

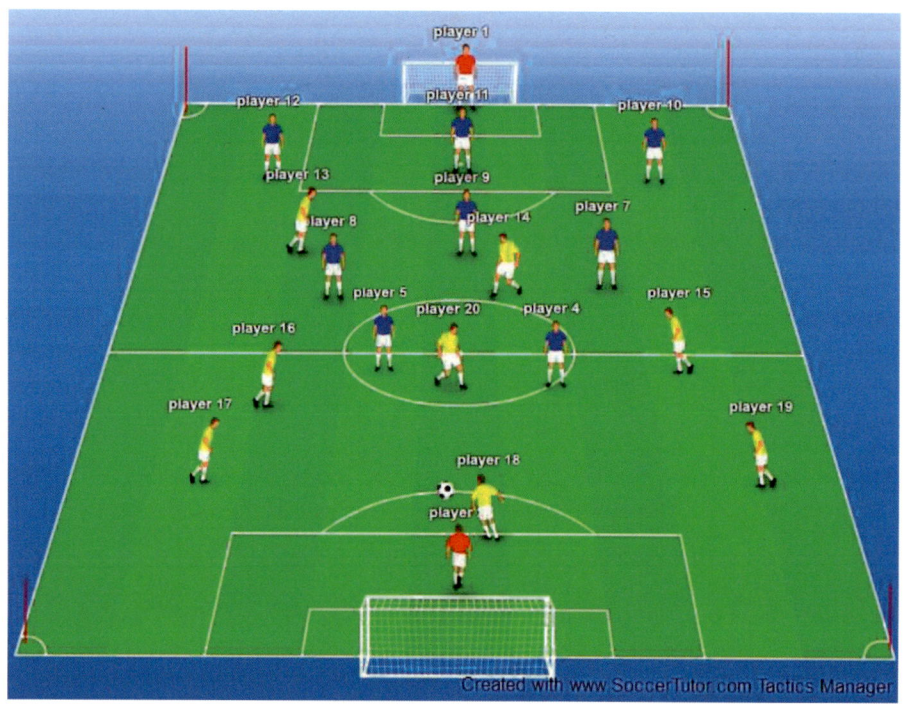

4.00-4.30 shooting finishing

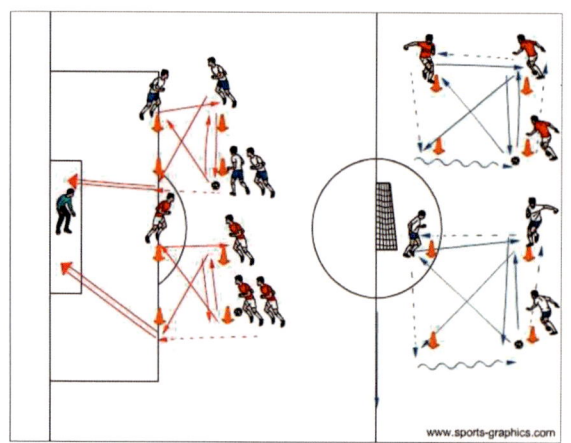
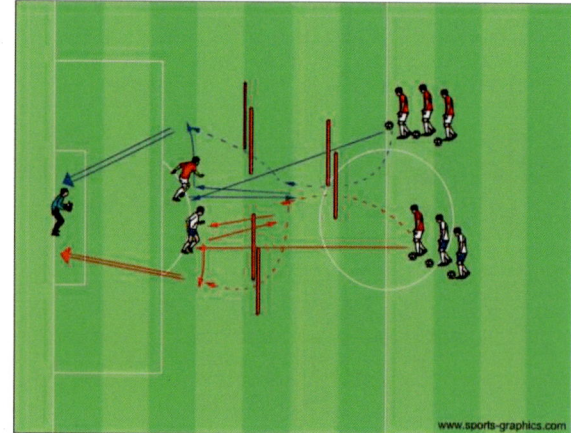

Offensive station ;

20 min

warm up great bosses two players one ball receiving with the inside food outside food crossing the body away from the boy before we push them all back to the partner trebling doing some turns fakes .

1. First tiki-taka passing 20 min

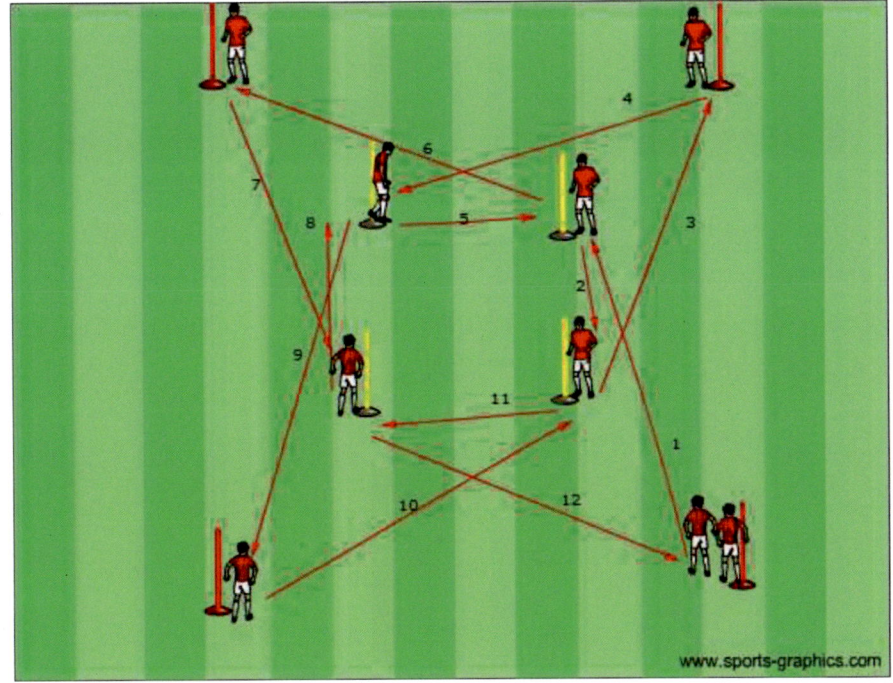

passing row following the numbers on the picture .

2. offensive high pressure. 30 min

Both teams have to practice and give 100% pressure try to double teaming the opponent and do not let the other team making any easy passing drill'

Re doing regular game with corner kicks tarrowin and free kicks.

3. corner kicks and free kicks ; 30 min

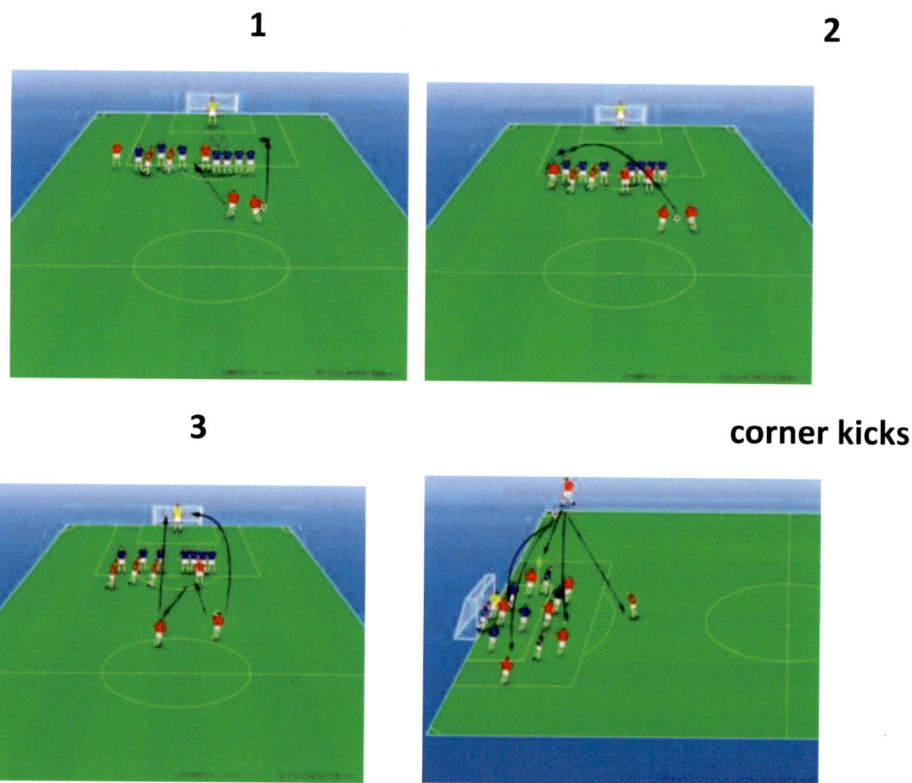

4.00-4.30 shooting finishing

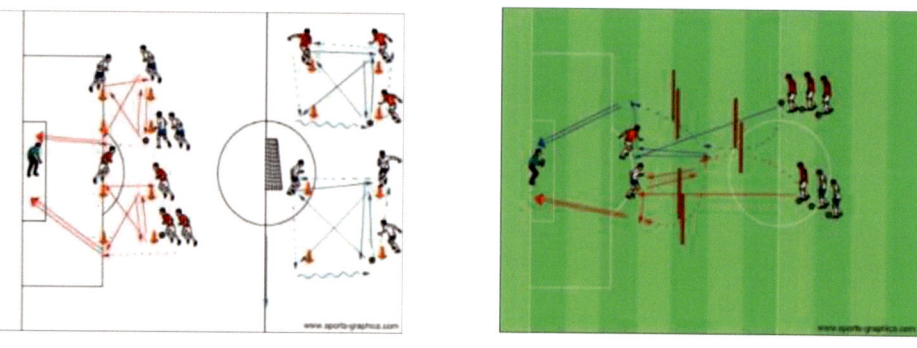

Thursday evening session;

6.45 -7.00 pm warm up

7.00-7.30 pm Shooting finishing

7.30-8.30pm evening small sided games; 4 v 4; 5 v 5; 6 v 6; 7 v 7;8 v 8 and 9 v 9

Could be the best if we have a team 12 players and evening, they play 6 v 6 and

Every night can switch teams and players. Monday to Wednesday then

Thursday and Friday 8 v 8 and 9 v 9 games.

Friday morning session ;

6.15-7.00 am

Soccer Aerobic if it is indoor, or fitness and technical sessions

Start the morning session:

8.45-9.00 Group warmups funny warmups make the kids ready for the focus on the sessions 9.00-11.30am start main training session

Defenseive station ;

1.Positioning diferent formations; (English style)

4-1-3-2   30 min   Line-up;

1. Defenders and midfielders generally stay on their side of the field (zone). 2. RD & LD challenge attackers on their side, cover for RD & LD, overlap when attacking. 3. CD & CD mark central attackers if play is in middle. 4. MFR& MFL are wingers when attacking, defend against overlapping defenders or outside midfielders. 5. DCM plays defensive, OCM is playmaker setting up attacks. 6. F1 & F2 make runs to near/far post or to wings.

In Defense; 30 min

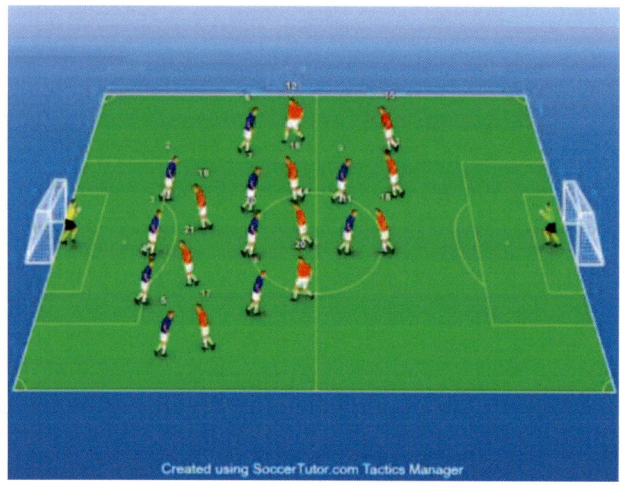

1. D4 challenges overlapping midfielder. 2. D5 provides support to D4 3. D2 marks central attacker. 4. D6 shifts to mark second central attacker. 5. M4 marks overlapping defender. 6. M2 & M3 pick up central midfielders. 7. M8 marks outside midfielder. 8. F1 & F2 cover remaining three defenders

Throw-in ;

1. Defense zone;

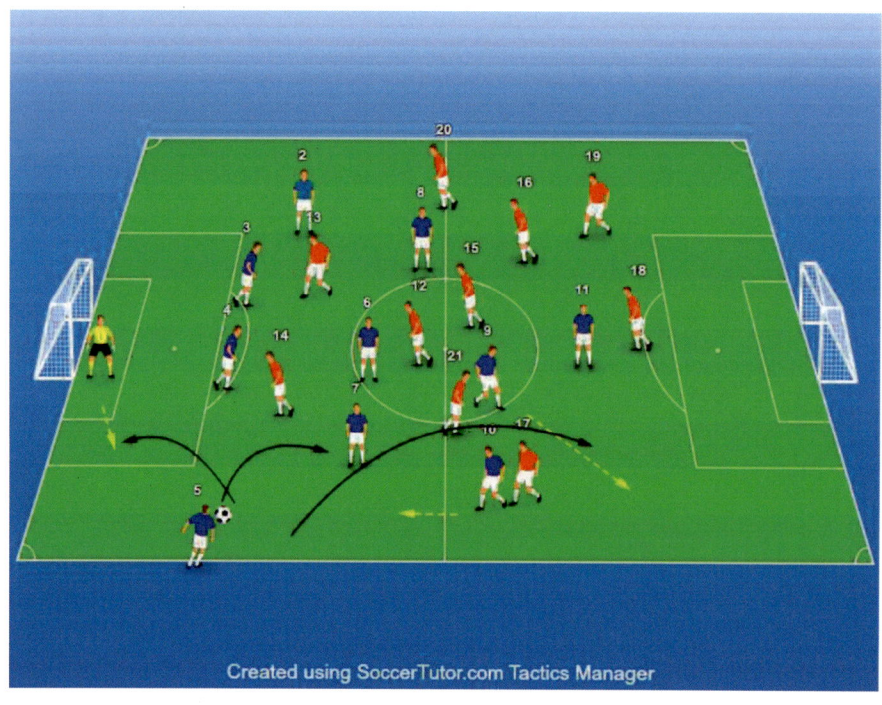

Player can throw it closest player orto goalkeeper or on the line the player checking to you and behind another player from inside coming out and throw it over the head this is very powerful variation.

2. Midfield zone :

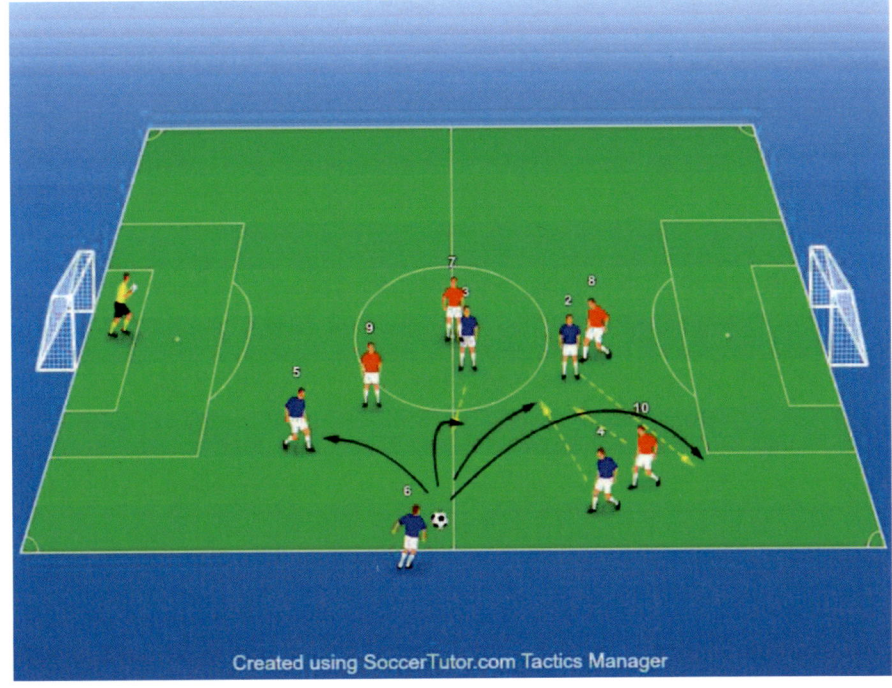

Play a throw-in to the Defender or from inside player checking to you or from the right outside player move inside then from the inside player move outside into the open space and you're going to throw over the head into the space .

3. Offense zone ;

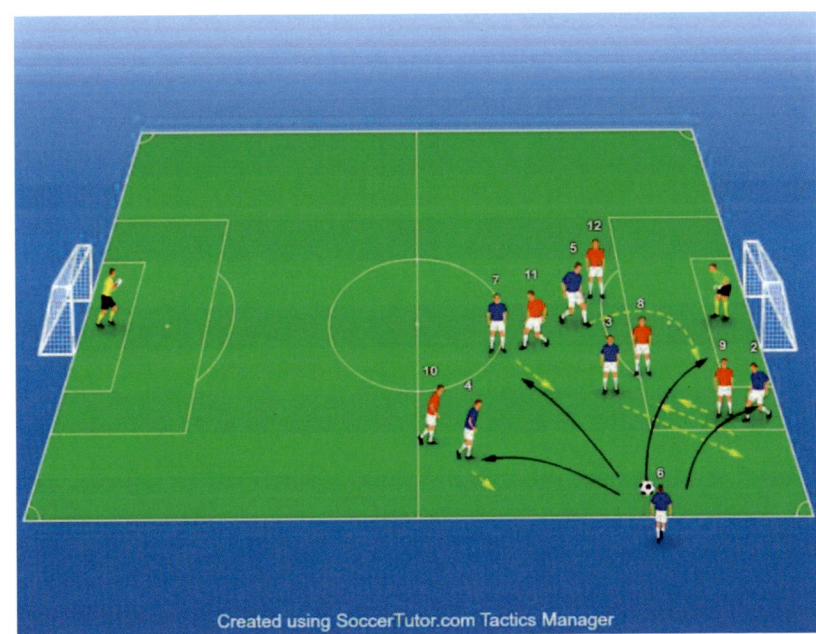

#6 has a choice to throw the ball to number 4 or #7 who is checking to him the number two from the goal line running inside #3 from inside running outside into the goal line between #5 from the center running into the open space close to the six yards this is more powerful in that case this would be the best option.

Finish the session with 8 v 8 plus GK game

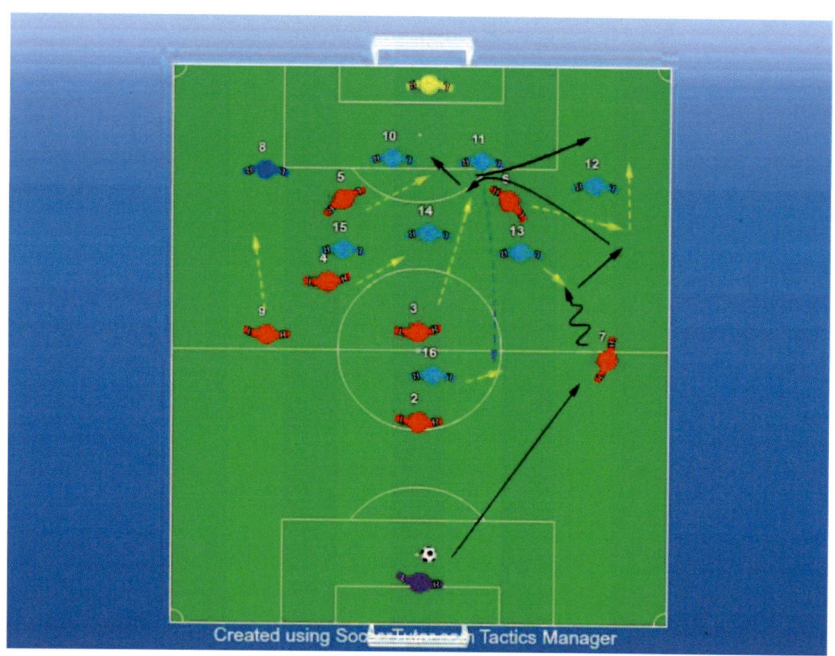

coach could ask the players to create and repeat nobody Asians what they learned from Monday until Friday .

Midfield station ;

1, Goodnight kicks free kicks variations. 50 min

Freekick # 1

One forward stay on the wall 1 yard away from the wall the shooters showing he gonna shoot right away to the goal but he running to the ball and pass the ball straight behind the wall into the space the player from the center close to the wall turn quick run to the ball and shoot or dribbling to the goal line and Pass the ball back .

Freekick # 2

Shooter kick the ball over the players to the left side left forward Is ready to run to the ball head it or kick and tried to score if the pass is too long the player have to control the ball shield it, dribble and try to cross in or play the the ball back .

Greekick # 3

Shooter pass the ball left side to the open player who kicking over the wall the right side into the space the shooterAfter when he passed the ball run straight to the ball and try to finish or try to create chances to score pass back.

2. Transitions; 50 min

1. M4 gets ready to make overlapping run. 2. F20 gets ready to make diagonal run. 3. M9 is primary target for a pass from defenders. 4. D4 supports D5 for a back pass. 5. D6 has option of passing to D4, M9 or deep to right. Depending on where on the field the play is, the player in possession should have at least three passing options to players either coming towards the ball or making runs into space

Ask the players to show what they learned positioning this week Monday to Friday ask improvisation from the players London movement good first touch good ball control Communication is key in in team work.

Free kicks and corner kicks variations in corner kicks far post near post back to the D short corner kicks.

Offensive station ;

Practice the free kicks;

Is more technical exercise the players have to eat them all right find the right position behind the ball grab the ball if they have to hit the ball power depends what they trying to do;

Free kicks technique;

1. Curve the ball over the wall

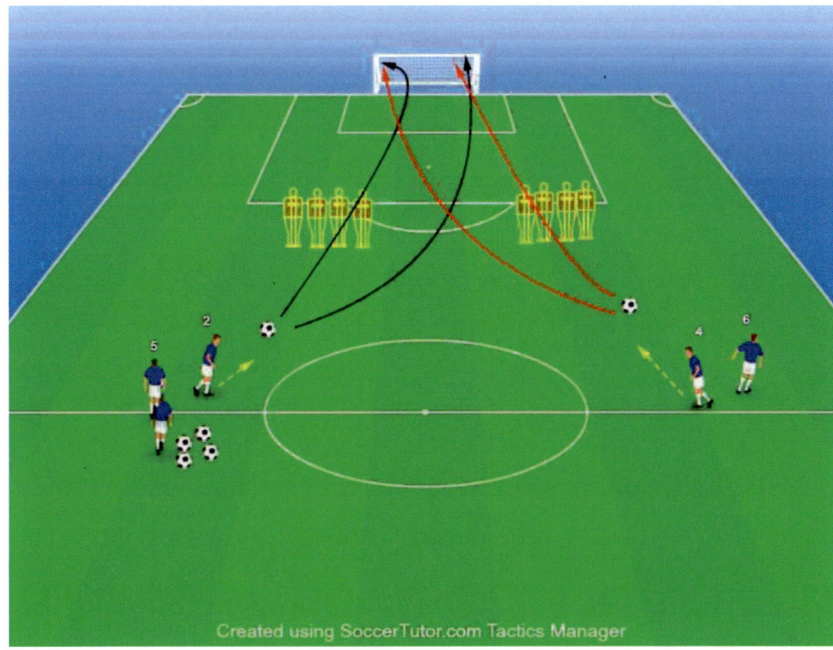

Both side every players can try it curve the ball with the inside foot to the near post or to the fahr post

How much you Lying back with your body. Every players is different the coach have to correct the misstakes from the players. Important how much you curve the ball, how much power you need to kick the ball put it over the wall?

2. After short service kick it with power, or do curve it to the corner.

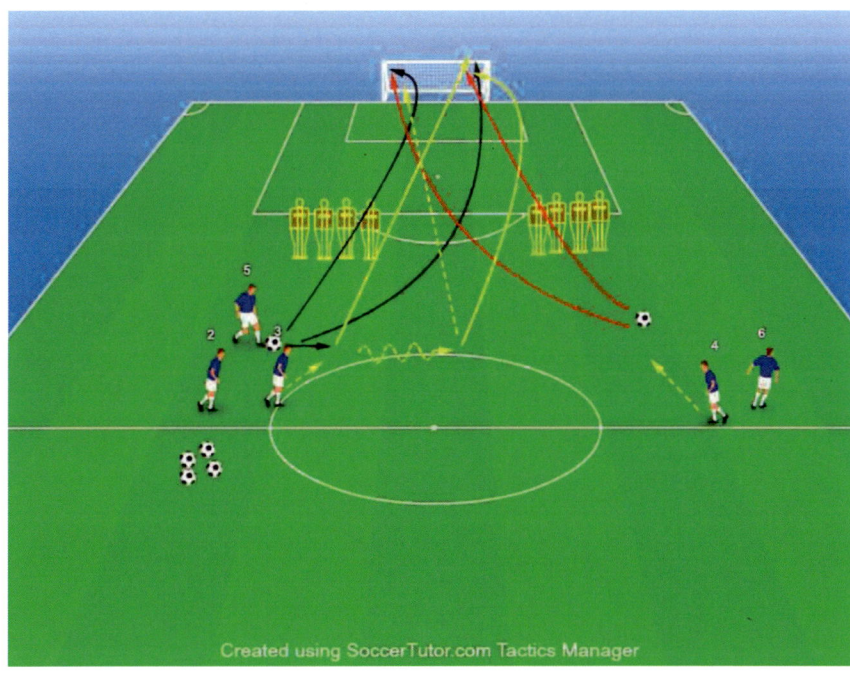

Every players is different the coach have to correct the misstakes from the players. Important how much you curve the ball, how much power you need to kick the ball put it over the wall? Here the partner make a short pass and the shooter run to the ball and hit it with power, or curve it to the corner. Is the yellow line on the picture

3. Freekick from the center and from outside.

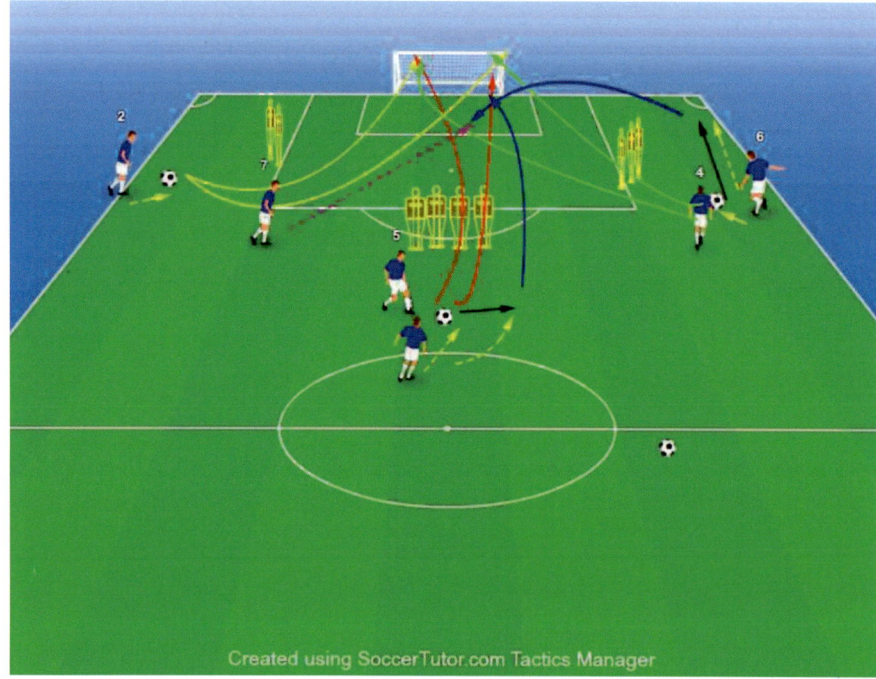

Free kick from outside left you curve the ball into the near post or to the far post, in the center position curve the ball like before into the near post or into the far post, you can bring it over the wall straight to the corner or the left corner or you make a short pass and your partner run to the ball and hit the ball straight to the goal ,from the right side with the left foot U curve in to the near post or curve it to the far post or make a along pass forward your partner running to the ball crosses in and in the center coming a center forward and tried to put the ball into the net

4.8 v 8 plus GK. Game with trying all what you did learned the week.

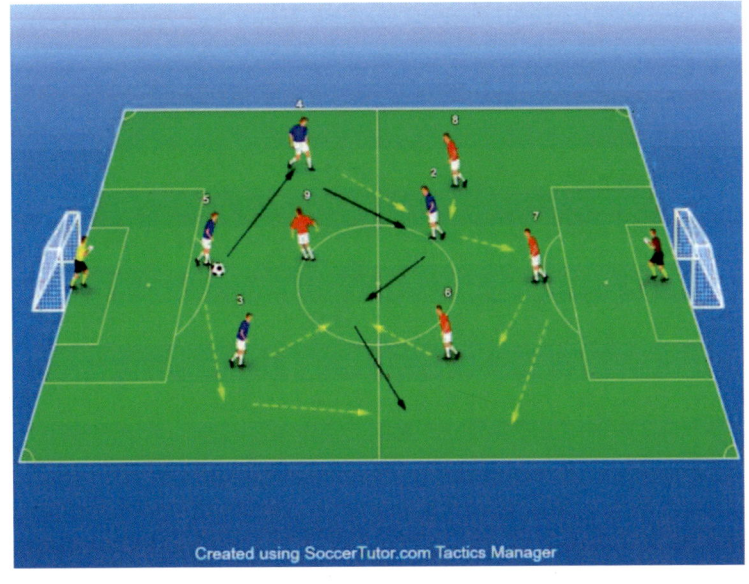

Afternoon session ; 3 positions working together defense , offense and midfield.

1.45-2.00 pm Group volume up for the volume up make the kids ready for the main session

2.00-4.30pm Start the main training session

1. Start with small side 3 v 3 D + FW

Coaches fallow the work from the defenders and the forwards to. Keeping the zones and try to go thru and finish, defense still the ball they became the offense team and try to score.

2. 4 v 4 keeping the ball in position but going to finish.

Coaches fallow the work from the defenders and the forwards to. Keeping the zones and try to go thru and finish, defense still the ball they became the offense team and try to score. Let the players improvise and create something from self.

3. 6 v 6 defense offense;

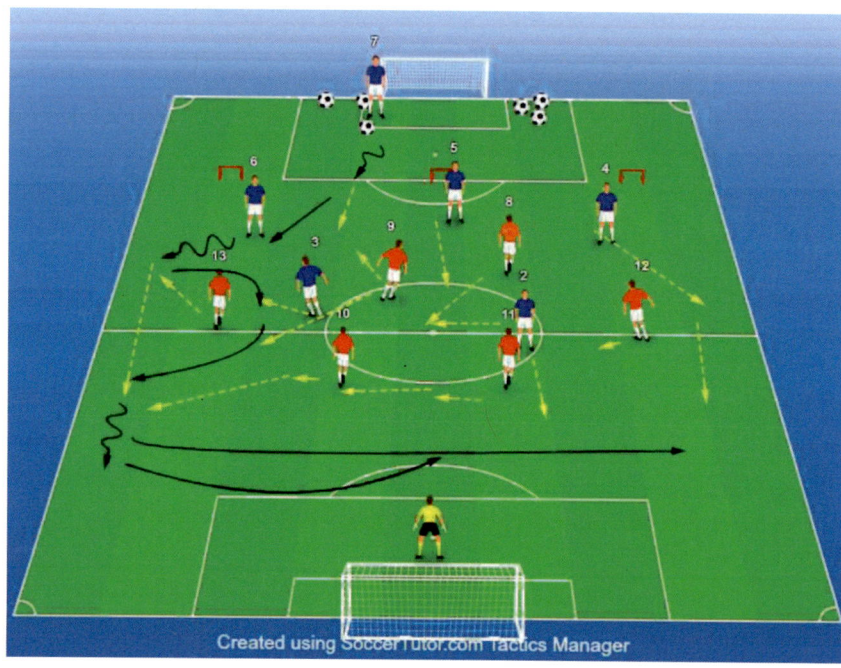

Coaches fallow the work from the defenders and the forwards to. Keeping the zones and try to go thru and finish, defense still the ball they became the offense team and try to score. Let the players improvise and create something from self.

4. 9 v 9 Free soccer games with free kicks corner kicks, Penalty kicks. Everywhere on the field, defense, offense, and midfield.

Friday evening session:

Teams going to practice the Saturday competitions, then depense the number of the players do a mini tournament.

Create so many fields how many players you have and play a small tournament. With time 5- 10 minutes halves.

Saturday Session.

8:45 am - Warm-ups

9:00-10:00 am Team competitions

10.00-10.30 am Final competitions

10:30 – 11.30 am games

12.00 noon Players Check-out

1.Team competitions

Teams going, they field with the evening coaches and doing the competition

6. Penalty Kicks
7. 18 yards shooting (ball must land behind the goal line in the air)
8. Heading
   Competitions 1-2-3 going for point system

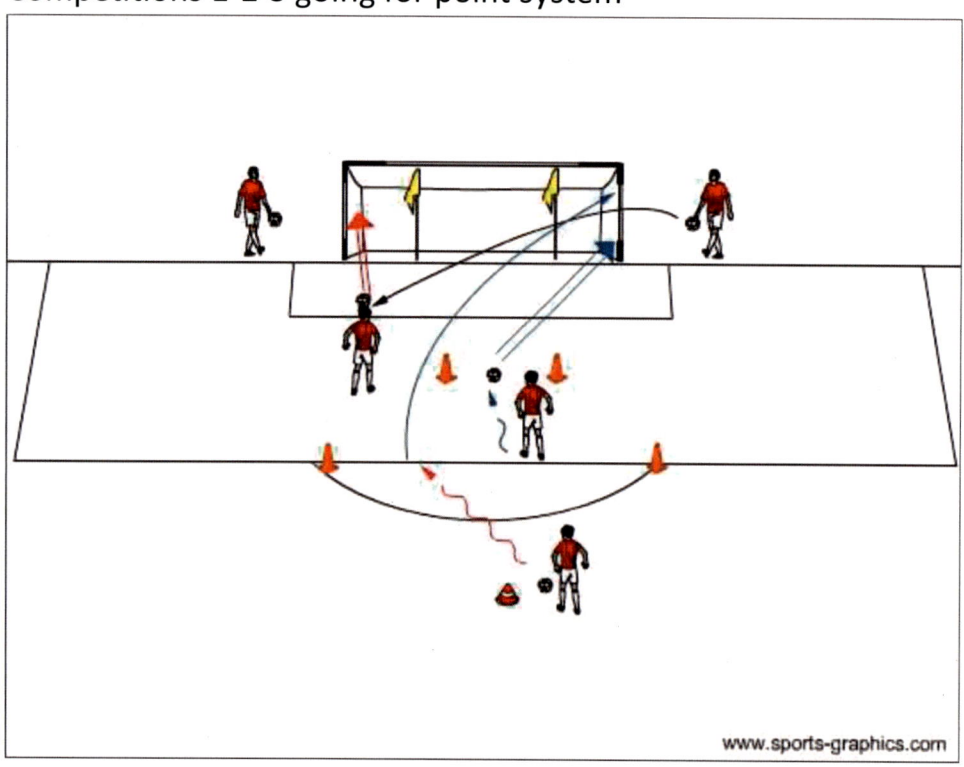

Competition 1-2-3 the ball must land behind the goal line.
In the side net is 3 point-between the flag and the post is 2 points
And in the center is 1 point

9. **King of the hill:**

Players dribbling with the ball individually and shield it because they must kick out somebody's ball. The players who is last standing in the field is the winner.
Players must move with the ball they cannot standing who does not move
Get warning second time is out from the competition.

You cannot leave your ball and kick somebody's ball out you must always in contact with your own ball.

10. **Juggling.**

Players starting in the same time and who is the last juggler is the winner. Players must keep touching the ball they cannot holding the ball on the foot or on the back. Continuing Juggling.

11.15 Price giving for the winners!!

11.30-12.00 noon Small sided games. Closing ceremony after the games

6 Coaches taking they own teams and starting very quick with the games Using small numbers (4 v 4; 5 v 5; 6 v 6) So the kids have a lot of touches and the parent's and family members can see what they kids did learned in the week.

The teams -Depense the numbers from the players.

135

12.oo Noon players checking out orientation on the field after the games

We are starting the third performance week. Witch is all week Team technique, team skill and team tactic.11 v 11

All day we are working us a team, of course we do defense, offense, and midfield situations.

Monday Morning Sessions: -We talk about the most team formations.

1-4-4-2

1-4-3-3

1-4-1-3-2

1-4-2-3-1

1-3-5-2

1-5-3-1-1

1-4-1-4-1

1-4-5-1

1. Improve Passing, receiving, penetration passes, thru passes, in defense, midfield and offense.

- Ball warm up in pairs, 1 ball each pair 18 min-

The players they move Without the ball and with the ball taking positions ,important the pass go through the gate and they Receive it players using one gate the next you have to use an different gate, important communication, look up see where is your partner and passthe ball when you partner call for it you can spin it over the turns before you post the ball,enjoy the warm up,First pass go to the players next pass go to the space.

-Diagonal and outside runs; 22 min 6 v 4 + 2

Passing receiving in movement, switch point of attack penetration passes first parts the defenders give only body pressure den the defenders going to be active, offensive team scores against keeper, the Defenses team score find the two blue target players.

-

-defense and midfield; 40 min

Defence focus on the midfield, midfield players in compact with the forward, I contact forcing with movement and passing take the opponent out of shape. With penetration passing going behind the defense line if the defense is good in position do not force it.

Breaking the deep ends with outside runs overlap and giving go.

-In 9 v 9 offense and defense creating positions, coaches asking the players to do what they learned, outside defenders making the run, the middle players talking and asking for the ball, making penetration passes ,players making crosses, but coaches expect from the players to improvise.   40 min

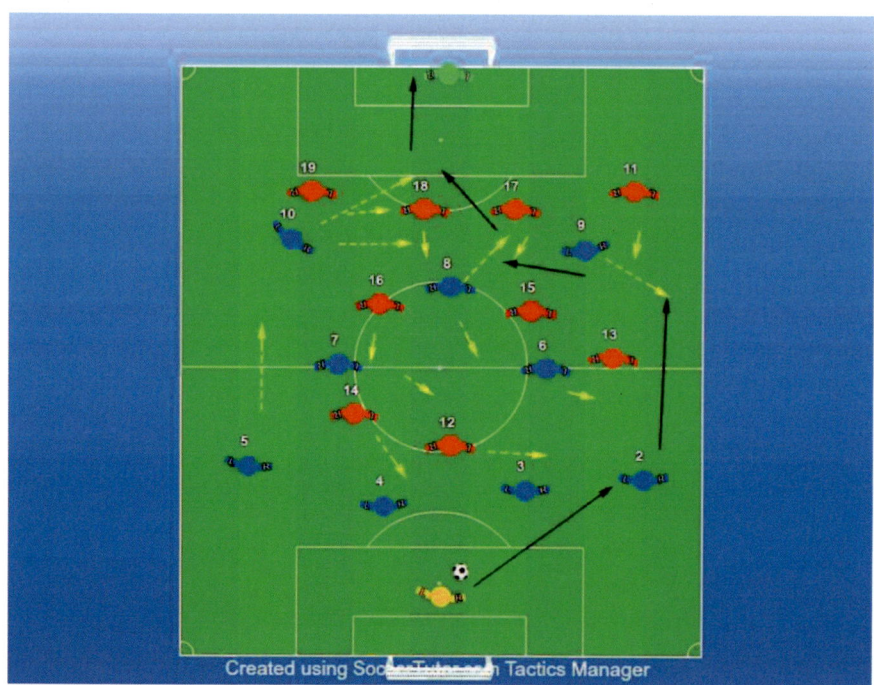

Monday afternoon session.

1.45-2.00 pm Group volume up for the volume up make the kids ready for the main session

2.00-4.30pm Start the main training session

3-5-2 Tech-Tach position and play 20 min

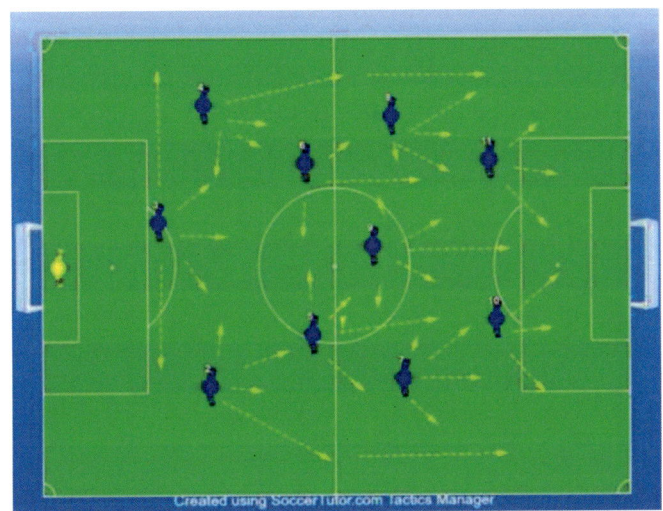

Players movement in offense

Improve positional play in for 3-5-2 team play 40 min

Create shape pressure cover ,lateral movement, Ball in front stay in contact, communication, wide midfielder Overlap, force website attack, Losing the ball try to get position and pressure get the ball back.

11 v 11 one team is 3-5-2 the other team is 4-4-2 (COACHING THE 3-5-2 MOST) 70min

In modern soccer the movement without the ball is very important ,the players have to understand lot of movement could be improved the positions and helping beat the opponent ,would like to see in that game a lot of movement overlaps Cross runs, through passes, wide midfielders and outside defenders runs into the space, forwards doing cross runs ,defensive center mid forward and cross runs, we would like to see in the third line helping in the offense ,counter attack ,line of pressure, losing the ball in that case take the position very quick And getting high pressure on the opponent .

Of course, is a real game we have thrown balls we have corner, kicks we have free kicks.

Monday evening session.

6.45 -8.30 --11 v 11 side games 2 times 45 min. – warm- up with the teams

Try everything what we did practice combination plays, penetration passes, outside runs, crosses. Free kicks, corner kicks, throw-ins.

Every night switching opponent it is possible. After the numbers of players.

The camp number is not big enough then change players in the teams, of course this change going to be helping for the players. development

Tuesday Morning Session:

6.45 am Soccer Aerobic if it is indoor, or fitness and technical sessions

Start the morning session:

8.45-9.00 Group warmups funny warmups make the kids ready for the focus on the sessions 9.00-11.30am start main training session

High Pressure-Ball recovery 40 min

Red team: tempo on the ball, good support, good communication, quick movement, get open, correct good passes.

Blue team: right moment to press on the ball, aggressively attack the player in possession, work together to close out the passing lanes. Keep the shape on position. Goal you can score only if you get in the 18 yards without pressure. Then the teams switch position.

8 v 8 plus keeper-High pressure – ball recovery 50 min

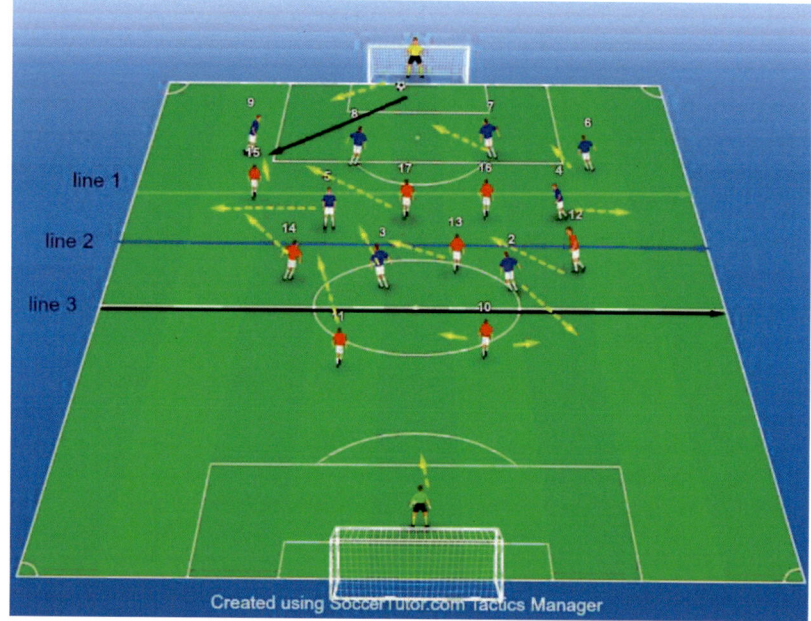

when the team lost the ball, they try to get the ball back with high pressure. We have 3 lines witch we give numbers, Winning the ball in the first line is the best because close to the goal and can right away attack or shoot. Of course, any line is good to win the ball. Extremely important the communication and the aggressiveness to working good together. Team did win the ball, then if passible quick play and movement, but not to force over anything.

11 v 11 positioning games focus on the high-pressure Offense is 1-4-1-3-2 Defense is 1-4-4-2 formation   30 min

Practice in full size game focus on the high pressure.

Tuesday Afternoon session

1.45-2.00 pm Group volume up for the volume up make the kids ready for the main session

2.00-4.30pm Start the main training session

1. Position defense offense

4-1 defense v. 1-3-2 offense 50 min

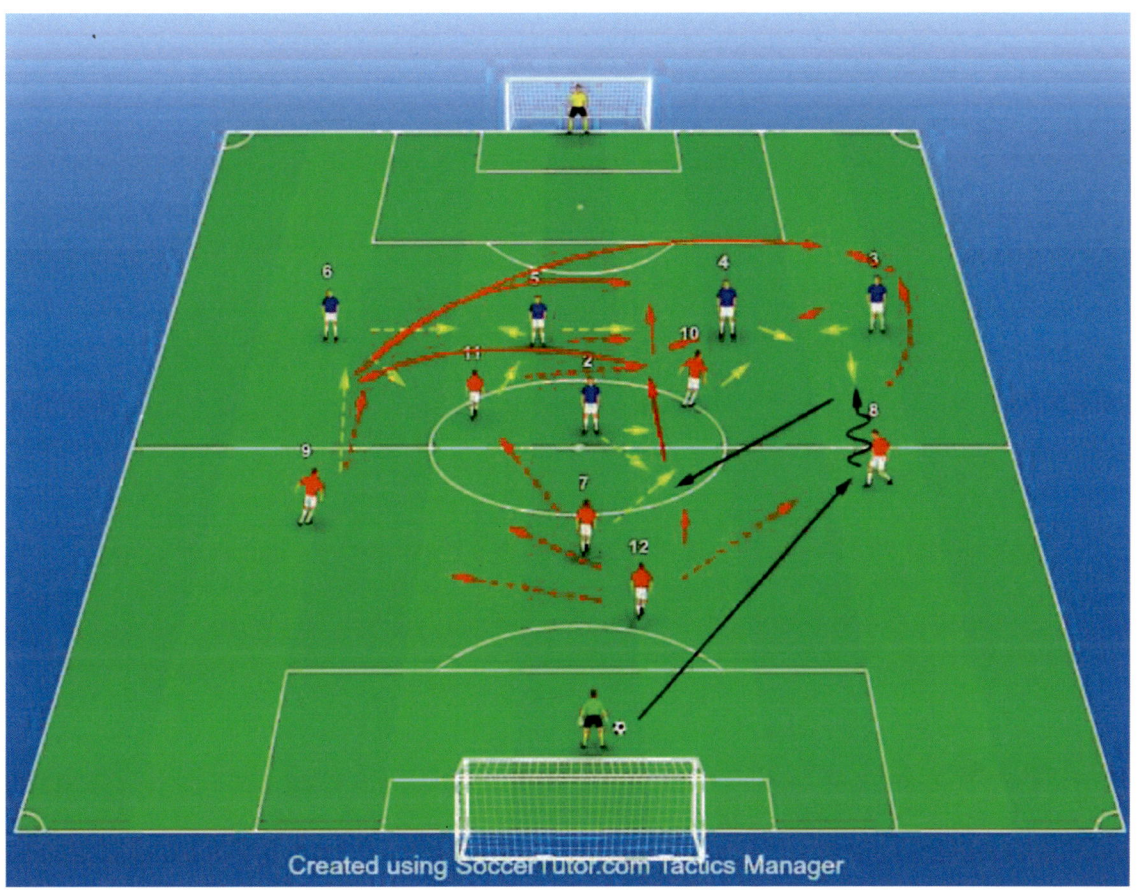

Keeper kick the ball to number 8 right offensive midfielder who start dribble against the left defender, after play the ball back in the center to number 7 who is passing the ball straight to number 11 who did move from the left side into the middle into the middle, Between #9 the left side coming forward ,#7 pass the ball to number #9 who is coming forward and he behind the defense line curve **the** ball to number 10 or to #8 they running forward into the space.

Coaches trying to make different variations and let the players improvise.

Defense still the ball – start the counterattack 50 min

Left defender did read the game he still the ball played back to the keeper in this moment the right defender giving option to the keeper who played the ball to him the number 5 center defender Cedars and starts running on the line #6 post about to him restart dribbling forward with speed and #2 in the middle maker on give an option for #6 who passed the ball to him they doing a given goal had #6 take a shot.

Coaches trying to make different variations and let the players improvise .

11 v 11 Game 30 min (free game after players improvisation) formation 4-4-2 and 4-1-33-2

Tuesday evening session:

6.45 -8.30 --11 v 11 side games 2 times 45 min. – warm- up with the teams

Formations; 4-4-2 and 4-1-3-2

Wednesday Morning session.

6.45 am Soccer Aerobic if it is indoor, or fitness and technical sessions

8.45-9.00 Group warmups funny warmups make the kids ready for the focus on the sessions
9.00-11.30am start main training session

1. Attack in Central and sideline.

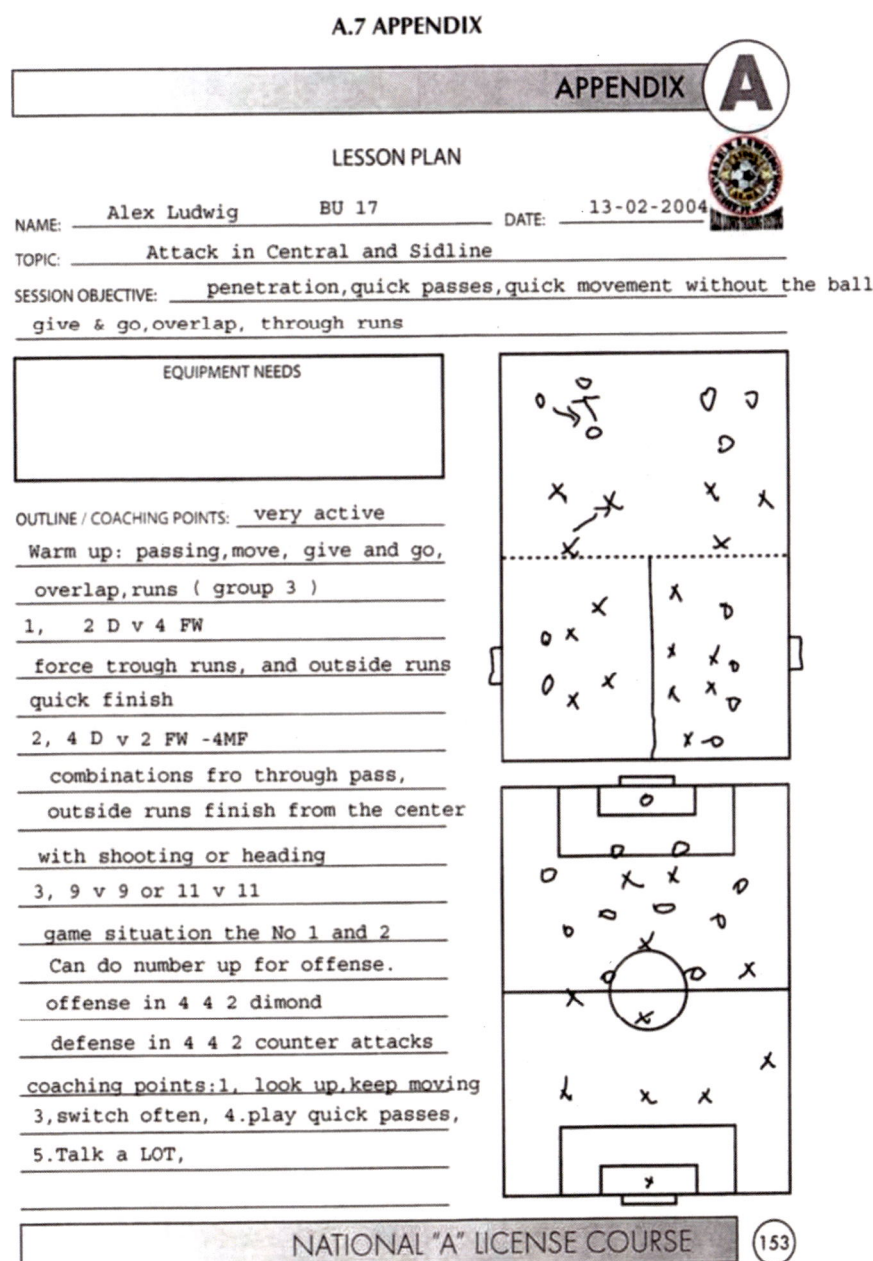

Here I would like to show you, how can you example make a day practice plan. B 17 training was in Los Angeles before a state cup game.2004 (4-4-2 in diamond and flexibility to 4-1-3-2)

Warm-up: in group 3, passing, quick move, give and go, overlap runs 10 min

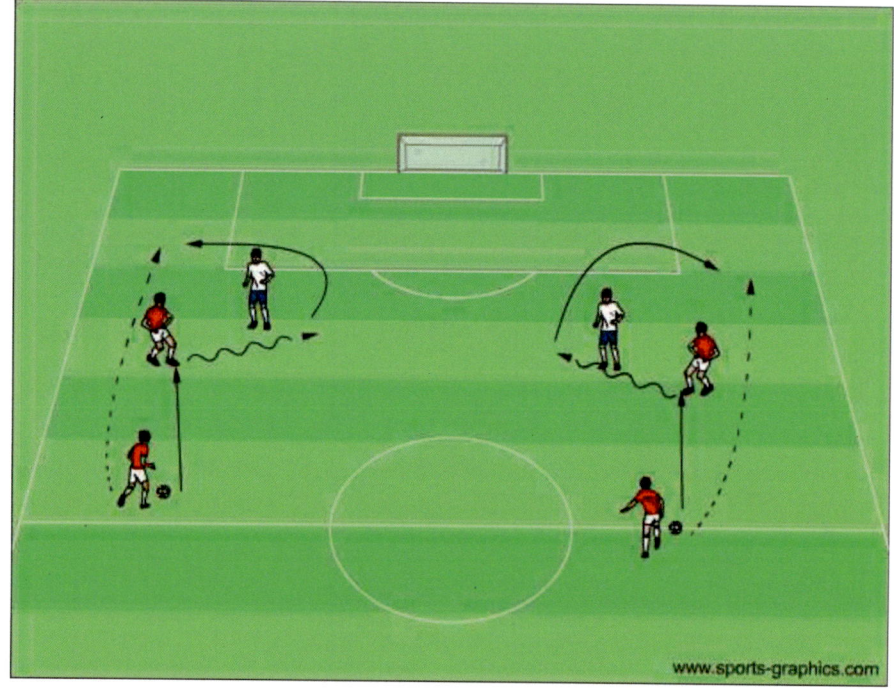

players focus on the movement, communication, making give and go and overlap runs. Stretch particularly good.

1. 2 Defender plus GK, versus 4 attackers 20 min

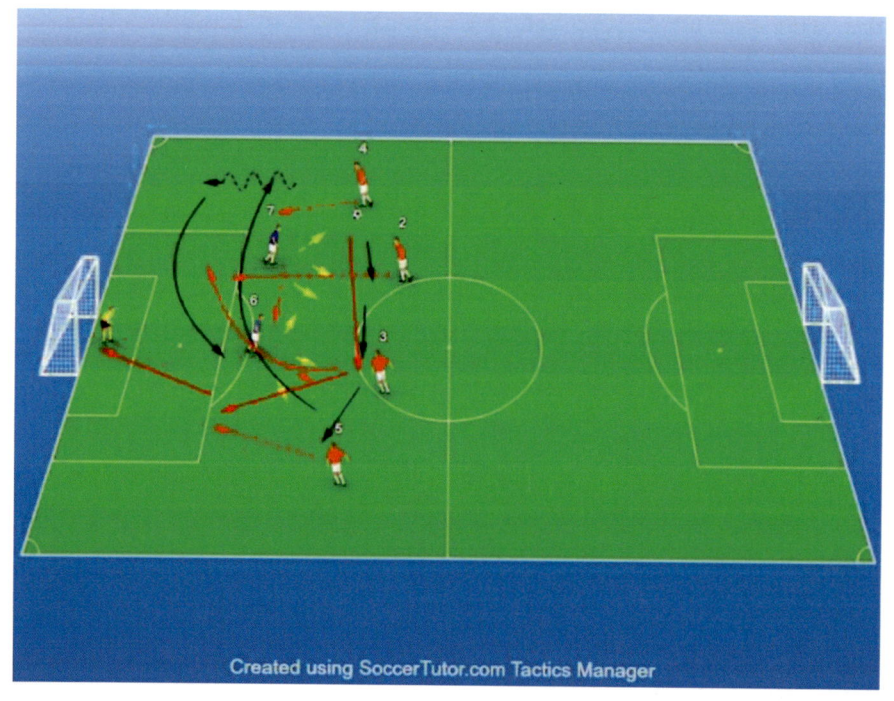

force thru runs, penetration runs and passes, outside runs, quick breaking the defense and finish.

Defenses win the ball -clear it or try to go thru the half line (Red lines for defense)

146

2. 4 Defender v. 2 forwards and 4 midfield players 20 min

Combinations for thru pass ,outside runs, finish from the center, with shooting or heading after crosses the combinations must be very quick, organized, and high-level communication.

Defender has the ball quick running out, lived forwards an offside and try to score the small goals with quick passes and runs.

3. 11 v 11 Offense is flexible from 4-4-2 to 1-4-1-3-2 defense is 1-4-4-2 formation 50 min

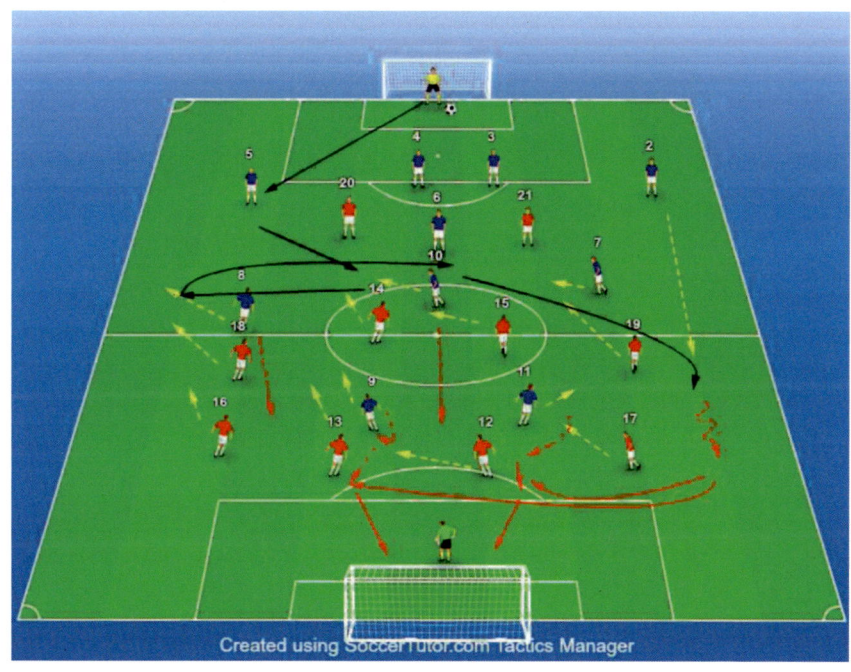

Goalkeeper kick the ball to right defense #5 who passing the ball to number 10 in the middle between #8 go to the sideline in the right side get the pass receive it and pass the ball back to number 10 in the middle between #2 left defender very quick go up make the nice run #10 pass the ball into the space front of #2 the he dribble down allaway down close to the 18 yards,between the two forwards turn and made their run in the center, number 2 do see this and cross the ball in the middle, and one of the forwards take a shot try to finish.

11.30 Lunch

Wednesday Afternoon Session:

1.45-2.00 pm Group volume up for the volume up make the kids ready for the main session

2.00-4.30pm Start the main training session

A.7 APPENDIX

APPENDIX A

LESSON PLAN

NAME: Alex Ludwig DATE: _____

TOPIC: Offensive organizations in 5 man midfield

SESSION OBJECTIVE: To improve shape of 5 midfielders when in position of the ball.

EQUIPMENT NEEDS

Ball, cone, bibs

OUTLINE / COACHING POINTS: in 3 warmups of tree short-short-long, support ball, look overheat ball poses.

2, 6 v 4 (5 MF + 1 FW) attack on sideline, recieving the ball and see held and pass quickly.

3, 7 v 6 introduce 1 other FW and more Defenders fro more presure 2 holding MF support in behind ball, switch point of attack. attacking MF must be mobile to find position, open players, get the ball, to attack sideline, create true pass, penatration, movement to the front.

4, 11 v 11 game

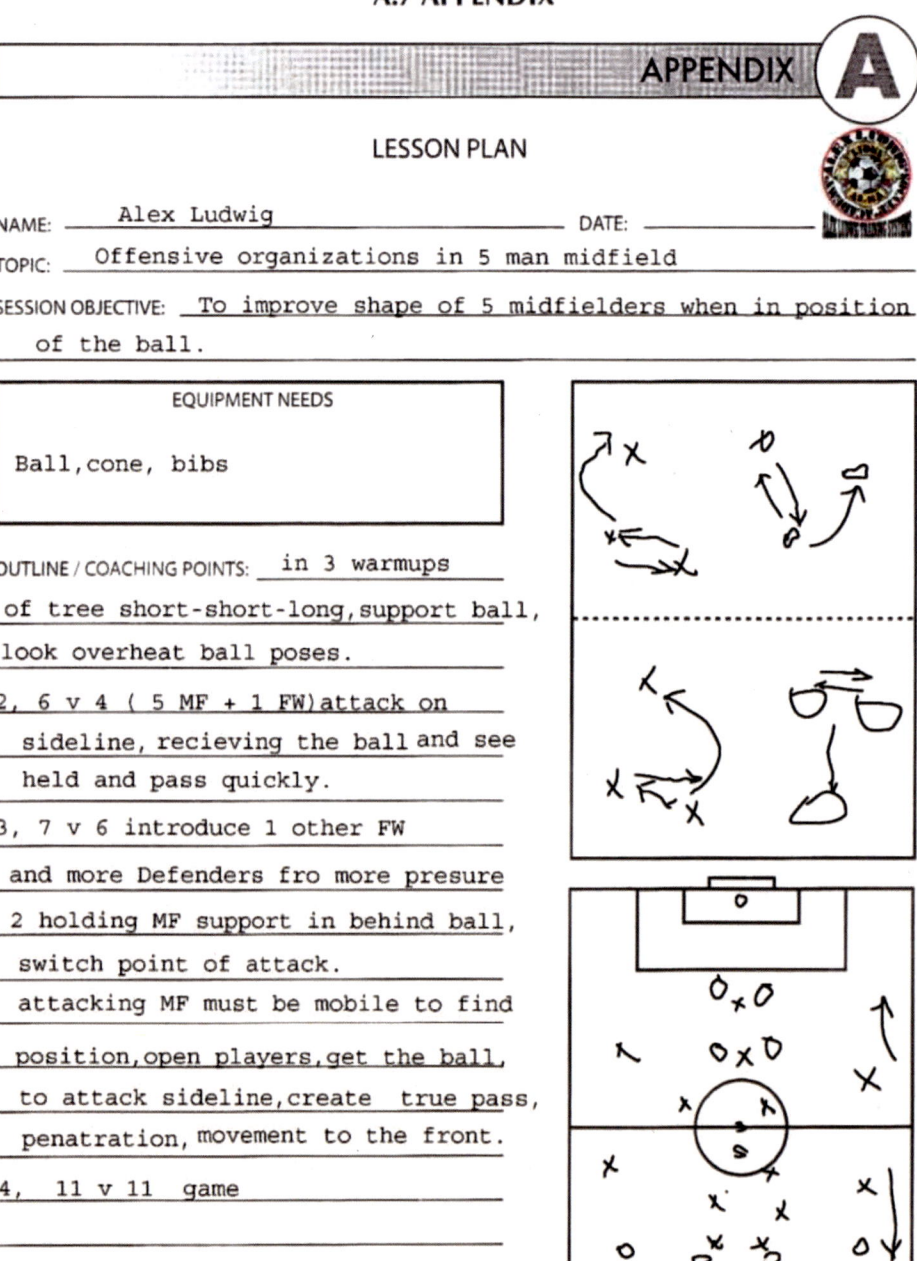

NATIONAL "A" LICENSE COURSE

Offensive game style in 4 and 5 Midfilder;

1. Warm-up in group 3, 15 min

Passing reciving, short, short then long pass, move with the ball and without the ball, receiving the ball then excelerate, communication, call for the ball.

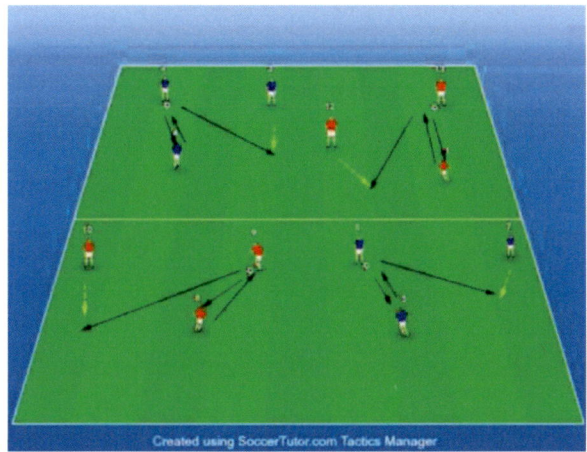

2. Combination play in 6 v 4 (5 MF and 1 FW) v 4 defenders 45 min

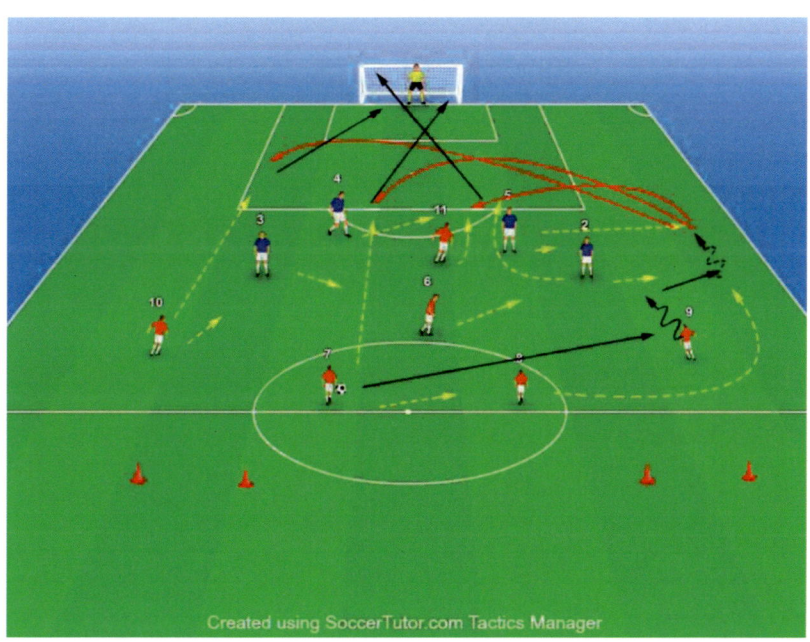

Five midfielders plus one forward against four defenders, the advantage is big for the offensive team Be'cause of the number. #7 offensive players passing the ball to to the right to #9 Who started dribble a little bit inside get the number 2 defender on him, Between #8 overlap him #9 make a site pass to number 8 who start dribbling forward intensive getting the defenders out from the middle, that moment number 11 and #7 start running in the center towards to the goal, and #10 the in the wite side make the lon run that case if the ball too long he can reach it. #8 has three opportunity to cross the ball one is to number 11 the other opportunity is numbers 7 other number 10.

3. 11 v 11 game, focus on the outside offense and the 5 midfielder working together. 50 min

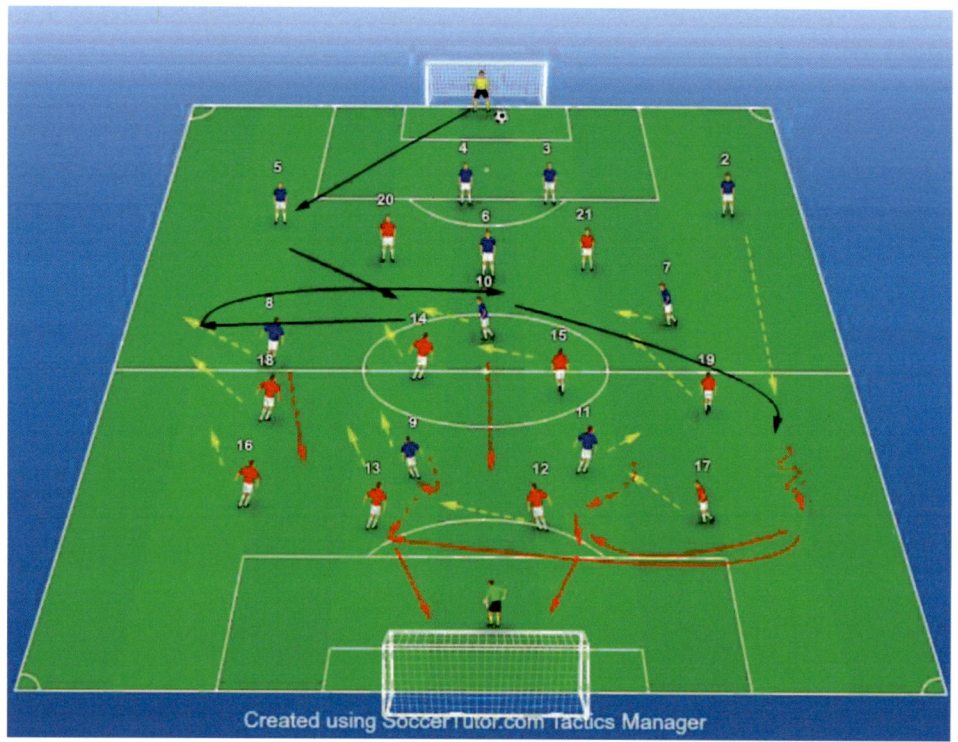

From lot of movement ,running, cross running, deep and wide,Creating positions to beat the opponent possible on the sideline with crosses and in the center the offensive players midfielders forwards coming to the opportunity to finish .

4.30 Finish go to Dinner

Wednesday evening session:

6.45 -8.30 --11 v 11 side games 2 times 45 min. – warm- up with the teams

Formations; 4-4-2 and 4-1-3-2

Try everything what we did practice combination plays, penetration passes, outside runs, crosses. Free kicks, corner kicks, throw-ins.

Every night switching opponent it is possible. After the numbers of players.

The camp number is not big enough then change players in the teams, of course this change going to be helping for the players. development

Thursday Morning Session:

6.45 am Soccer Aerobic if it is indoor, or fitness and technical sessions

Start the morning session:

8.45-9.00 Group warmups funny warmups make the kids ready for the focus on the sessions 9.00-11.30am start main training session

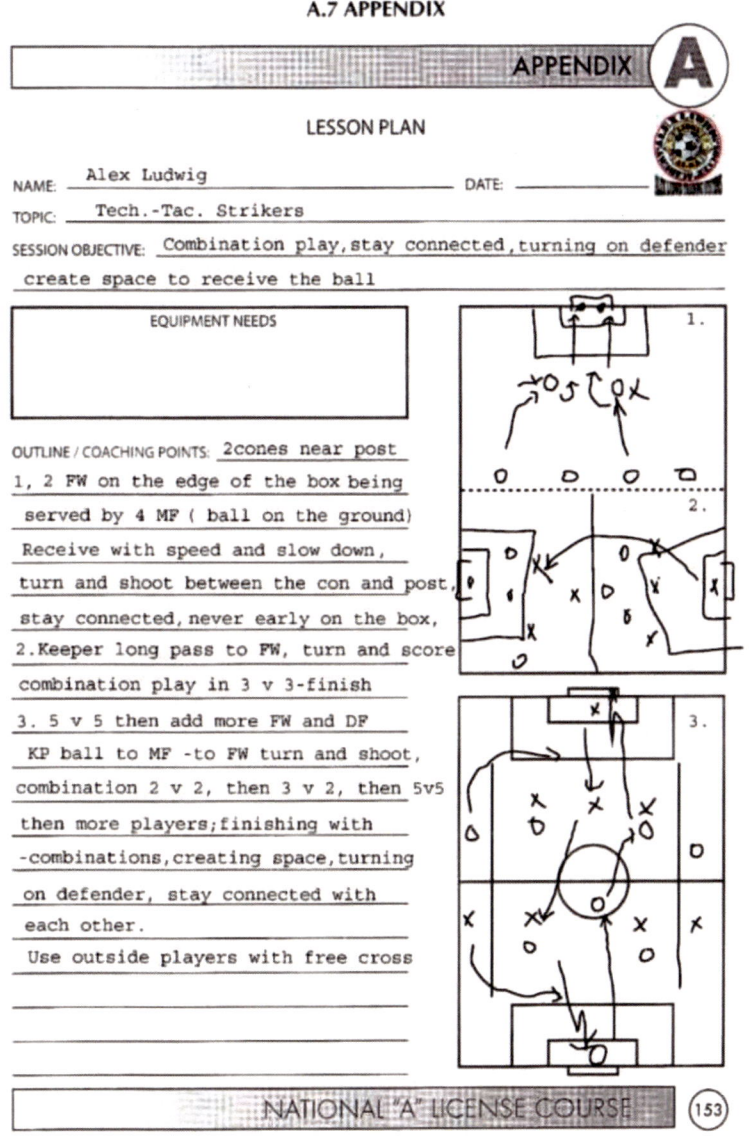

Technical-Tactical Strikers. 20 min

Physical warm-up, then 2 players with the ball passing receiving in movements

They put cones to the two goalpost one yards away from the goal post we have two forwards They are close to the 18 yards, and four midfielders.the midfielders passing the ball to the forwards the forwards go to the ball with speed receive it turning quick around the cone then slowdown dribble to the 18 yards line then shoot, how goal count only when the ball go between the goal posts and the cone into the net. Later the defenders goanna be active we're going to take that comes away and the defenders giving the pressure switching over 1 defender two defenders the forwards when the defender Active they can play the ball back to the midfielder and get open and the midfielder passing the ball back to the forwards he going to beat the defender and try to finish stuff.

2.3 v 3 both sides, GK kick the ball to FW turn and shoot, combination play 35 min

Keypads send a long pass to the forward he turning take a shot play combination passing with the partners same time the other goalkeeper made a long post to the other

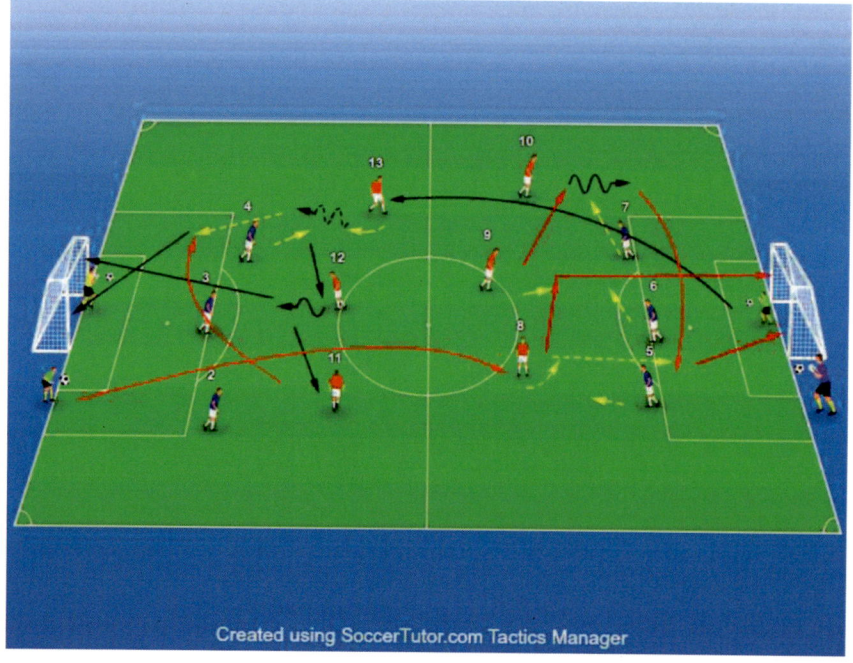

side both side playing three versus 3, 3 defender three forward. The forward receiving the ball they try quick turn and try to finish if the different their giving pressure do not play combinations with the partners. They have two extra goalkeepers making the game faster.

3. Combination play 5 versus 5 with 2 outside players 40 min

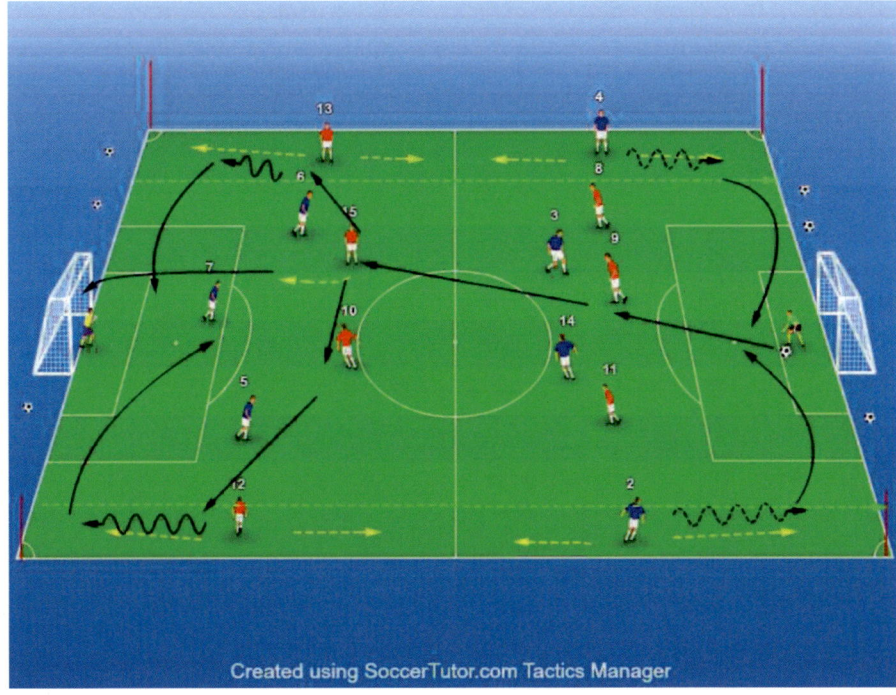

Goalkeeper throw the ball to the centre midfield he kicking the ball quick to the forward forward turn and take a shot if the defender give pressure then making pass site to the outside players he is free, they don't have pressure they can dribble all the way down until the goal line and cross the ball in, the two forward helped to come and finish the ball. Defenders stealing the ball they can right away too big contractors apples using the forwards oh using the outside players who can dribble down free and cross the ball in.

4. 11 v 11 with combination plays and outside crosses, and panetration passes, and dribbling in the mieddle with finish. 45 min

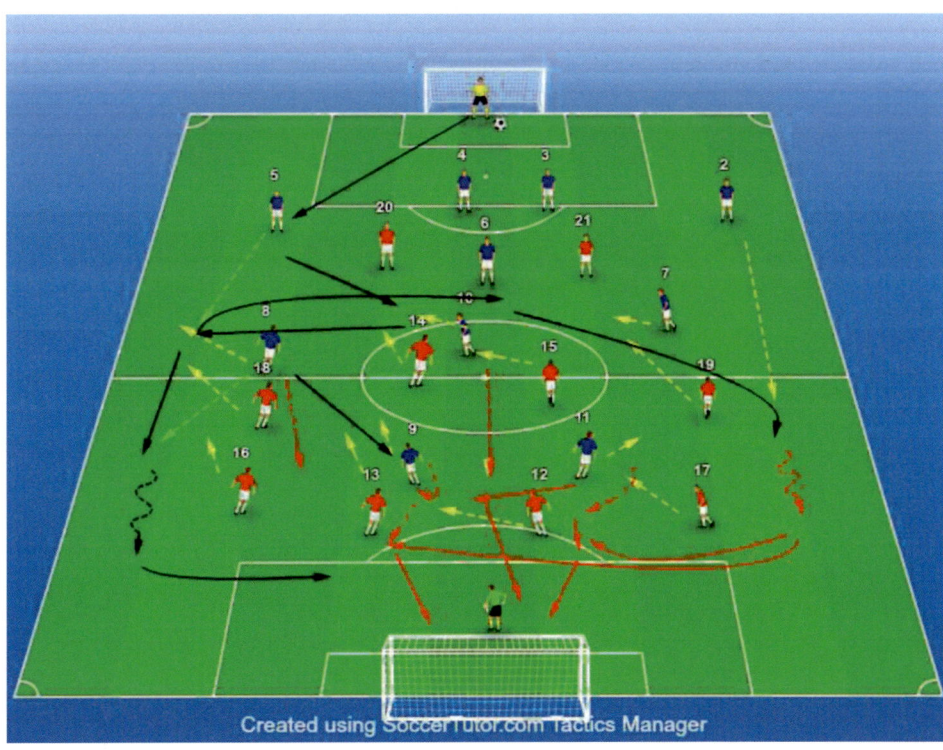

Try everything what we did practice combination plays, penetration passes, outside runs, crosses. Free kicks, corner kicks, throw-ins.

Thursday Afternoon Session.

1.45-2.00 pm Group volume up for the volume up make the kids ready for the main session

2.00-4.30pm Start the main training session

Warm-up: short-short long pass, give and go, take overs lot of movement 15 min

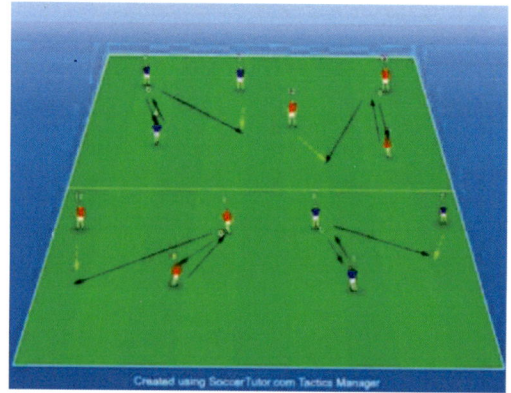

1 Attack in central, penetration, aggressive offense in the middle, through runs defense in 4-2 offense in 3 v 3 formation 50 min

Combinations you can follow the lines, the black lines, red lines and white lines, all different movements different passing. Aggressive offense and movement great ball control, you have a chance to score from the middle and going through the defense line. Throw in, free kicks and corner kicks, penalty kicks.

11 v 11 with combination plays and outside crosses, and panetration passes, and dribbling in the mieddle with finish. 45 min

Same way as we did in the morning session.

Try everything what we did practice combination plays, penetration passes, outside runs, crosses. Free kicks, corner kicks, throw-ins.

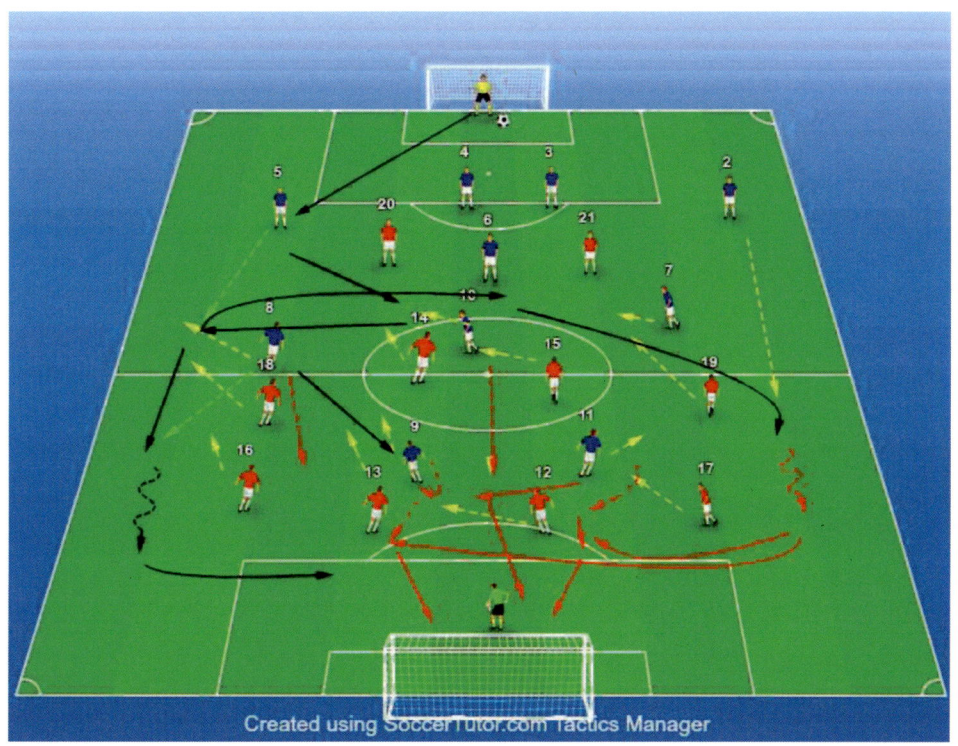

4.30 finish and Dinner

Thursday evening session:

6.45 -8.30 --11 v 11 side games 2 times 45 min. – warm- up with the teams

Formations; 4-2-3-1 and 4-1-3-2

Try everything what we did practice combination plays, penetration passes, outside runs, crosses. Free kicks, corner kicks, throw-ins.

Every night switching opponent it is possible. After the numbers of players.

The camp number is not big enough then change players in the teams, of course this change going to be helping for the players. development

Friday Morning Session: Speed of Play

6.45 am Soccer Aerobic if it is indoor, or fitness and technical sessions

Start the morning session:

8.45-9.00 Group warmups funny warmups make the kids ready for the focus on the sessions 9.00-11.30am start main training session

---

A.7 APPENDIX

APPENDIX A

LESSON PLAN

NAME: Alex Ludwig   DATE: 02-20-2011
TOPIC: Speed of Play
SESSION OBJECTIVE: increase insight pressure, awareness to provide quick circulation of the ball, penetrations

EQUIPMENT NEEDS

OUTLINE / COACHING POINTS:
warm up; address quality passing, receiving, force-speed of play
pass to men-pass to front-pass early
preapar the ball positive way.
Pozess support play: body position, hip alighnment, vision, move as the ball is,
Mobility, moving, maintain-shape:
play the way you are facing, the simple pass is the right pass, (quick pass)
speed in transition, shape in transition
10 v 8 = 10 going to score, alignment, the 8= get the ball to target
circulation of the ball, play away from pressure, find players who has a space,
speed the attack to goal when the play open, VERY QUICK PASS AND MOVE

8 v 7

10 v 8
11 v 11

+ target

NATIONAL "A" LICENSE COURSE   (153)

1. quality passing 25 min

Physical warm up, then passing, focus on the pass quality, receiving, force speed and first touch

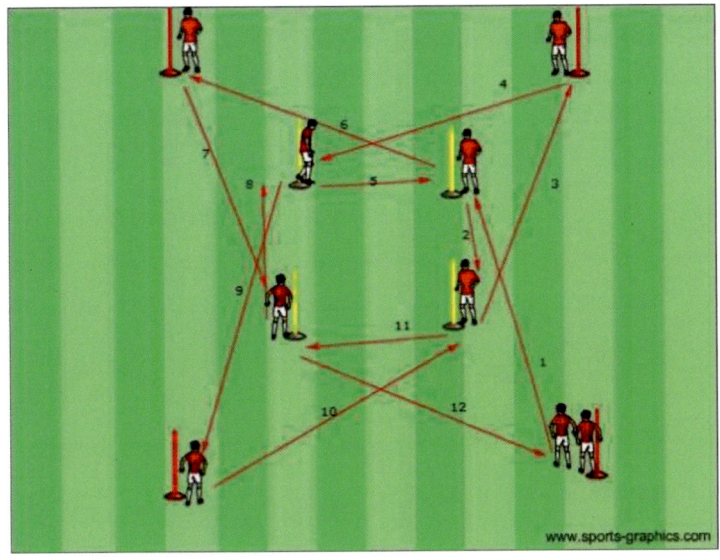

Address the players does it really have to focus on the first touch this exercise is great for speed and agility if the first touch is not really good then maybe can do two touches the spouses in that case probably the exercise slowing down .Players following day passing direction.

2. 8 v 7   8 v 7 passing drill mobility movements 35 min

Prepair the ball positive way, pozess support play ,important body position ,hip alignment ,vision, move quick without the ball, mobility, maintain shape . Passing to partner, pass to the man, Pass early Prepare you to receive the ball correctly.

3. Increase inside pressure awareness to provide big circulation of the ball penetrations 40 minutes

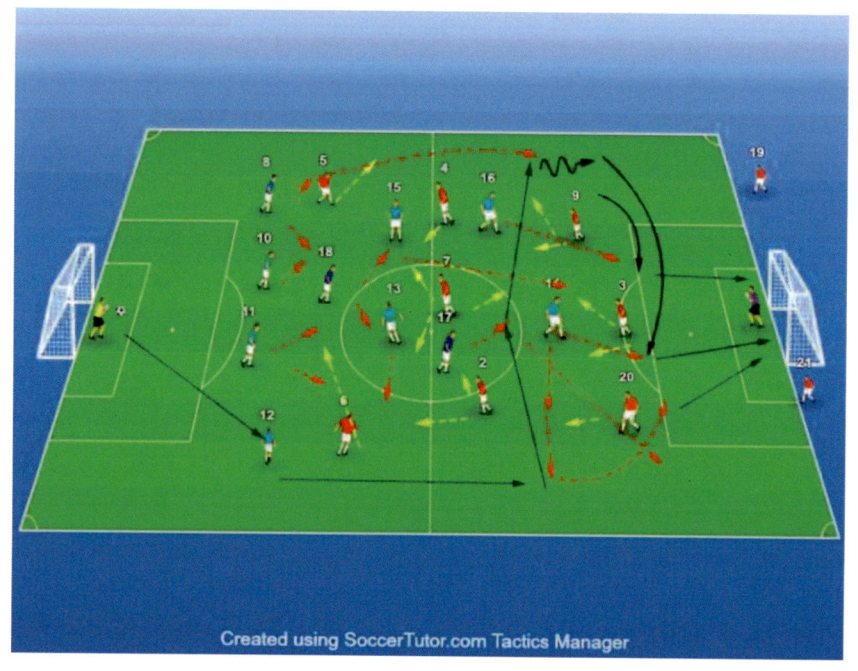

Maintain shape play the way where you facing ,the simple pass is the right pass Quick pass speed in transition, shape in translation, finish to score force in the middle. get the ball to the target create circulation for the ball, play away from pressure, find players who has the space, speed the attack to the goal ,open the play ,open very quick pass and move

4.11 v 11 Fallow the speed of play how just learned 40 min

11.30 Lunch

Friday Afternoon Session: Offside Traps

1.45-2.00 pm Group volume up for the volume up make the kids ready for the main session

2.00-4.30pm Start the main training session

1.Warm up with a hand ball game but the pass coming with the foot. 15 min

The ball is in the hand and you passing the ball with your feet in the air who is the ball cannot have a high pressure but the opponent in the air can steal the ball anytime you scoring with the head this two points you score with the fit is one point you score from volley is 5 point,

2 Offside trap -Center Deffense ; 3 MF-2 FW v 2 CD 30 min

Work on the relationship between the two central defender, pull level, recognize queues from servers step out on top the ball. Try to read the passing and the possible movement from the forwards.

3. offside trap 1 CD and 2 outside D and 2 DM 40 min

The key is defenders have to work together they have to understand the line, where they standing ,the two center defenders calling their movement ,pulling out possibly the other two center MF, than the last the outside Defender move a little earlier ,the main thing somebody have to attack the ball,Outside defenders and the 2 center midfielders they have to understand each other, important who is pressing the ball and who is marking the runners, Timing to set the trap, Work on recovery if it's not on ,convert on restarts traps.

4, 11 v 11 offside traps training game 40 min

Give a defensive team more space to practice the trap leader must good communicate, and everything what we just learned and practiced .The defense still the ball, then very quick counterattacks good long pass or great dribbling ,stay on the ball if nobody open ,need other players good timing in the runs, movement strong center pressure and outside runs, use the weak site if that you can see it..

4.30 finish and Dinner

Friday Evening session

6.45- 8.30 11 v 11 with formation changes. The team try to play every 3o min different formation

4-4-2; 4-1-3-2; 4-3-3; 3-5-2; 4-3-2-1; 3-4-3;5-3-1-1

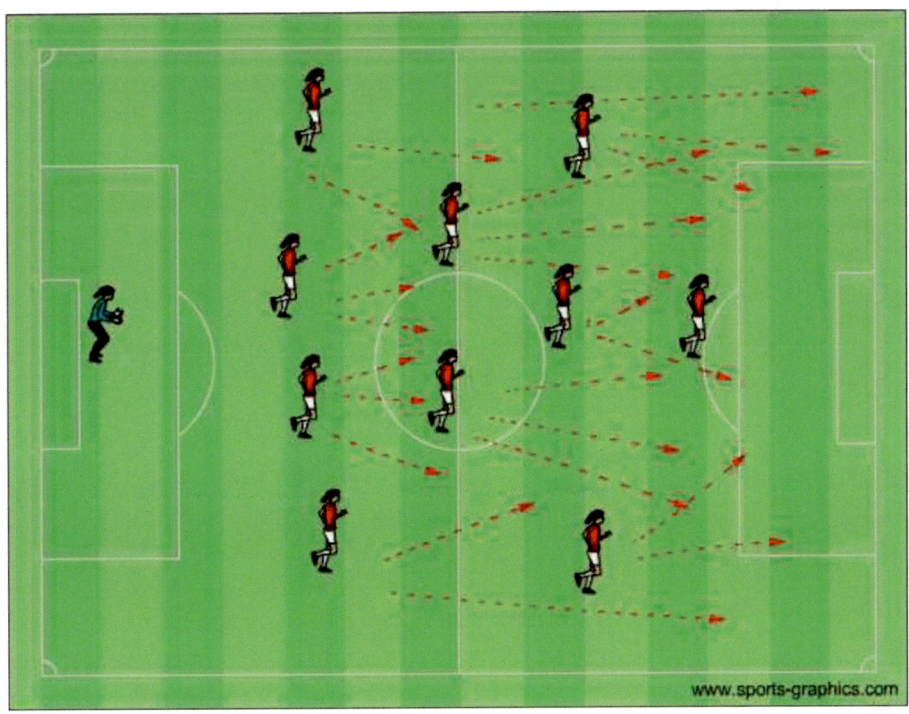

Saturday Session

8:45 am - Warm-ups

9:00-10:00 am Team competitions

10.00-10.30 am Final competitions

10:30 – 11.30 am games

12.00 noon Players Check-out

1.Team competitions

Teams going, they field with the evening coaches and doing the competition

    11. Penalty Kicks
    12. 18 yards shooting (ball must land behind the goal line in the air)
    13. Heading
       Competitions 1-2-3 going for point system

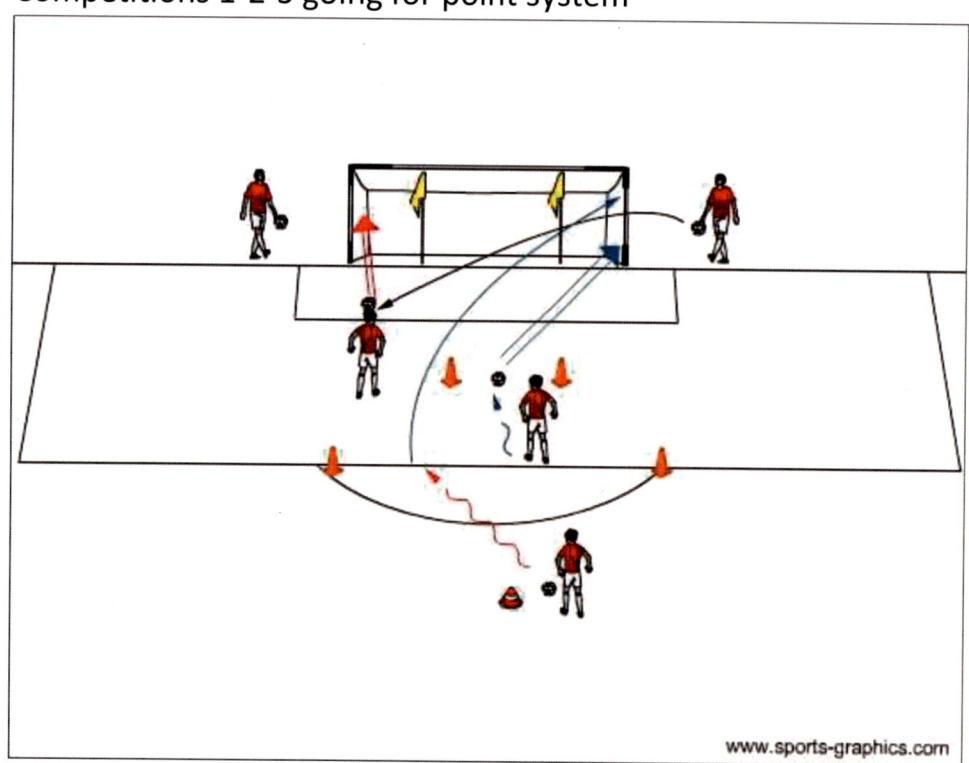

**Competition 1-2-3 the ball must land behind the goal line.
In the side net is 3 point-between the flag and the post is 2 points
And in the center is 1 point**

14. King of the hill:

Players dribbling with the ball individually and shield it because they must kick out somebody's ball. The players who is last standing in the field is the winner.
Players must move with the ball they cannot standing who does not move
Get warning second time is out from the competition.

You cannot leave your ball and kick somebody's ball out you must always in contact with your own ball.

15. Juggling.

Players starting in the same time and who is the last juggler is the winner. Players must keep touching the ball they cannot holding the ball on the foot or on the back. Continuing Juggling.
11.15 Price giving for the winners!!

11.30-12.00 noon Small sided games. Closing ceremony after the games

6 Coaches taking **the teams and play 11 v 11 – 30-40 minutes.**

12.oo Noon players checking out

Goalkeeper Training Performance Program

Monday Morning Session

DAILY SCHEDULE RESIDENTIAL CAMP):

6:15-7:00 - Soccer aerobic (technical 7:30 am - Breakfast

8:45am - Warm-ups

9:00-11:30 am   Training

1. Goalkeeper technique: 45 min – Rotation

Physical warm up, stretch particularly good

1. coach throw the ball over the net and GK catch it and throw it back. GK move side to side and jump to catch the ball.

2. Coach stay diagonal from the goal with the Ball, GK from the middle sideways shuffle to the goal post touch it, and shuffle back ,then the coach kick the ball to his hand he catch it then throw the ball back to the coach then repeat it.

3.GK jump over the small gates with one leg, after the last gates coaches pass the ball and keeper diving and catch the balls and throw it back to the coach. Repetition and switching sides.

Every 15 min change stations

2. GK training technique 2 - 40 min

jump over the gates, dive catch the ball throw it back

and quick jump to the other side and catch the ball again

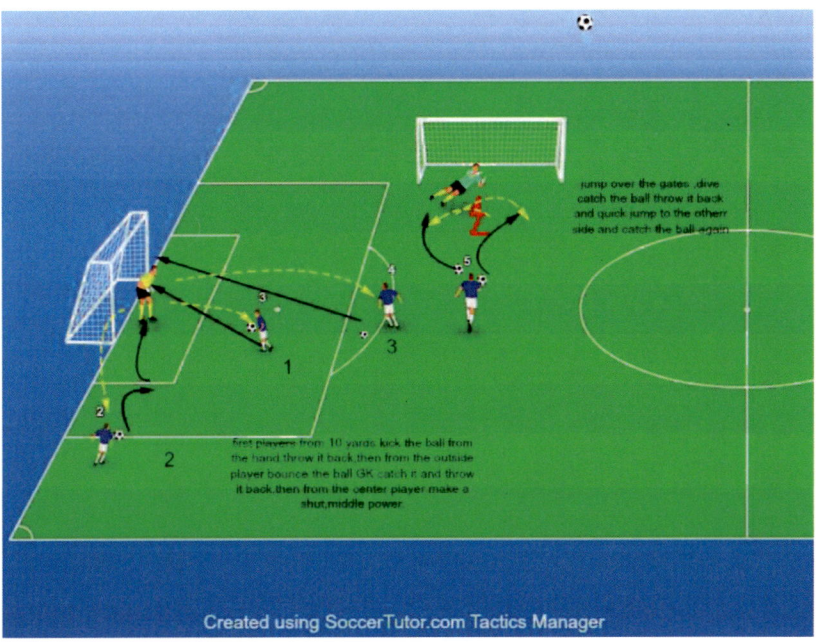

first players from 10 yards kick the ball from the hand, throw it back, then from the outside player bounce the ball GK catch it and throw it back, then from the center player make a shut with middle power.

Group switch stations after 20 min.

3. Fake steps the dive and save the shut 35 min

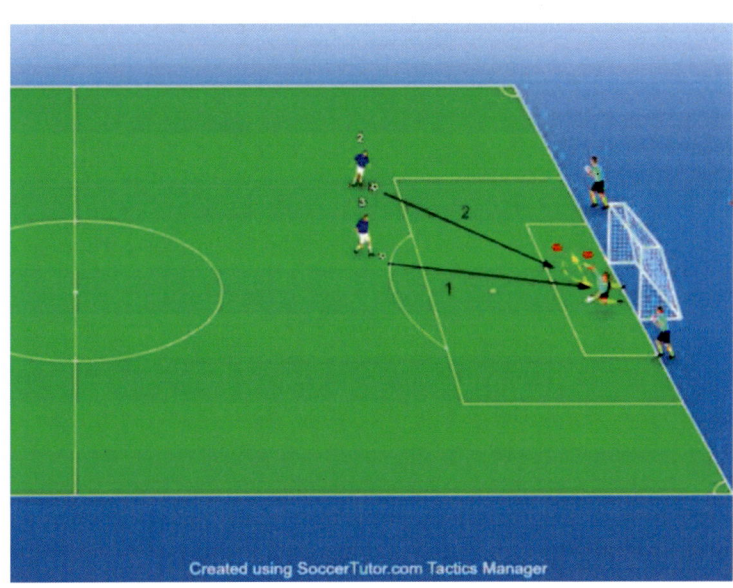

By the goal is 2 cones the keeper does some steps (3-4) to the cone then the shooter takes a shut, GK step back and dive to save the ball.

GK switching in after 4-5 shuts.

11.00-11.30 Keepers going to teams and receiving shuts.

Monday Afternoon Session:

1.45-2.00 pm Group volume up for the volume up make the kids ready for the main session

2.00-4.30pm Start the main training session

Goalkeeper Technique; 45 min - Rotation

1. Footwork stepping over the ball facing the coach then after the last cone coach kick the ball GK catch it throw it back move start position. Then same but GK go over the cones sideways.

2. Start position ball in the hand run put the ball into the ring then get back take one other ball and put it into the next ring. Compitation!

3. 3 cons in triangle Coach kicking the ball GK step diagonal forward, direction where the ball coming then dive and catch the ball, throw it back. Important the step forward diagonal and dive not sideways better diagonal forward.

Stepping sideways the forward over the cone 35 min

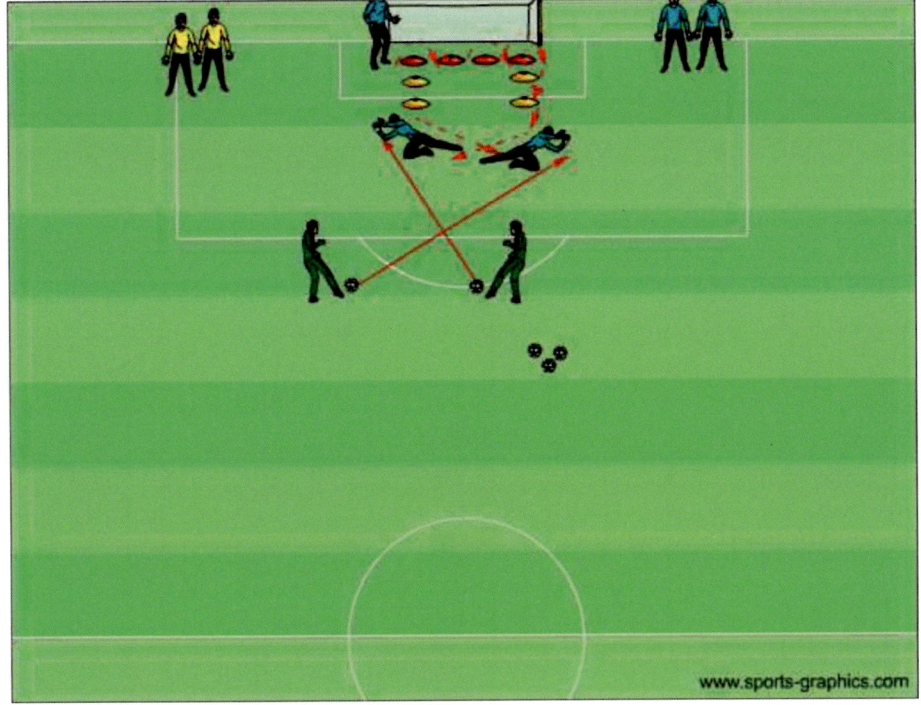

Stepping sideways then over the cones then step sideway the other direction and look for the shut then catch the ball and throw it back to the coach

Reflex and quickness development 30 min

GK stay in the Middle of the net, coach standing 10 yards from the goal keeper, the keeper and the coach has a ball in hand, throw it each other, then the keeper drop his ball, coach shooting GK sideways diving have to step and catch the ball, or punch it out. Going for both ways.

4.00-4.30 pm keeper going to the teas shooting finishing

Monday evening session:

6.45 -7.00 pm warm up

7.00-7.30 pm Shooting finishing

7.30-8.30pm evening games; **Depense the week, first and second week- smallsided games in the thrid week camp 11 v 11 every day.**

Thuesday Morning session;

6:15-7:00 - Soccer aerobic (technical 7:30 am - Breakfast

8:45am - Warm-ups

9:00-11:30 am   Training

GK Training Technique; 45 min

1. conse in triangle,GK start from the red con run to the black cone thhen go backwards to the red and coach pass the ball GK runto the ball and pass it back,then backwards and going to the left side to the white con and same way backwards and other coach pass GK run and pass the ball back.

2. two conse GK go figure eight coach kick the ball to his hand , catch it and throw it back.Figure eght and other coach kick, catch and throw it back. Next GK catch the ball dicin forward ball in the hand close the the body, jump up and roll the ball back on the ground.

3. 7 cones in one line, GK steping over every cone and the and coach pass the ball GK go down grab the ball and one going down.Next GK going thru the cone same way and the end coach kick the ball sideways, GK dive and hold the ball cole to the body, or punch it out if he cant hold it.

Footwork, sedways running and diving; 40 min 15 min

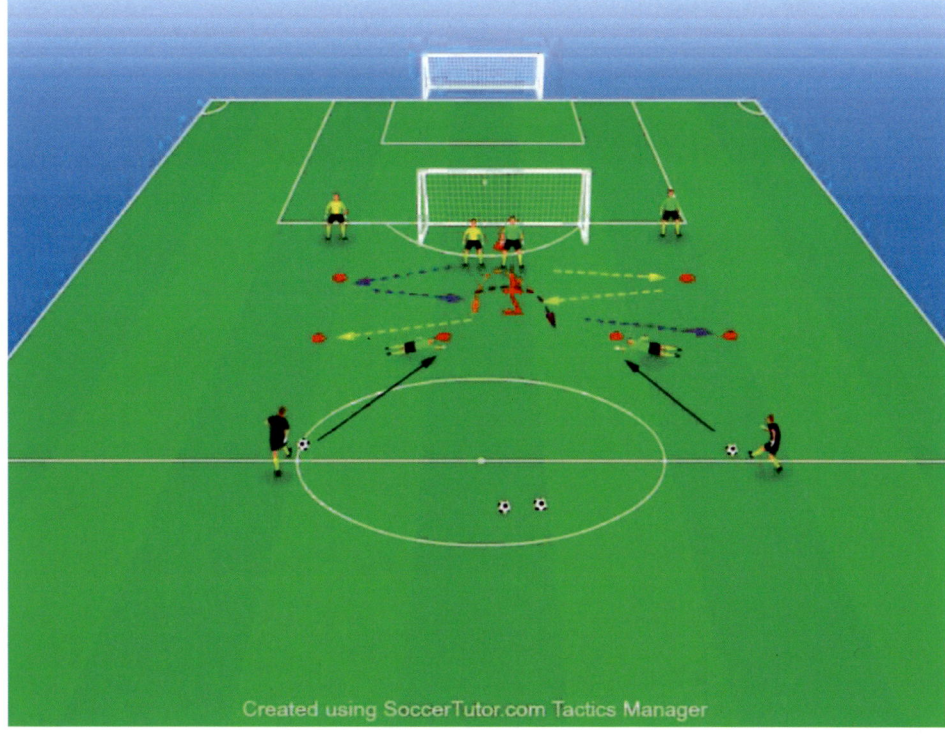

Green Keeper running diagonal sedways to the first cone then other dirction to the gate, jump over then diagonal sedways to the far cone, coach make a shut GK divin and Catch the ball. The the yellow GK start same way bot the other directio. Controll the body position and good ball catch, keep the ball in the hand. GK switching sides every time.

Throw the ball from center, and shooting from sideways

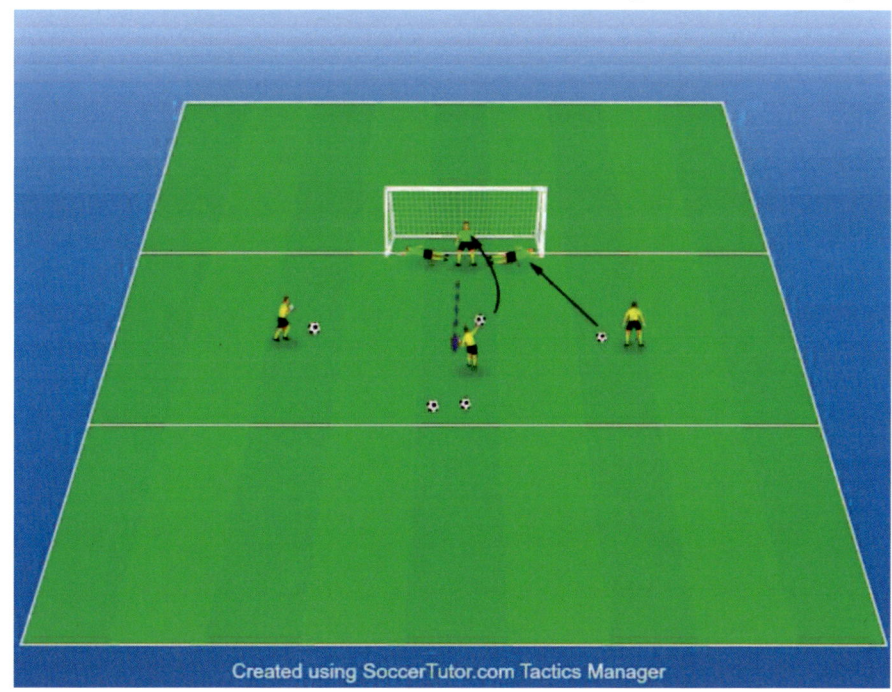

GK in the middle of the goal, player throw the ball from 10 yards, roll it back then playrs shootin from outside, catch it and throw it back or punch it out if you cant catch it.

11.00-11.30 shootin finishing with the teams

Tuesday Afternoon Sesiion:

1.45-2.00 pm Group volume up for the volume up make the kids ready for the main session

2.00-4.30pm Start the main training session

Goalkeeper Technique;

Passing GK using the foot; 45 min

1. GK staying Between 2 cone and behind him is forgone ,the coach passing the ball to the keeper people push the ball back to the coach right away turn around back touch one cone who's going to car yellow or red cone then going forward to the two cone and passing the next ball back to the coach very intensive exercise ,using both feet.

2. Goalkeeper need an between two corn ,the coach throwing the ball to him with one hand he pudding up and throw the ball back to the coach,between his legs stretching out sideways front of the cone. repeating it both ways.Important goalkeepers I have to focus when the ball came in the air and punch it back to the coach the foot that moment stretching out have to work together the hand and the feet .

3. Goalkeeper between two cones bending the knee down ,coach shooting middle power boss direction to the cone ,goalkeeper have to kick the ball before the the ball touched the cone.Intensive exercise need a lot of focus keep us help to pick up the rytmus.

GK combination Training; 70 min

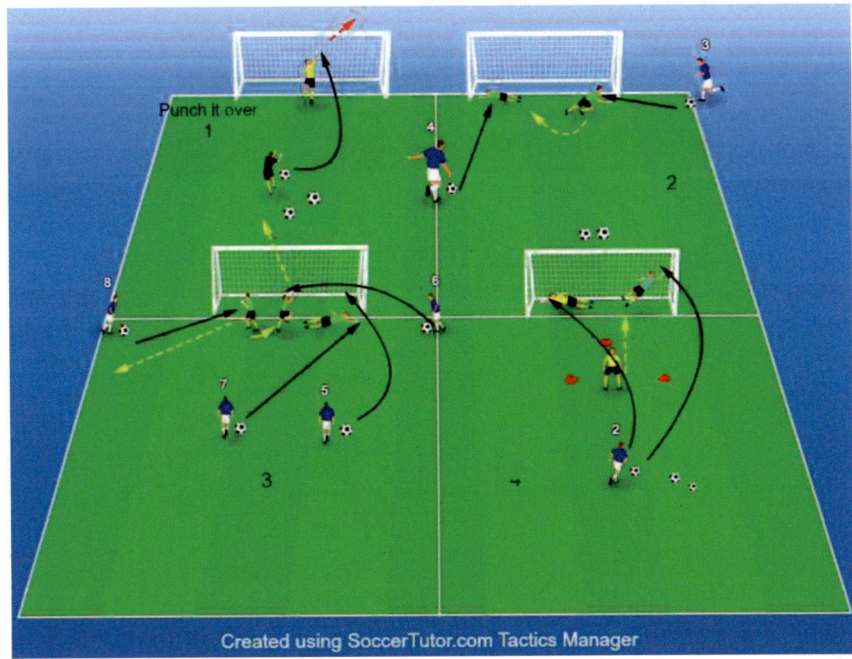

1. Coach kicking the ball to the goalkeeper from the hand from the ground powerful ,Keeper must Punch the ball over.important the keeper must be ready for every ball because it's powerful need a lot of focus '

2. Goalkeeper getting a powerful cross from the right side punch it over punch it out then turn another player shooting on the right corner have to punch it out or gadget .the two forwards have to give time for the keeper to be ready for both shot .

3 the exercise we have 4 shooters the keeper from the left side coming shut have to punch it out the same direction where the ball came ,then from the right side coming highcross the keeper have to punch it over ,then from the center coming a shot to the left corner he has to punch it out, then very quick jump up because from the centre coming a high shot to the upper corner he has to punch it out .

4. It has three cone in triangle keeper start going backwards from the two coins and when he arrived the goal line coming a shot to the right corner he has to punch it out then quick jump up because the next shot coming in the left upper corner he must punch it out..

4.00-4.30pm Team shooting and finishing

6.45 -7.00 pm warm up

7.00-7.30 pm Shooting finishing

7.30-8.30pm evening games; **Depense the week, first and second week- smallsided games in the thrid week camp 11 v 11 every day.**

Wednesday Morning Session;

6:15-7:00 - Soccer aerobic (technical 7:30 am - Breakfast

8:45am - Warm-ups

9:00-11:30 am   Training

Goalkeeper Technique; GK TRaining 11 fowork with diving rytmus; 60 min

1.Go keep going sideways over the cones Gorge kicking the ball high in the hand he go both ways back and forth.the red arrow shows a second time the coach giving a lowball.

2.Next exercise goalkeeper get some area signed area coach kicking the ball to people diving this is low balls both side left and right side .

3.exercise 3 just the same like exercise 2 but the coach kicking high balls and the did goalie diving and try to catch the ball in the air ,if they can't catch the ball in the air they have to punch it out .

4.Did the goalkeeper start jumping over with double X the gates then they posted 3 gates coach kicking the ball first highball goalkeeper diving and catch the ball in the air and second time kick it low ball.

Ball all exercise very important the goalkeeper footwork his body coordination his secular hand pull the ball in the hand possible don't drop it, and all together the rytmus-tempo is the big key.

Coach have to explain the goalkeeper how to catching the ball ,they have to charge and read the ball speed,and if he drapes the ball they have to cover with possible the whole body.

GK Training Tempo quickness, and high focus   30 min

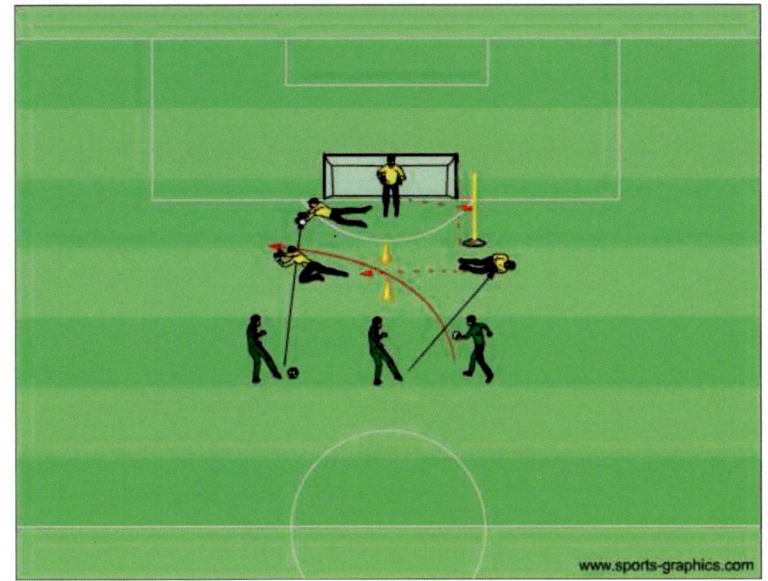

Keeper first dive the right side catch the ball get up quick, then go run to the pole touch it, then the shot coming dive to the left side, get up go thru on the gate, then high shut coming catch it, throw the ball back.

Then do it the same excercize but the other way.

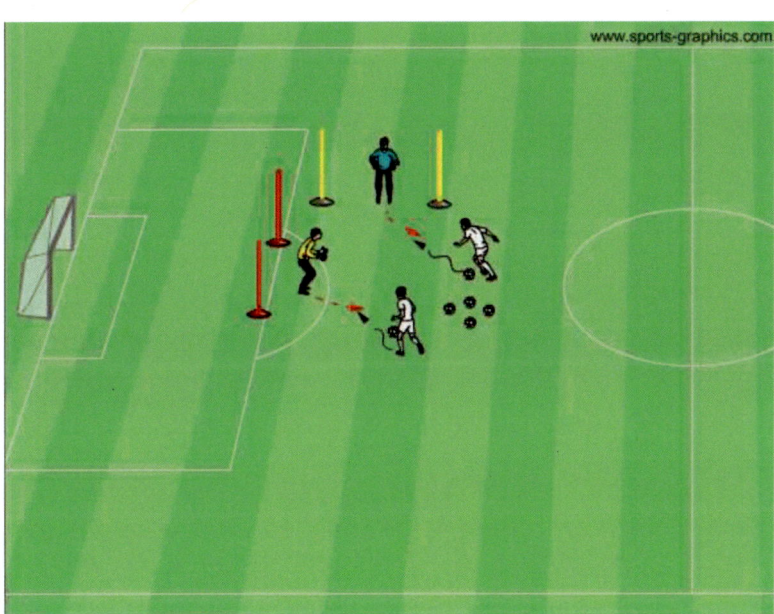

GK TRaining dribblig lot of shut GK have to save it. 30 min

Creating two goals from pole close to each other, two goalkeepers two forwards lot of balls, the forward stribling and tried to score any goal goalkeepers have to pay attention and stop every ball kick it away and be ready for the other more be'cause the four of us has a lot of balls and they can take anymore anytime and start dribbling and tried to beat the goalkeeper. very intensive exercise good practice for the goalkeepers to learn focus 100% reflex and good hands, they can stop with the hand they can stop with the body they can stop with the feet.

11,00-11.30 am Team shooting-finishing

Wednesday Afternoon Session;

1.45-2.00 pm Group volume up for the volume up make the kids ready for the main session

2.00-4.30pm Start the main training session

Goalkeeper Training;

Goalkeeper technique, lot of movement ; 55 min

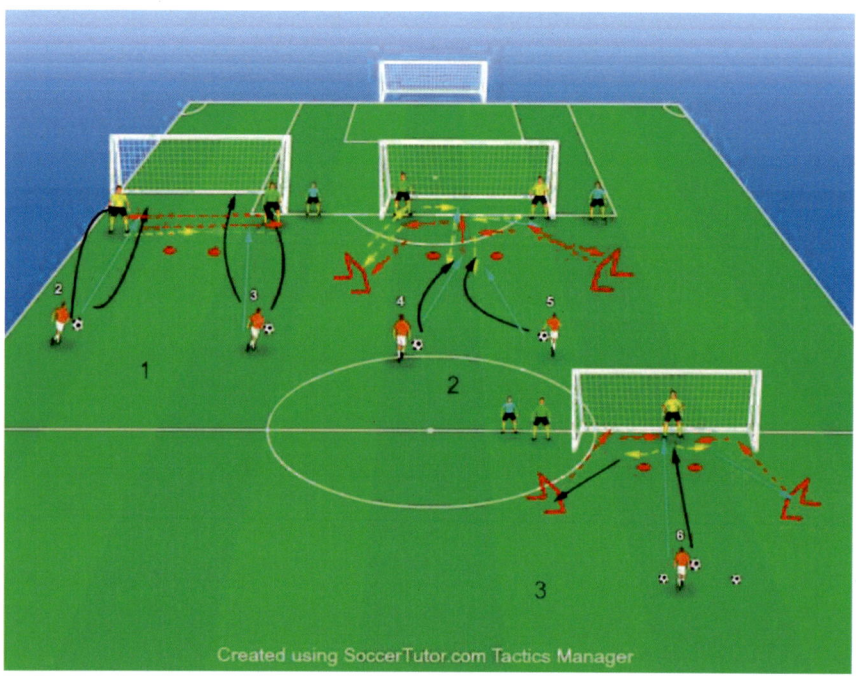

1. Yellow gold goalkeeper start #2 forward shoot key pair catch the ball throw it back and go sideways in the middle between green goalkeeper catch the ball goes sideways don't go back showboat goalkeeper going side to side and between catching the ball highball global. Second parts the green goalkeeper start catch the ball heibel watch the ball back the loebel then going to the other post side base ,yellow goalkeeper doing the same .

2. Green goalkeeper start running to the gate touching the gate backwards to the goal line sideways in the mirror forward running to the cones catching the ball throw it back to number 4 ,between yellow goalkeeper start sideways in the middle around forward between the two cones sketched about throw it back go backwards then going to the other goal post. And from the other goal posts running forward to the gate touching the gate and go backwards and repeat the same exercise one time they got global one time data table.

3. One goalkeeper in the middle #6 kicking the ball GK did receive it sideways,then Passing the ball through the gate, go backwards sideways the middle, receiving the next pass ,the other direction pass the ball through on the other gate then backwards and sideways in the middle and receiving in the center the other pass, and keep continuing like that , 2 or 3 minutes switching the goalkeepers.

GK TRaining 15 Speed and decision-making; 60 min

1. Two goalkeeper passing the ball each other ,coach call go! then the goalkeeper who is on the goal line running forward past the redpole and curve running too the small gate between #2 FW take a shot and the goalkeeper have to save before the ball go through the small gate.Switching site and switching goalkeepers to.Speed and decision-making very important.Goalkeeper from the red porn going to the goal line another goalkeeper from outside going between two the redpole.

2. Here we start the number FW 4 who taking a shut the goalkeeper diving punched the ball out then jump up very quick run to the goalpost touching the goalpost then coming outside and forward #4 passing the ball to him he pass the ball back to the number 4, then running sideways #4 making a long pass and the goalkeeper had to save the ball before they're rolling out from the field .

4.oo-4.30 Team finishing and schooting, lot of 1 v 1 against the GK.

first 1 v 1 against the keeper , intensive hard work

other field still 1 v 1 but 1 extra FW help to get the keeper focus the highest level.

Evening Session;

6.45 -7.00 pm warm up 7.00-7.30 pm Shooting finishing

7.30-8.30pm evening games; **Depense the week, first and second week- small sided games in the thrids week camp 11 v 11 every day.**

Thursday morning session ;

6:15-7:00 - Soccer aerobic (technical 7:30 am - Breakfast

8:45am - Warm-ups

9:00-11:30 am   Training

GK Training 16 reflex, quickness, focus, ball security 50 min

1. GK go sideways over the cone, catch the ball throw it back, then diagonal run direction to the flag, the shut coming to the flag GK catch it or punch it out. Then go back and start the a other direction.

the next time coaches throwing the ball with bounce it one time GK have to catch throing back, then run to the flag, save the ball, then go backwards and start again. switch keepers.

2. GK in the center from the goal, start steping over the cone, then run around the pole, run direction to the figur , the coach shut the ball, GK has to catch it or punch it out. Going backwards then start the other direction. Seitch keepers.

3. GK start jumping over the gates, after the last gates the coach left side roll the ball to the cornel from net. GK have to dive and punch the ball out. ThenJUmp up quickly run to the figure touch it and the other coach make a shut to the corner in the air and GK must catch it or punch the ball out.

Goalkeeper Training 17

High Intensity GK Practice: 25 min

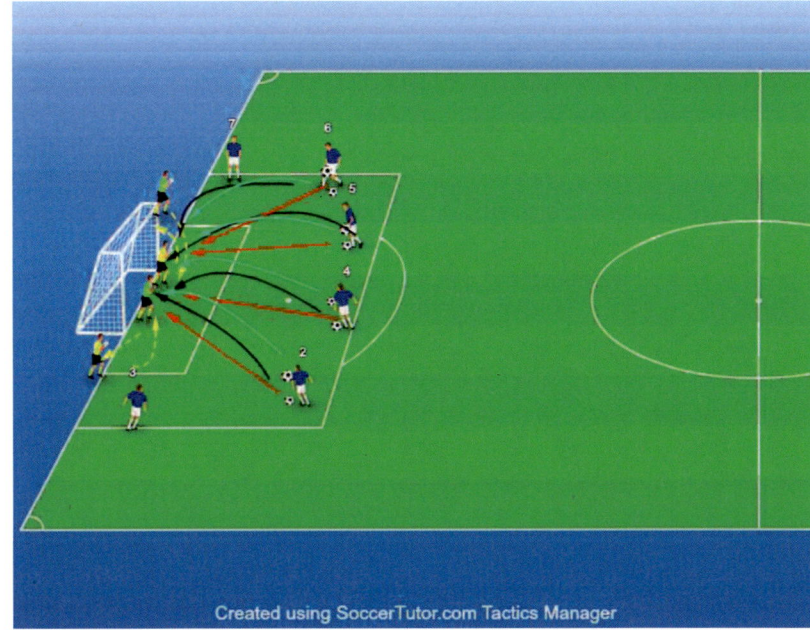

Same time 2 GK in the net, 4 forward start shuting from the hand,(Black line), then they start shooting from the ground(red line), then start thowing the ball (bue line) and very quick shooting from the ground high or low.

Keepers have to switch 3-5 minutes.

Goalkeeper Training 18

High Intensity 2; 25 min

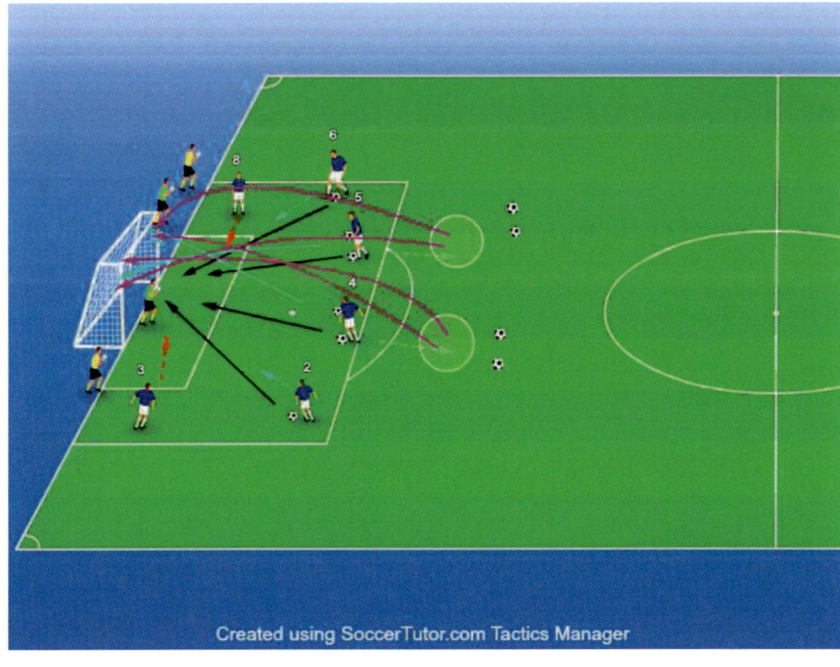

here is only 2 GK in the net, 4 FW shooting the 2 outside FW shoot low ball the 2 inside FW shoot high balls,they can change the shooting high, if The GK drap the ball, one of the outside forwards (Red arro) can come and shoot the rebound.

Later the 2 center FW nove back to the circle and shoot from there ,like a free kicks, most high ball ,target the upere corners.

11..00-11.30 Team shooting finishing-formation coaches decision

Thursday Afternoon Session;

1.45-2.00 pm Group volume up for the volume up make the kids ready for the main session

2.00-4.30pm Start the main training session

GK Training 19; quick catching - diving and quick up and go to next 60 min

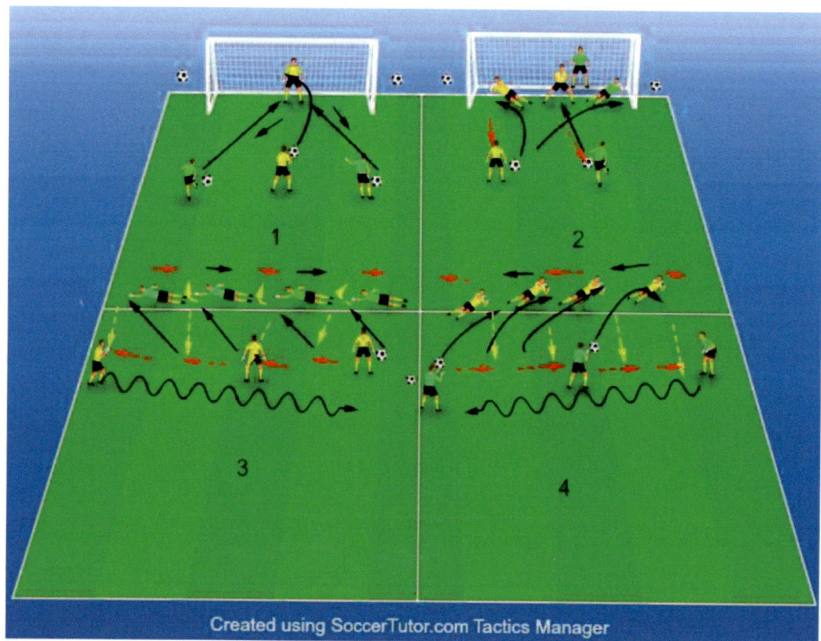

1. start from the right side player pass the ball Gk pass back and Looking for the center, from there coming a high ball, then from the left pass,and going to back to the center,switching th GK every 2 minutes,

This must very quick and good middle stron balls.

2. GK in the center, low pass from the right side,throw it back then quick move to the othe side the high ball diving catch it or punch it out, then go again to the center high and next low ball. Very intensive, grea for focus and ball handeling.

3GK start from the righjt side , pass is diagonal half high ball cach itthrow it back and get up quick go sideway again because the nex ball coming , and so 4-5 times.change GK, then all down to the left then goin to the other direction.

4. Here The goalkeeper starting from the left side banana bus coming in the half air he threw the ball back get up very quick and go right there across the next ball coming for five times diving then switch goalkeeper when everybody done then same way going to the other direction,Quickness focus ball handling it's very important .

6.45 -7.00 pm warm up

7.00-7.30 pm Shooting finishing

7.30-8.30pm evening games; **Depense the week, first and second week- smallsided games in the thrid week camp 11 v 11 every day.**

Friday morning session ;

6:15-7:00 - Soccer aerobic (technical 7:30 am - Breakfast

8:45am - Warm-ups

9:00-11:30 am   Training

GK Training 20 combined with warm-up   40 min

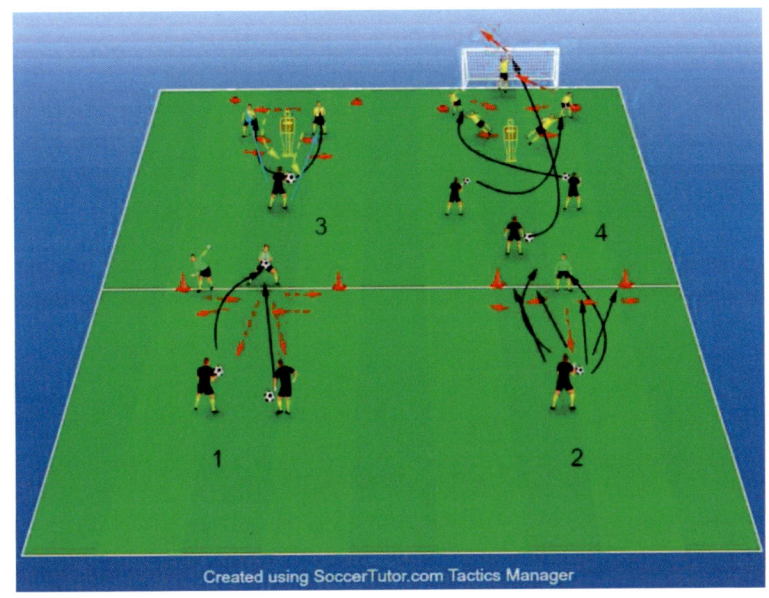

1.Goalkeeper start from the centre gold right side shuffling touch the cone coming in a center catch the ball throw it back go to the left side budged account come in a center catch the ball throw it back and going back and forth sometimes highballs sometimes lobel.switch the goalkeeper.

2.Similar exercise like the number 1 here he catching the ball then always going to dive forward and covered the ball with the body, then get up and go sideways touch the cone look for the next ball, every single time when you're catching the ball you have to dive forward and put the ball under you body and hold it to your chest .

3.Hit the goalkeeper stay behind the figure then go sideways the coach throw the ball goalkeeper catch it and go to the other side behind the finger very quick catch the ball again throw it back ,one time highball one time lobel intensive exercise focus on the ball handling and every time highball coming hold about close to your chest .coaches have to kick the ball really hard when you draw it you can throw 1 bounce too.

4Here we have three coaches they serving the ball GK start behind the figure go the right side first ,touched the cone run back catch the ball go to the other side touched the cone catch the ball throw it back, then move very fast, GK are switching positions very short time be'cause very intensive exercise ,highball diving low ball diving ,every single time touched the cone .and the last from the coach who is in the center, kicking the ball little bit from far in the middle ,keeper have to come ,jump and punched the ball over the net .

GK Training, 21 technique and skill; 30 min

1. People start behind the con line we have two lines with four 4 cone, keeper start running to the right side do the first corn touch it then they're gonna run to the second line the last corn between the coach kicking the ball keeper catch it dive throw the ball back and run back in a start position, dim start the other direction same way. Switch the keypad after 2 minutes.

2. We have two flags and one bending war keeper standing facing the bending words two coaches behind the Cooper kicking the ball on the wall the ball coming to the goalkeepers hand catch it through it done turned out the side and the player rolling the ball on the ground who threw it with bounce, the keeper catch it and turned back to the bending wall and keep going very intensive 2 minutes then switch to keeper.

coach have to really care the turning and the holding body position, it's very important by the bending wall example the ball come always different angle, different direction, people have to try to read the ball way, and if it is this possible do not drop the ball after the turn have, to pay attention to the player throwing the ball, sometimes bounce it, sometimes higher sometimes low ball, he needs to extra focus to.

GK TRaining 22 diving front of the body figure; 20 min

Gooch is kicking the ball front of the body figure people have to touch the goalpost then come diona forward and try to save the ball catch the ball before the boy body finger touch it.have to do it for both side very quick if they can't catch the ball they have to punch it out but by owner away from the goal.gorgeous kick the ball low balls high bars strong balls slow balls Facebook important they challenged goalkeeper.

GK Training 23 shooting ,Body figure in center and from outside 20 min

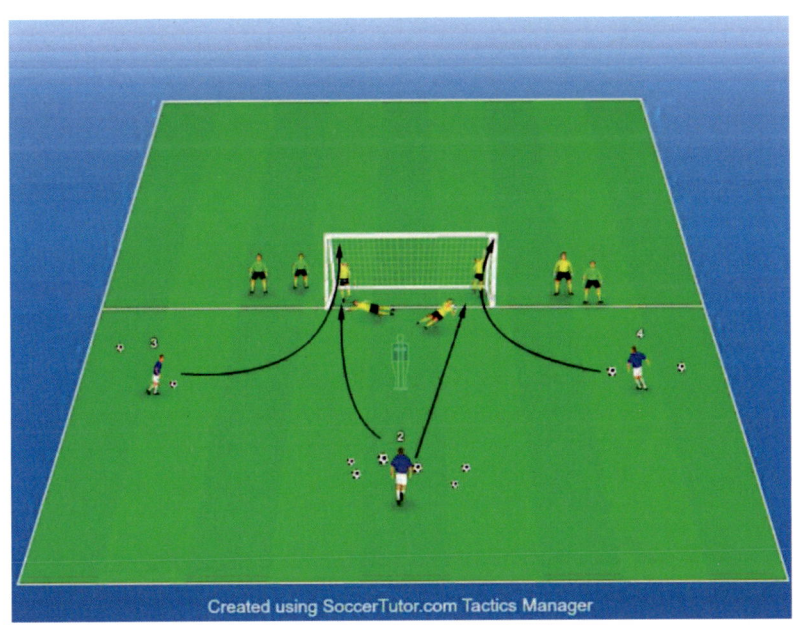

Good body figure innocent that goalkeeper stayed behind from the center coming the shooting the right and left side keep it diving on the left up quickly and go to the right side up quickly then coming right and left outside to the upper corner curving the ball keeper help to punch it over the net.is very intensive change the keeper after 2 minutes .because the keeper loaded times on the ground they have to get up very fast.

11.00-11.30 team shooting finishing,

Friday afternoon session ;

1.45-2.00 pm Group volume up for the volume up make the kids ready for the main session

2.00-4.30pm Start the main training session

GK Training 24; Speed and Reaction Training; 60 min

1. Goalkeeper is in the middle on the goal facing another person who is over the head throwing the ball and the goalkeeper over the head catch it and throw it back ,3 four times then from the right side and left side throwing the ball to the keeper and he with one hand punch it out 1st from left and after right.

2. 1 player has two balls in the hand put it in the air and drop it one time right hand ,one time left hand he going to drap it, the goalkeeper must react and he will catch in the air or Diving can catch it.

3. Goalkeeper stay in a small goal, the other players stay with the ball facing him 6 -Seven yards one ball in the hand one ball in the front by the foot ,he throwing the ball in the air goalkeeper punching out, then the player kick highballs GK catch it, then kick low balls GK kick it back.

4. Goalkeepers and the players standing between the four pole ,the players has the ball, one player in the hand the other player in the feet Proximately at the same time through the ball and kick the ball to the GK on the ground ,and the keeper have to react with the hand and with the feet in the same time ,start kicking and throwing slow balls then you can speed it up a little bit.Keepers switching all for stations.

GK Training 25; Speed and Reaction 40 min

1. GK between 2 pole and on the knies,coaches kicking the ball first low,GK have to punch it out,then coaches kicking the ball high he must get up quick and catch it or punch it out.Swtch the keeper every 2 minutes.

2. we have 4 poles and 1 keeper between 2 ploes. Coaches kicking the ballthe first GK he has to pinch it out and run diagonal to the cone tuch it and go back the position punch the second ball,the go and toch the con the other side.Then the coaches kicking the ball to the second GK who doing the same exercises.Between the 2.nd GK working the other coach can start with the 1.st GK again. Swich the goalkeepers 2-3 minutes.

GK Training 26; small sided games 3 v 3 small goals

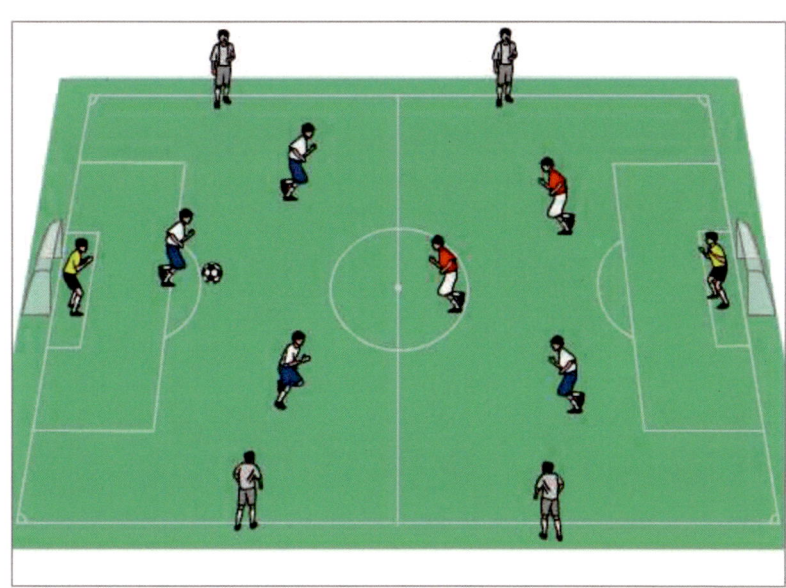

Friday evening Session;

6.45 -7.00 pm warm up

7.00-7.30 pm Shooting finishing

7.30-8.30pm evening games; **Depense the week, first and second week- smallsided games in the thrid week camp 11 v 11 every day.**

Saturday Session.

8:45 am - Warm-ups

9:00-10:00 am Team competitions

10.00-10.30 am Final competitions

10:30 – 11.30 am games

12.00 noon Players Check-out

Penalty kicks; 5 or 10 times each   **18 yards shooting; 5 or 10 times each**

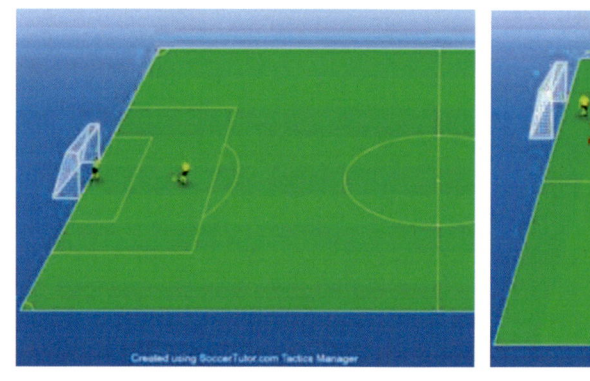
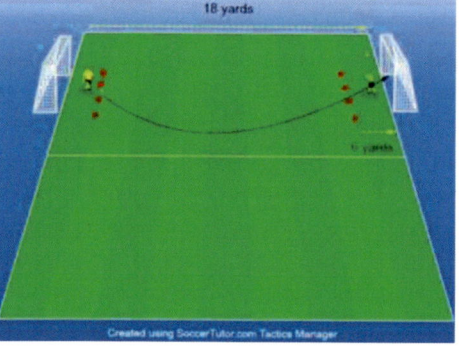

12 yards throw balls 5-10 goals

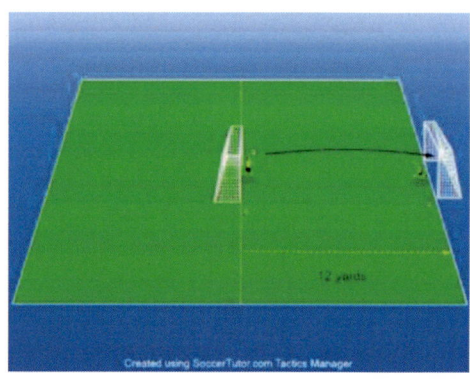

Alex Ludwig Master Coach, Coaches Curriculum

Years/ 6	8	10	12	14	16	18
		Development of large-scale ability			Development of small scale-ability	
Shaping the technique of rough coordination		Shaping the technique of fine coordination			Apply the technical level to that of growing speed and power	
			Development of speed with technical-tactical exercises			
				Development of sped with dynamic leg-strength combination		
					Development of speed with other power combination	
				Dynamic leg-strengthening		
					Development of power speed and Special Stamina	
			Large-scale development of basic stamina		Small scale development of basic stamina	

Implementation of Age Group-Related Training - Tactics: parallel with the technique, with one step delay

Alex Ludwig
Director of Coaching

You can learn a brilliant book of coaching drills by heart, but the ability to act at the right moment, to make an accurate analysis, and to show how things should be done, is much more important. That is the heart of the matter! - Alex Ludwig

"Winning is not everything but not winning is nothing " - Alex Ludwig

Alex Ludwig age related technical system

Prepare Age (6 – 10 years)	Basic technique -skill (10 – 14 years)		All technique and skill Special period (14-18 years)	A
	Level-up technique (6 – 12 years)	**Specific technique period One (12-14 years)**		
Passing (ground) -inside foot -outside foot -instep **simple receiving:** -inside foot -outside foot -chest **Dribbling:** -strait line -slalom -change direction -stop and start -inside & outside foot **Simple fakes:** -stop the ball -passing by -roll and turn **Simple heading:** -short throws -self throws **Passing in the Air:** -inside foot -instep	**Repeat technical exercises (in move)** -building technical drills -shooting 1 v 1 -ball control -heading -chest, thigh, head combinations -dribbling and finishing -passing with turns -passing in the air -passing on touch -using, chest, high, head combination shooting in the air -defensive exercises -slide tackle -long passing ground -long passing air -combinations fakes (program 1 to 10) **All exercises with and without defender**	**Repeat knowing exercises** -bouncing ball kicking -inside foot -outside foot -instep -long ball receiving -long ball in the air -shooting –inside-outside and instep in different angels (18 and 25 yards) -Volleys -difficult ball control -heading on the goal -Jumping heading -free kicks -cornel kicks -shooting 1 v 1 -finishing 2 v 1 - control the ball with all body parts -quick and strong ball passing -in move lot of one touch passing **All exercises with and without defender**	**In this age all technical and skill drills must know, and they must use it in game situations!** Every technical drill must practice in: -quick movement -in game situations -under pressure **Never in stay position!**	T E C H N I C A L P E R I O D
Goalkeepers: -basic standing -rolls -footwork -using hands -short throws **and technique like the field players**	**Goalkeepers:** -repeat exercises -diving low ball -diving middle high ball -ball punching - ball from side -coming out from the goal low and high ball -shooting -goal kicks **Communication!!!**	**Goalkeepers:** -Repeat technical exercises in under pressure -long throws -long kicks -punching -diving high balls -crosses - 1 v 1 shooting	**Goalkeepers:** -All technical drills repeat In quick move and reaction speed. -under pressure-	

Prepare Age (6-10 Years)	Basic Tactical skill (10 14 years)		Special tactical period (14 – 18 years)	AGE
	Level-up tactic (10 – 12 Years)	Specific tactical period (12-14 years)		
-Players on the field -position - not all going for the ball -move on the field -position in defense -position in offense	-The basic soccer rules - understand the position defense, Middlefield, and offense -Building offense -Building defense -transition -pressure -marking -communication	-All rules from soccer -Team work in defense and offense -Understand deep and wide positions -understand –shifting -marking -zone defense -communication	Person, group, and team tactic -fallowing marking defense -mixed defense (marking and zone defense) -communication	THEORITICAL tactic
Simple and short passes -move without the ball in small area -technical and tactical exercises -1 v 1; 2v1;2v2;3v3; 6v6 **Goalkeepers:** Position Short throws Direct the defense	-Going to the ball -deferent ball control -good first touch -switching positions -take over -overlap -give and go -open space- -free kicks -cornel kicks 1v1 to 10v10 games **Goalkeepers:** -Specific talk for defense -Long passes-throws	-long passes -transitions (defense, Middlefield, offense) -group and position tactic - 1v1 to 10v10 games **Goalkeepers:** -Specific talk for the defense -Long passes-throws	-person, group, and team tactic practice -position tactic -in the game use improvisation -communication **Goalkeepers:** -leading person and group tactic -understand using long and short goal kicks -communication	PRACTICAL TACTIC

Alex Ludwig Age related Tactical developing program

Alex Ludwig
Master Coach

Psychological and mental teaching

Prepare Age (6 – 10)	Basic mental period (Age 10 – 14)		Special Mental Period (Age 14 – 18)	AGE
	Basic mental fitness (Age 10 – 12)	Special mental period (Age 12 – 14)		
-group truly integration -how you are acting with team meets -visiting the practices -practice discipline -trying your best always -mistake is part from any game -focus - more interest after sport - how important the school -communication with the parents	- Time important -make your staff ready -responsibility for sport and team meets -How you are acting in the field -how you are acting in the game -respect team meets and adults -Respect your Club - how important the school	-Personal Tate -appurtenance -courage -hardiness -Respect your Club -Respect opponent - how important the school -passion for the game	-Special Personal Tate -volitional quality developments -right way of living -respect opponent - how important the school - be ready for the life -be ready for conflicts -passion for the game	M E N T A L strength

Alex Ludwig
Master Coach

Prepare Age (Age 6-10)	Speed, agility, and stamina development (Age 10 - 14)		Special Period (Age 14 – 18)	AGE
	Level up period (Age 10 – 12)	Specific Period (Age 12 – 14)		
basic exercises -gymnastic (simple) -small ball games -speed and quickness competition -simple stretching exercises -games with the hand (skills) -body contact	-Gymnastic (more difficult) -ball games - games with the hand (skills) - speed and quickness games(skills) -special speed and quickness exercises -quickness and speed exercises -competitions different body contact	-Gymnastic (special exercises) -ball games (special) -games without the ball (skills) -speed and quickness (with the ball) -special speed and quickness without the ball -special skill and speed exercises using all parts from the body -quickness and speed exercises -special body contact	-special quickness and skills -special gymnastic -special games with the ball - ball games using all parts from the body -quickness and speed exercises -competition -special body contact	SKILLS
-Speed exercises -short sprints -running technique -footwork -simple technical exercises with quickness -three touches games	-short sprints -running technique -technical exercises with quickness -dynamic leg-strengthening -jumping exercises -one and two touches games	-short sprints -long sprints -running technique -one and two touches games with quickness - dynamic leg-strengthening -technical fitness	-short sprints -long sprints -technical fitness -one and two touches exercises	Speed and Quickness
-No special strength exercises -gymnastic - 85 % with the ball	-Gymnastic -technical strengthening - 70 % with the ball	-gymnastic -special technical strengthening -exercises with partner -dynamic leg-strengthening	-Dynamic leg-strengthening -All muscle strengthening -develop power exercises -special stamina	strength
-Basic stamina -long distance jogging -long distance running with the ball	-long distance running 10 – 15 min -swimming	-long distance running 20 min or more -swimming -uphill downhill running -bicycle -development power and stamina	- development of basic stamina -speed and power stamina -switching large and small development of basic stamina and power -long distance running 20min and more	Stamina

Age related   Development of Speed and stamina with technical-tactical exercises

Alex Ludwig
Master Coach

Coach Alex Ludwig Team Building

*"The team building process is the tool the coach uses to develop the
soccer concept, the style of play, as optimally as possible
with the aim to achieve success"*

*"In the land of the blind, the one-eyed man is king,
but he still only has one eye"*

Soccer is a game with certain elements. There must be a **ball**, **teammates** and **opponents**, a **field with boundaries**, **goals opposite each other** and **soccer rules**.

-The plan is the collective understanding and agreement as to how the team will approach the game. It involves the distribution of tasks and responsibilities so that the team stands the best chance of winning.

-It is what we must do, how we will do it, who is responsible, and when it will be done.

-Parents, spectators and the referee can have an influence on the match. The coach and players must keep in mind which of these factors they can influence, and which ones they cannot. **Control the controllable.**

-Today children are not as well suited for the increased demands as their parents were.

-Thirty years ago a coach had a whistle, a few cones and players with a higher level of interest in the sport, as there were fewer distractions

-A clear understanding about how the team will play in order to achieve the desired result. This includes an understanding of the tasks and responsibilities.

-Support for the coach and the vision from the team administration. In youth soccer this includes the parents.

-A high level of **communication** must be developed inside the team.

-An understanding that team building is a process and not a thing. It is not a team bonding activity like a pizza party.

-The benefits of team building are long term. They are not specific to a team or season. They can be carried along throughout a career.

-The ultimate objective of team building is winning. Development without winning is like reading without understandings. (At the youth level winning should be associated with performance. It is important that players develop their qualities to their highest **level** and this effort is what constitutes a winner.)

It is voluntary. Children play soccer because they want to
Behind every action must be a thought
You do not know what you do not know

Alex Ludwig-

Cover